AFGHANISTAN AND ASIAN STABILITY

AFGHANISTAN
AND
ASIAN STABILITY

Edited by:
V.D. CHOPRA

GYAN

GYAN PUBLISHING HOUSE
NEW DELHI-110002

on behalf of
INTERNATIONAL INSTITUTE FOR ASIA-PACIFIC STUDIES
New Delhi

AFGHANISTAN AND ASIAN STABILITY

(*International affairs, Politics, History, Culture, Religion*)

ISBN: 81-212-0585-9

Published in 1998 by
Gyan Publishing House,
5, Ansari Road, Darya Ganj
New Delhi-110002

Laser Typesetting at A.S. Printers, Delhi.

Printed at Mehra Offset Press, Delhi.

CONTENTS

List of Contributors 7

Preface 9

Introduction 13

1. **Geopolitical Importance of Afghanistan** 23
V.D. Chopra

2. **Specific Feature of the Development of Feudalism in Afghanistan** 37
Igor Reisner

3. **Afghanistan's Independent Development** 49
An Afghan Scholar

4. **The Taliban Takeover in Afghanistan** 63
Kalim Bahadur

5. **The Russian and Central Asian Response to Taliban Takeover of Kabul** 71
Devendra Kaushik

6. **Russian Perception of the Afghanistan Crisis** 79
O.N. Mehrotra

7. **American Role in Afghanistan** 89
Chintamani Mahapatra

8. **The US Renewed Interest in Afghanistan** 101
P. Stobdan

9. **The Afghanistan Crisis and its Impact on South Asia and South-West Asia** 117
Uma Singh

10. Taliban Poses a Dilemma to Muslim World 133
Jagdish P. Sharma

11. Weapons and Narcotics in Afghanistan: Strategies and Ambitions in a Light Weapon War 147
Tara Kartha

12. Afghanistan Crisis: Geopolitical Aspects 183
Nasser Saghafi-Ameri

13. Oil Factor in Afghanistan Crisis 187
V.D. Chopra

14. Religious Fundamentalism and Ethnic Conflicts 197
V.D. Chopra

15. Common Heritage of India and Afghanistan 203
V.D. Chopra

16. India's Stand on Afghanistan Crisis 213
V.D. Chopra

17. Contemporary Afghanistan 225
Fred Halliday

Index 235

LIST OF CONTRIBUTORS

V.D. Chopra: Vice-Chairman, International Institute of Asia Pacific Studies, specialises in politics and economy of the Asia-Pacific Region.

Igor Relsner: He is a well-known Russian scholar.

Afghan Scholar: He is a scholar from Afghanistan and presently living abroad.

Kalim Bahadur: Professor of South Asian Studies and Chairman, Centre for South, Central, South-East Asian and South-West Pacific Studies, Jawaharlal Nehru University. A leading expert of India on Pakistan and Afghanistan.

Devendra Kaushik: Professor, Centre for Russia and East European Studies, Jawaharlal Nehru University, New Delhi. An outstanding specialist of India on Central Asian Republics.

O.N. Mehrotra: He is a Research Associate of the Institute for Defence Studies and Analyses, New Delhi. A prominent expert on international affairs with main focus on the erstwhile USSR.

Chintamani Mahapatra: Fellow, Institute for Defence Studies and Analyses. A well-known specialist on the United States.

P. Stobdan: Fellow at the Institute for Defence Studies and Analyses, New Delhi.

Uma Singh: She is an Associate Professor, Centre for South, Central, South-East Asian and South-West Pacific Studies, Jawaharlal Nehru University.

Jagdish P. Sharma : Reader in History, University of Delhi, expert on West Asian and North African Studies.

Tara Kartha: Research Officer at the Institute for Defence Studies and Analyses. A leading Indian expert on weaponisation of Afghanistan.

Nassar Saghafi-Ameri: Charge d'Affairs, Embassy of the Islamic Republic of Iran.

Fred Halliday: Prof. Fred Halliday is a well-known author on international affairs. His publications include Iran (1978), with Maxine Molyneuse, The Ethiopian Revolution (1982) and Second Cold War.

PREFACE

Afghanistan and the heroic struggle of the Pushtoons of the North-West Frontier Province (now in Pakistan) would fascinate anybody, who knows these areas and the people. To me these areas and their people have a special attraction because it is in this area that I had my political baptism as a young boy. I was present in Kissa Kahani Bazaar of Peshawar in 1930, when armoured cars were sent to cow the angry and peaceful masses. It was a period of the rising tide of the anti-imperialist movement throughout India, after the Lahore resolution of the Congress for complete independence. The mass movement which developed in April 1930 took a new dimension. The working class strike movement, no-rent campaign throughout the country, the famous Chittagong armoury raid in Bengal and above all the incident of Peshawar reflected the temper of the country.

For ten days this city was in the hands of the people. But there was something more significant than this. Following the arrest of local leaders, armoured cars were sent to suppress the popular movement. The indignant demonstrators in the bazaar, the centre of trade in the entire region, set on fire one armoured car and its occupants ran away, in broad daylight before thousands of people, all Pushtoons. Thereafter, wholesale firing was started by the British soldiers. This led to the death of hundreds of people and thousands of casualties. Later, two platoons of the Second Battalion of 18th Royal Garhwali Rifles appeared on the scene. In stead of firing on the people, these Hindu troops mixed with the Pushtoon crowd and refused the order to fire. After this incident the military and police were completely withdrawn from Peshawar: from April 25 to May 4 the city was in the hands of the people, until powerful British forces, with air squadrons were concentrated to recapture Peshawar. I was one of those young boys who were present in Peshawar during these epoch-making days. This not only left a deep imprint on my impressionable age but changed my outlook for the rest of my life. Therefore, when I write about Afghanistan and the Pushtoons, I do so with passion to discharge my debt partially.

It is this inspiration, rather a torch of light which has always been a driving force for many of us who come from that part of the sub-continent. That is why the tragedy of the Pushtoons and Afghans has always touched the conscience of Indian people deeply.

We have, however, compiled this book to present an objective picture about Afghanistan to the entire international community. The rich contribution made by scholars in this book has its own academic value. Though a large number of books have been written on Afghanistan both by Indian and foreign scholars, yet this book has its own merit. It evaluates the various internal and external factors which are operating in this country and retarding the process of a peaceful solution.

What is more painful is that in a section of the print and electronic media, the people of Afghanistan are being projected as a 'backward' and 'tribal' people. However, the history of nations cannot be erased. Afghanistan once was a cradle of civilization. Let us not forget this fact.

The authors of the various articles in this book specialise in diverse academic disciplines. They have made a valuable contribution in this book after a two-day national seminar organised by the International Institute for Asia-Pacific Studies. If there is a strong continuity in their analyses and conclusions, it is neither by design nor chance. Indeed, it reflects an important confluence of critical perspectives resulting from independent research based on an estimate of the factual data.

That is why this book has been brought out to meet the needs of policymakers, researchers and analysts interested in a comprehensive and detailed knowledge of society, of factors moulding the course of events in Afghanistan.

This country has been aptly described as on the "crossroads of Asia." This shows how the future of this country will have a bearing on the whole of Asia. The internal dynamics of Afghan society have been ignored by some scholars and there are others who have minimised the role of external factors in deepening the crisis in this country. In this book an attempt has been made to bring about a synthesis between these two aspects. That is why the institute believes that this book will be an important critical contribution to the existing literature on Afghanistan.

Finally, I must thank Mr. M. Rasgotra, the Chairman and Prof. K.P. Misra, General Secretary of the Institute for working out the main framework of this book.

I must also thank senior members of Gyan Publishing House for their cooperation in bringing out this book.

V.D. Chopra

J-1882, Ground Floor,
Chittaranjan Park,
New Delhi-110019

INTRODUCTION

Social science cannot be equated with astrology or for that matter with any discipline of physical sciences. Therefore, no precise prediction cannot be made about the future course of development in any country or region and that too in a period when equations and relations among the various nations and their internal developments are in a state of change. If one keeps this basic postulate in the forefront, it becomes clear that no firm prediction can be made about the future of Afghanistan. Therefore, it is relevant to point out that any study of Afghanistan in the last three years of the present century will suffer from this constraint. This aspect is being highlighted to bring out all that the articles included in this book have analysed the present developments in Afghanistan, the policies of the various states on the basis of the empirical data and trends as they are available now. In the post cold-war period particularly after the demise of the Soviet Union—a political and economic structure which appeared to represent an alternative to the American and western models—a basic shift as taken place.

There is another aspect which too should be kept in mind. Both in geo-political and geo-economic terms the centre of gravity has already shifted to the Asia-Pacific region. In this change Asia has come to occupy a strategic position for various reasons, including its natural resources, manpower, expanding markets, biggest reserves of technical and scientific talent, rapid expansion of new middle and upper middle classes and above all the emergence of some of the Asian states as major factors in the world economy. If Japan, for instance has already assumed the role of a super economic power, China during the next one decade is likely to become a superpower, economically, politically and militarily. ASEAN has already carved out a unique place for itself and India has the potential of becoming a major world power.

That explains why the American and Western policymakers have begun to evolve long term policies for this region. The US Under Secretary of State Thomas Pickering came to India on a dual mission in the third week of October, 1997. He wanted to set the tone for a 'strategic dialogue'—defined by him as "thinking in the future rather than discussing the past"—following the successful Clinton-Gujral summit in New York to prepare the ground for the future visits of Secretary of State Madeleine Albright and President Bill Clinton. However, on this trip Pickering still had to reckon with divergent perceptions on national interest and security between the world's single superpower and Asia's growing regional power, particularly on such contentious issues as non-proliferation and the Comprehensive Test Ban Treaty (CTBT). Although the US is committed to nuclear Non-Proliferation Treaty (NPT), it evidently did not want the evolving Indo-US strategic partnership to become hostage to an inflexible nuclear stand considered unacceptable by India.[1]

There are clear indications that the strategic alliance with Islamabad will be elevated to a higher-level. How Washington will strike a balance between 'strategic partnership' with New Delhi and 'strategic alliance' with Islamabad is anybody's guess.

Recently, the US recognised trans-border terrorism directed against India and blacklisted the Pakistan-based Harkat-ul-Ansar. This is particularly welcome in view of the numerous irresponsible references to Kashmir by senior American diplomats in the past.

Nevertheless, what is intriguing is that so far Washington has not given any indication about its policy on arming and training of religious fanatics of Kabul by Islamabad and its indirect support to the Taliban. Have the policymakers in Washington begun to re-examine their stand on religious fundamentalism including Muslim fundamentalists who have become a real threat to democratic and secular political structures in countries like Algeria, Egypt and Sudan? Has the United States a dual policy on this basic question? Is it still following the old policy of backing such forces? There are no readymade answers to these questions. Nevertheless, USA's commitment to democracy and human rights will be tested in this region, particularly in Afghanistan in this sub-continent and central Asia. Let us leave this question at that.

The policy makers of the United States have candidly admitted that they have deep geo-political and geo-economic interests in this region. US Deputy Secretary of State Strobe Talbott in a speach at John Hopkins University's Central Asia Institute on July 21, 1997, three months before his visit to India admitted that "the United States has a stake" in the economic reforms in Caucasus and Central Asia. He did not leave at that. He said "if reform in the nations of the Caucasus and Central Asia continues and ultimately succeeds, it will encourage similar progress in the other new independent states of the former Soviet Union, including Russia and Ukraine. It will contribute to stability in a strategically vital region that borders China, Turkey, Iran and Afghanistan, and that has growing economic and social ties with Pakistan and India. The consolidation of free societies, at peace with themselves and with each other, stretching from the Black Sea to the Pamir mountains, *will open up a valuable trade and transport corridor along the old Silk Road, between Europe with Asia."* (Emphasis added) He did not leave at that.

He underlined that if economic and political reforms in the countries of Caucasus and Central Asia do not succeed and if internal and cross-border conflicts simmer and flare, the region could become a breeding ground of terrorism—a hotbed of religious and political extremism and a battle-ground for outright war.[2]

This announcement sums up the American policy in this region. On the basis of this assessment two major decisions have already been taken by the United States as far as this region is concerned.

Firstly, the Clinton administration has sought a 40 per cent increase in foreign assistance funds for the nations of this region. Secondly, in September, 1997, the Central Asian peace keeping battalion, made up of armed forces from Kazakhstan, Uzbekistan, and Kyrgyzstan, hosted troops from the United States, Russia, Turkey and other nations in a joint peace-keeping exercise.

These two steps in the oil-rich region have a long term significance and need to be watched very carefully.

These developments have been mentioned to make out that the developments in Afghanistan and even on Indo-Pak border cannot be delinked from the new strategic thinking of the USA. That being the position, resolution of conflicts and new modes being evolved to resolve inter-state and intra-state conflicts should be kept in the forefront.

Whatever may be the objective and subjective reasons for Nagorno-Karabakh conflict in Azerbaijan, the conflict in Caucasus about which Shevardnadze has so often spoken and the conflicts in Tajikistan, one thing is certain that all these conflicts are paving the way not only for foreign intervention but also for the presence of foreign military forces. But there is something more to it than meets the eye.

These conflicts are being used as a political instrument to influence both the internal and external policies of Russia. Notwithstanding the fact that the cold war phrase of 'menace of communism' has lost its relevance, now Moscow, particularly the new Russian elite is being given guidance on how to restructure its economy. It is also been advised about its political role in the countries of Commonwealth of Independent States (CIS). Prejudices against Moscow for its acts of omission and commission are being blown up. Washington has been advising Moscow that a great power can promote patriotism without expansionism. Obviously the pressure on Russia is that in stead of integrating CIS it should allow its neighbours to function more independently. There are some critics of American experts who feel that a weak Russia alone will enable other countries to penetrate into the economies of the oil-rich Central Asian republics.

Developments in Afghanistan, therefore, have a wider implication than what appears on the surface. Let us look at this problem from another angle.

In the post cold-war period, multi-religious, multi-ethnic and multi-cultural societies and nation-states are facing new challenges from religious fanaticism, ethnic conflicts, and organised terrorism. The developments in Afghanistan including the intensification of proxy war by the ISI of Pakistan in the recent weeks and what is going on in some parts of India, in Jammu and Kashmir in particular, confirm this conclusion.

The rise of religious fanaticism, intensification of ethnic conflicts and above all organised terrorism are the burning problems which are disturbing the developing nations. This phenomenon has erupted with a new intensity in the Asia-Pacific region, though in the Balkans, it continues to lead to blood-shedding. Yugoslavia has already been split. Nevertheless, the question arises why these conflicts are appearing in the Asia-Pacific region?

This question can neither be answered in simplistic terms nor can it be explained within the framework of old dogmas. However, one thing is certain that when the centres of economic power have already shifted from Europe to the Asia-Pacific region. As has been mentioned earlier, the nation-states in Asia-Pacific region have become the main target of geo-political and geo-economic strategies. Nation-states, big or small, which have the potential of becoming major economic powers or can become geographical links do not fit into the geo-political strategies of the developed nations, and are nations which are faced with serious economic problems and growing resistance among their people. The recent political developments in Europe and the United States confirm this conclusion.

It goes without saying that the nation-states of the East have not only rich cultural heritage and their own history, notwithstanding the fact that during the colonial period the direction of the political, economic and cultural developments of these states were changed by the colonial powers. The cradles of human civilisations were systematically decimated.

There is one more aspect to the problem. It is said that for the past 200 to 300 years, the supremacy of Europe and the United States over their Asian and African colonies subsisted in a more advanced mode of production. This is correct, but not an exhaustive explanation. About a hundred backward eastern countries, basically remaining peasant ones, with predominantly pre-capitalist economies whose level of development of production, science and technology were incomparable with that achieved in the western countries, managed to liberate themselves from the political domination of colonialism. Why did this happen? In what way did these backward nations surpass their oppressors? Not, of course, in the mode of production, nor the productive forces, nor the level of technology and organisation of the economy. It was the anti-imperialist, democratic nationalism that aroused the peoples of Asia and Africa. This became the organising force behind the struggles waged by hundreds of millions of oppressed people of these countries.

This anti-imperialist consciousness among the people of the

former colonies and the semi-colonies increased manifold during the last five decades and they have began to demand an equitable economic order through the non-aligned movement and the United Nations. To weaken this rising tide, religious, ethnic and tribal conflicts were promoted by the elite of some of the developed countries. Thus a new social force was created in a large number of these countries though this is not the place to make a detailed review of this trend. Let us look at some facts with an open mind.

Whatever may have been objective and subjective factors for the disintegration of the Soviet Union, one cannot ignore the fact that even after dismantling of the old political and economic structures of Russia, threat to its unity and integrity continues to grow. Above all, attempts are being made to weaken the CIS. Let us take the example of Chechnya.

The separatist forces in Chechnya are demanding independence from the Russian federation. They are pressing the demand for their international recognition. Alsan Maskhadov during his negotiations with Moscow has rejected the proposal that Chechnya should be given a status like Tatar Republic.

The separatist forces in Chechnya have declared that they would sign international agreements with other countries as an independent state and may join Islamic organisations. This speaks for itself. More significant than this development is that the separatist forces in Chechnya are being supported by Saudi Arabia, Pakistan, Jordan and Sudan.

What is most intriguing is that these separatist forces are being given moral and material support from outside their own countries. Both in the electronic and print media the conflict in Chechnya, Balkans and in other areas are being blown out of proportion to make out that these nation-states are facing a serious crises. There are reasons for this. If Chechnya for instance gains the status of an independent state as has been designed by religious revivalism and the west, it will have a chain reaction on Caucasus, Central and South Asia. This will threaten the unity of the whole of Asia, because this development will have its own fall-out on the entire region. It is in this sense that the developments in Chechnya, Jammu and Kashmir and Afghanistan have some common features.

It is relevant to mention here that the rise of religious revivalism in most of these countries have certain specific features.

The religious revivalist movements including Islamic militants are being liberally financed from outside their respective countries. These financial resources are increasing tremendously by illegal drug and arms trade.

In Egypt, Algeria, Sudan and Afghanistan, large amounts of external money, especially, from Saudi Arabia, has been pouring in. Even the western scholars have admitted this fact. They point out that these forces are being strengthened to influence the course of history in the Muslim world. "Iranian pretensions to the leadership of Islam" has to be destroyed, they advocate.

Whatever may be the element of truth in this assessment, one interesting fact has recently come to light. Some 2000 Algerians were recruited by the Saudi-based World Muslim League for training in Sudan and Pakistan. They were recruited for operations in Afghanistan. Now they are operating in Algeria and heading the fundamentalist movements. This fact has been mentioned by Graham E.Fuller in his book entitled *Algeria: The next Fundamentalist State*.

There is sufficient evidence to prove that armed militants are being trained in Pakistan for promoting religious fundamentalist forces. What concrete shape it is taking in India has yet to have investigated and analysed, though Indian Intelligence may have compiled material on this sensitive question. This shows that the rise of religious fanaticism, intensification of ethnic conflicts and state-sponsored terrorism indeed are new instruments of destabilisation in this entire region.

The studies included in this book deal essentially with the multi-faceted dimension of the Afghanistan problem arising out of its geo-political location, its history, and currents and cross-currents within this landlocked country, the role of the major world powers and the fall-out of the prolonged civil war in Afghanistan on Asian stability.

There are three sets of articles included in this book. The first set deals with geo-political importance of Afghanistan, specific features of development of feudalism in Afghanistan, problems facing

Afghanistan in following the policy of independent development, religious fundamentalism and ethnic conflicts and the common heritage of India and Afghanistan. These studies analyse the internal situation of Afghanistan which is rooted in its history and its geo-political location.

There is another cluster of studies which examines the geo-political aspects of the Afghanistan crisis as it has developed in the post cold-war period. This study has been contributed by the Iranian diplomat, Nasser Saghafi-Ameri. However, this aspect has been examined in various other studies also. A critical analysis has been made of geo-economic aspect of the Afghanistan problem in the chapter on 'oil factor'.

In the second set Prof. Kalim Bahadur has brought into focus the factors which led to the takeover by Taliban of Afghanistan. Prof. Devendra Kaushik has made a critical estimate of the Russian and Central Asian response to the rise of Taliban in Afghanistan. In the same set-up Dr Jagdish P. Sharma has attempted to bring out the impact of Taliban on the entire Muslim world and how it has become a threat to the democratic structures of a large number of Muslim majority countries.

In her study Dr Tara Kartha has made an estimate of weapons and narcotics in Afghanistan.

The articles of the third set includes the role of big powers in Afghanistan. This covers a study on the Russian perspective of the Afghanistan crisis by Dr O.N. Mehrotra. There are two other studies which examine the American role in Afghanistan. These studies are by Dr Chintamani Mahapatra and P. Stobdan. Dr Uma Singh in her study has made detailed analysis of the impact of the Afghanistan crisis on South Asia and South-West Asia.

There are two other studies which essentially deal with India's relations with Afghanistan. One examines common heritage of India and Afghanistan in historical terms. The other makes a study of India's stand on Afghanistan during the last two decades.

This goes show that the study in which contribution has been made by an Afghan scholar and an Iranian diplomat makes a comprehensive analysis of Afghanistan crisis. The International

Institute for Asia Pacific Studies is grateful to the distinguished authors for their contributions and hopes that this book would be found useful to all those who are interested in objective analyses of the problems of Asian stability in the context of the crisis in Afghanistan.

V.D. Chopra

References

1. The Times of India, editorial, October 20, 1997
2. USIS, Wireless File, July 22, 1997.

Institute for Asia Pacific Studies is grateful to the distinguished authors for their contributions and hopes that this book would be found useful to all those who are interested in objective analyses of the [illegible] of Asian stability in the context of the [illegible] Afghanistan.

V.D. Chopra

References

1. The Times of India, editorial, October [illegible], 198[illegible]
2. [illegible] Weekly [illegible] No. [illegible]

I

GEOPOLITICAL IMPORTANCE OF AFGHANISTAN

V. D. CHOPRA

Long before the current developments in Afghanistan, beginning with the Saur Revolution of April, 1978, the Soviet intervention, the withdrawal of Soviet troops after one decade and the prolonged civil war, Afghanistan has been a focus of attention of the great powers, the Czarist Russia and Great Britain during the nineteenth century and of the United States, Pakistan and Iran after 1947.

Afghanistan, a secluded and mountainous country with a backward economy, occupies a very important strategic and political position in South-West Asia.

The boundaries of the country were established in the nineteenth century by an agreement between the two imperialist powers—Great Britain and Czarist Russia. It is bound on the west by Iran—boundary fixed in 1857 and 1904-05, with final corrections made in 1935; on the south by Baluchistan boundary fixed in 1896-97; on the north by Russia—boundary demarcated in 1886-87; and 1893-95; with minor adjustments in the 1920s, 1930s and 1948; on the east by North-West Frontier Province of British India (now Pakistan boundary) fixed in 1893-95; and China to the east of Wakhan Corridor—boundary fixed in 1895.

A land-locked and mountain-studded country, Afghanistan

has an area of 647,497 sq. kms.—249,995 sq. miles. The extreme length of the country from the north-east to the south-west is 700 miles, and extreme breadth from the Herat Frontier to the Khyber is about 600 miles. Afghanistan has no outlet on any ocean and the nearest sea—the Arabian Sea, lies 300 miles to the south. When communication was overland Afghanistan enjoyed the superiority of trade and cultural exchanges. The country occupied a momentous position at the crossroads of the shortest routes among India, Central Asian Khanates, East Iran, Sinkiang and West China. The military conquerors who marched to India passed through the Khyber and Bolan passes in Afghanistan. But it was isolated and left outside the mainstream of civilisation when the sea route to India was opened.

Hindukush—the chief mountain range of Afghanistan, covers three-fourths of the country. Its elevation is between 13,000 to 20,000 feet. The highest peak attains altitude of 25,426 feet above the sea level.

Afghanistan is considered one of the richest countries in Asia, though most of its natural resources are not developed. Northern Afghanistan is rich in copper, iron and lead. The slopes of Hindukush are rich in coal of fine quality. Crude petroleum is discovered in northern Afghanistan and Herat. Traces of gold and silver are found in the neighbourhood of Kandahar and Panjsher valley, respectively. Badakshan is the only area in the world to produce the famous lapis-lazuli—a beautiful azure-blue mineral, consisting of aluminium, sodium, silica and sulphur. It is used as ornament and for its medicinal value.

Sulphur deposits are also found there. The craftsmen of Afghanistan are famous for their jewellery work. Cotton and wool textiles, leather goods and beautiful woollen rugs are manufactured. It was after 1885, that a little more attention was also devoted towards the manufacture of arms and ammunitions in the country. Cotton, fruits, spices, tobacco, wool, rugs and Karakul lambskin rank first among the exports. Rearing of silkworm is carried on in the neighbourhood of Herat, Laghman and Kabul. Silk is used in the local looms and exported to other countries.

Some opinionated mineralogists declared that the oil reserves of Afghanistan are an important component of the oil belt extending from the hilly regions of Kangra area of Himachal Pradesh to Jammu and Kashmir in India and go right up to the Central Asian republics. This fact has been mentioned in one of the unpublished research papers of late K.D. Malaviya, the founder of the petroleum industry in India.

Equally important is the fact that both Afghanistan and India (particularly Jammu and Kashmir) are rich in strategic raw material like uranium. This in itself brings into sharp focus the geo economic importance of Afghanistan and Jammu and Kashmir, along with Central Asian republics.

The generation that has grown up in this country since World War II has little knowledge of how and why Afghanistan dominated relations between two empires—the British in the south and the Russian in the north—for well over a hundred years spanning three centuries. Modern Afghanistan, wrote Lord Curzon, is indeed a purely accidental geographical unit which has been carved out of the heart of Central Asia by the sword of conquerors or the genius of individual statesmen. Geography placed the Central Asian kingdom precariously between the competition and conflicts of two swelling imperial themes.

Historically speaking, in the nineteenth century after British imperialism established its domination on India, both economically and militarily, it had the ambition to further expand northward. On the other hand, the Russian empire was pushing southward through Central Asia Since Afghanistan was on the crossroads of Asia, it was but natural that these two imperial powers wanted to have directly or indirectly control over Afghanistan.

Though Britain dominated the sea, it wanted to protect its empire from the north-west. It also had an eye on Central Asia.

It was in this context that Afghanistan evolved a flexible policy towards Britain and Russia. However, to live in peace with Russia became an important principle of Afghanistan's external relations. In the 1870s the Russians wanted Britain to concede Afghanistan as a buffer state between the two empires. The British refused. In the agreement of 1873 Afghanistan was not recognised as a buffer state because Russia conceded that it was beyond its sphere of influence.

Britain wanted to keep the Pushtoons divided. The Pushtoons

in North-Western Frontier Province (NWFP) had very close ties with those living in Afghanistan.

Fearing an expansion of Russia influence to Afghanistan the British invaded the country twice as pre-emptive measures, but both the expeditions failed, and the British forces had to retreat. The fearful tribesmen who had turned back the mighty British from their motherland became the subject of legend.

Afghanistan only succeeded to some extent in easing out of the British sphere of influence after World War I. The process began with the coming of Amanullah to the throne in Kabul with his declaration that Afghanistan was no one's puppet, but a fully independent sovereign state. But British colonial rulers were not in a mood to accept this status of Afghanistan. As a complete contrast to this the Soviet Union recognised Afghanistan as a sovereign independent state.

In less than a month the British declared war on Afghanistan. Nearly 35,000 British troops, equipped with aircraft, heavy artillery and armoured cars were opposed by 50,000 Afghan soldiers. Even then victory eluded the British. The shortest of the three Afghan wars did not last more than thirty days. The armistice, signed on 3 June, 1919, led to a peace treaty on 8 August but the British did not formally recognise Afghanistan as a sovereign state. Afghanistan, however, signed a treaty of friendship with the Soviet Union on 28 February, 1921.

This shows how when the "Young Afghans" started the process of transformation of their country, they had to face a foreign armed intervention.

Following the agreement with the USSR, Afghanistan concluded treaties with Turkey, Iran, France and Italy. These treaties finally led to an Anglo-Afghan Treaty in which Britain renounced control of Kabul's external relations.

However, Afghanistan's relations with the Soviet Union were not smooth.

In 1929 Amir Amanullah fell from power because of strong opposition to his reforms. Amir Habibullah was the next in power for a short period. After Habibullah was deposed and executed on 15th October, 1929, Nadir Khan became King of Afghanistan. He concluded several treaties with the USSR. Soviet-Afghan relations improved considerably. Nadir followed a policy of non-intervention in Soviet Central Asia, and refused to allow northern Afghanistan to be used to promote Pan-Islamic, and Pan-Turkish activities. Under the next Afghan monarch, Muhammad Zahir Shah, who ruled Afghanistan for forty years from 1933 to 1973, Kabul's relations with Moscow improved considerably. Muhammed Zahir Shah renewed the Soviet-Afghan Mutual Assistance Pact concluded in 1931 and signed a new trade agreement in 1936. Russian exports to Afghanistan had doubled in volume between 1928 and 1933. Afghanistan signed an alliance in July 1937 with Iraq, Iran and Turkey. It is in this period that Afghanistan stepped up its efforts to become a modern state. A new modern political elite began to emerge.

Post Cold War Period

In the post Second World War period American political interests in this region enormously increased. Oil wealth of Arab countries became a focal point of Washington's policy as has been examined in this direction. Afghanistan had to adjust itself to this reality. For nearly one decade when the Soviet Union was rebuilding its economy, Afghanistan kept a low profile. In the post-war period the countries with which Afghanistan interacted most were the USSR, the United States, Pakistan and India, though Indo-Afghan relations were still on a low key.

If one looks back and examines all facts, it becomes clear that after 1947, the pivot of American policy was Pakistan. Afghanistan was a secondary factor. Pakistan appeared to be far more attractive to Americans than Afghanistan or even Iran in the late' forties as the most important nation that could make the United States a key lever in the Persian Gulf-South Asian region. In this major policy decision, the United States depended on the inputs of the British foreign office.

Afghanistan had a long-standing claim to the Pushtoon-speaking areas of Pakistan which bordered it. The dispute between Afghanistan and Pakistan cannot be seen in isolation from this basic fact—the division of Pushtoon in two areas—Afghanistan and Pakistan. In 1949, the Afghan ruler denounced the frontier agreement with the departed British, and demanded that the Pushtoon-speaking areas in Pakistan be given independent status as a sovereign state of Pushtoonistan. In response, Pakistan closed the border, on which Afghanistan depended heavily for imports.

It was this factor which moulded America's Afghan policy. It should be recapitulated the N.W.F.P. was never a strong base of the Muslim League. Pushtoons were anti-British and the powerful Red Shirt movement reflected this. American policymakers, therefore, could not trust Afghanistan which had at least 40 per cent Pushtoon population. Therefore, a policy to divide Pushtoons to destroy them was evolved. One cannot easily dismiss this theory.

In the mid-fifties, American policy in this region took a clear shape with the US-Pak pact of 1954. This marked a turning point in the geopolitics of this area. A year earlier, King Zahir Shah had appointed his first cousin, Mohammed Daud Khan, an ardent protagonist of Pushtoonistan, to the office of Prime Minister.

This development had its own impact on Afghanistan's foreign policy. It started strengthening its relation with the Soviet Union. A boundary agreement was settled in 1948. It was followed in 1950 with a four-year trade agreement. The Soviet-Afghan Treaty of 1931 was extended. The Soviets began to extend economic aid to Afghanistan. In 1955, Daud convened a *Loya Jirgah*—an assembly of tribal leaders—which approved his concept of a security treaty with the Soviet Union. A programme of development with the Soviet aid started.

Significantly, for development of petroleum reserves near Sherghan in north-west Afghanistan was started to develop Afghanistan's rich reserves of natural gas and minerals like iron, copper, lead and coal. The Soviet Union also started helping Afghanistan to strengthen its defence. In a period of twenty-five years up to December 1979, Afghanistan received from the USSR 2.5 billion US dollars in economic and military aid.

Till the Soviet intervention in Afghanistan, the United States had limited options. Its strategy was to build Pakistan and through it influence the course of developments in Afghanistan.

However, the USA's efforts to make Afghanistan sign a pact with Iran and Pakistan in 1953, providing facilities for US airfields, did not succeed. The Afghan-Pakistan conflict over the future of the Pushtoon tribe and the subsequent arming of Pakistan by the US finally resulted in the breaking off of diplomatic relations between

Kabul and Islamabad. The USA's military designs and the subsequent closure of the Pakistan-Afghan border forced Afghanistan to re-route its trade through the USSR and seek Soviet assistance to modernise its army.

Afghanistan passed through a period of uncertainty during the regime of Mohammad Daud, who came to power after overthrowing King Zahir Shah in a coup on July 16, 1973. Daud, who became the Prime Minister and head of the state on August 23, 1973 soon came under the influence of the Shah of Iran. This paved the way for repressions directed against the People's Democratic Party of Afghanistan (PDPA) at the instance of the newly-inducted Savak secret police of the Shah of Iran.

These developments, among others, gave rise to the April 1978 Saur Revolution, followed by the bringing in of a new regime in Kabul. The Revolutionary Council proclaimed the Democratic Republic of Afghanistan and elected General Secretary of the PDPA Central Committee Nur Muhammad Taraki, as the President and the Prime Minister. But the leader of the revolution, Nur Muhammad Taraki was overthrown and finally assassinated in a coup staged by Hafizullah Amin, who became the President and Prime Minister in September, 1979.

The internal chaos in Afghanistan, followed by the intrigues of rebels during Amin's dictatorship, finally led to Amin's downfall on December 27, 1979. The next day Babrak Karmal took over as the President of the Revolutionary Council and General Secretary of the PDPA Central Committee. This development preceded the entry of Soviet troops whose assistance had been repeatedly sought by the Afghan Government.

Thus another tragic phase began in Afghanistan. Foreign trained Mujahideens (holy warriors) were sent to Afghanistan. In 1979, the personnel of rebel combat units operating in Afghan territory all armed, equipped and trained by the US and its allies, had reached 100,000 men and 40,000 mercenaries.

Quite apart from this aspect, foreign interference in the region took a serious turn with the USA's espousal of the theory of an "arc of crisis", in the wake of the fall of the Shah of Iran. The Carter administration now began claiming that the USSR was out to grab the Gulf's oil. Ironically enough, the USA itself had opposed a UN resolution recognising the right of developing countries over their national resources, which was backed by the USSR.

In this connection, it is relevant to recall Indira Gandhi's statement in the Indian Parliament at that time that the Afghan developments were part of a *wider effort on the part of America to stir up tensions from the Atlantic to South-East Asia, not to speak of the Indian Ocean in between.* (Emphasis added)

The Afghan developments, moreover, were a blessing in disguise for Pakistan President General Zia-ul-Haq who used the pretext of a "Soviet threat" to obtain enormous US military and economic aid. By launching a successful insurgency in Afghanistan, he dreamt of establishing Pakistan's sway over that country.

The western countries and conservative Arab countries poured in one billion US dollars to the fledgling country by their activities against the Karmal regime. The astronomic sums of covert and overt financial assistance given to the extremist bands, their military training, their arming with the most modern and lethal weapons, such as "Stinger" missiles by the US and "Blowpipe" missiles by the UK, the despatch of spies to the territory of Afghanistan, all were a vivid proof of the interference of these countries in the internal affairs of Afghanistan. The USA had reportedly already spent over 3000 million dollars on the undeclared war besides the billions it had given to Pakistan as military aid in this period.

Dr M. Najibullah became General Secretary of the Central Committee of PDPA in 1986. He was elected President of the Revolutionary Council in October, 1987 and finally the President of the Democratic Republic of Afghanistan on November 30, 1987. He radically changed the internal policies of Afghanistan to bring them in tune with the new realities, hopes, aspirations and consciousness of the people.

Whatever may be the estimate about the Saur Revolution, the Soviet intervention and the subsequent withdrawal of the Soviet troops, the last units of the Soviet troops left Kabul on February 14, 1989. The Kabul regime almost single handed defended the country's independence. Najibullah took one initiative after another to resolve the internal crisis in Afghanistan peacefully and evolved a formula for the formation of a national government. Finally, on April 28, 1992 Hazarat Sibghatullah Mujaddedi, Chairman, Islamic Interim

Council, formally took over power from Najibullah. But peace still evades Afghanistan, notwithstanding the fact that Najibullah himself was assassinated. The crux of the matter is that the people of Afghanistan have continued to pay a heavy price for the geopolitical location of their country. In fact, after the disintegration of the Soviet Union, this landlocked country's geostrategic importance has further increased because the world power centres have shifted to Asia. It is this aspect which needs to be critically examined.

Historians have rightly described Afghanistan as a "unique country" because of its geographical location, being at the "crossroads of Asia". But in the post cold-war period, geostrategic position of Afghanistan has undergone a major change. The most important factor which has brought about this change is that the *centre of gravity* of world power is shifting steadily though surely from Europe to the Asia-Pacific. Four countries—USA, China, Japan, and Russia—are located here. Out of the seven nations or state systems that may emerge as major players in the world in the beginning of the next century, six are likely to be from this region—USA, China, Japan, Russia, ASEAN, or South-East Asia and India. This brings into sharp focus that in the geopolitical strategy of the USA, China, Russia, South-East Asia and India, geographical location of Afghanistan will be a key factor. Any critical examination of the prolonged crisis in Afghanistan from long term point of view should take into account this factor.

"Asia is the key to the economic health of the United States and to the everyday lives of Americans. It is the *most lucrative terrain for American* jobs and exports", according to the White House, a National Security Strategy of Engagement and Enlargement. (February 1995, pp. 28-29. (Emphasis added) This candid admission by the American policymakers speaks for itself and needs no comments.

The US economic penetration in the Asia-Pacific region is likely to grow at an even faster pace in the future. In the six years between 1987-92, US exports to the economy of the 17 members of the Asia Pacific Economic Cooperation (APEC) increased by at least 50 per cent.

Significantly East and South-East Asia remain an important

market for the US military exports. Foreign military sales in 1993 amounted to more than 10 billion US dollars.

Seen in this context, the geostrategic interests of the United States in Asia should be critically examined.

There are two clear indicators which should be taken into account.

Firstly, after the end of the cold war, US troop level in Asia-Pacific has remained steady at about 100,000 soldiers for the last three years. Compared to this, its military strength in Europe decreased by about 20 per cent annually in the same period. North Atlantic Treaty Organisation's (NATO) eastward thrust should also be seen in this context.

Secondly, the end of the cold war and highly degraded status of the former Soviet Union as an arms supplier has radically changed the arms trade pattern. While the United States remains the largest exporter of arms, the second position in 1994 was taken by France, with Russia a poor third, exporting arms worth only 1.8 billion US dollars during the year.

During the past ten years, *parties to 45 current conflicts and on-going wars, have imported arms worth 42 billion US dollars from the US alone*. (Emphasis added) In more than half of the current conflicts the United States has been a major supplier to one of the parties to the dispute including in the ongoing wars.

The US has also been the primary supplier of arms during the previous five years to governments which are involved in ongoing wars and armed conflicts. It is relevant to mention here that among the top ten arms importing countries, Turkey, Saudi Arabia and Pakistan are in the leading position. Can this not be described as a policy of divide and rule and that too when economic interests of the United States in this region are growing?

This analysis has a direct relevance to the current crisis in Afghanistan in more than one sense—Economically, politically and militarily China is emerging as a super power Russia has begun to rediscover itself and is asserting her nationalism. India has all the potentials of becoming a major world power. Political and economic interests of Iran, Iraq, Libya and possibly of some other West Asian countries come into conflict with the United States.

In this situation Washington needs new instruments to reverse these trends. This leads one to the tentative conclusion that the crisis in Afghanistan is one of these instruments. The crisis in Afghanistan has certain new features.

One of these features in the recent past is the rise of Taliban as a major factor. At one stage it appears that the fundamentalist outfit Taliban had almost succeeded in establishing its domination in the strategic areas of Afghanistan. However, this turned out to be a short-lived development. The Taliban faction now seems to be facing one setback after another, though one should not draw hasty conclusions.

However, one thing is certain that in geopolitical terms India, Central Asian republics and Iran have deep interest and stake in the stability of Afghanistan, particularly in terms of security, territorial intergrity and success of a free independent and sovereign nation. Obviously, India's geopolitical integrity and geostrategic stakes in South-West Asia and South Asia are closely tied with Afghanistan. This has been so in the past. After the emergence of the fundamentalist Taliban, it has assumed a new dimension. The reason is obvious. Islamic Republic of Pakistan has soft, porous and contiguous frontiers with both India and Afghanistan. This is the hardest reality.

India and Pakistan have fought three non-nuclear wars during 1948 and 1965, over the state of Jammu and Kashmir and in 1971 over East Pakistan, which emerged as the free independent and sovereign nation of Bangladesh.

After the withdrawal of Soviet troops in spring 1989 from Afghanistan, Pakistan has trained, equipped and deployed tens of hundreds of Afghan Mujahideens to fight what it called a "holy war" in Afghanistan.

For countless centuries the world had known the Afghans, as a proud and independent nation who did not accept outsiders (foreigners) as their superiors. As history demonstrates Afghanistan indeed has been a graveyard of diplomatic political, military and racial interventions from outside. Notwithstanding the fact that Afghanistan is a multi-ethnic country with two religious sects, Shias Sunnis, this national characteristic of Afghan has always moulded this small nation.

This explains why even after the creation of Pakistan in August 1947, Pakistan and Afghanistan could not develop cordial relations. Islamabad had its own ambitions in Afghanistan. The two countries were antagonistic towards each other. Conflict over the Durand Line surfaced between Afghanistan and Pakistan after the British withdrawal from the sub-continent in 1947 to quote one instance. Afghanistan has been an exponent of the demand that an independent Pashtoonistan should be created and that Pushtoons east of the Durand Line be given the choice of independence.

Pakistan, therefore, evolved a policy of "divide and rule" over Afghanistan. It began to create its own base in this country. After the withdrawal of the Soviet troops it almost had a free hand in subverting this country.

There are some other aspects of the development in Afghanistan.

Firstly, Afghanistan is almost equal is size to the territories of France, Belgium, Netherlands and Denmark, put together. This landlocked country shares a border with Central Asian republics. There is something more to it. Ethnic population of Afghanistan, such as Uzbek and Tajiks have close affinity with their counter parts in Central Asian republics.

Secondly, Afghanistan's proven reserves of natural gas, oil, iron ore, tin, coal and above all strategic materials like uranium should not be minimised as has been mentioned earlier.

Thirdly, Afghanistan and the Central Asian Republics are landlocked countries. Therefore, they require an access to sea for the growing trade commerce and industry. Pakistan has the option to provide this outlet to them. Seen in this context one cannot ignore the fact that the major communication routes from Pakistan to the Central Asian republics lie through Afghanistan. These routes however, have remained blocked because of the civil war in Afghanistan. A Pakistani thinkers believe that "Afghanistan remains they key to Pakistan's geo political access to Central Asia" (Emphasis added). The Central Asian republics are just a few hours by road from North-West Frontier through Afghanistan. "The future of our geostrategic access to Central Asia and Afghanistan are interlinked" according to Pakistani experts.

Fourthly, Pakistani military and strategic interest in

Afghanistan and Central Asian's get a new thrust in view of its hostility towards India.

The civil war in Afghanistan has wider implications than appear on the surface.

The Talibans are armed, promoted and patronised by Pakistan both overtly and covertly. There are no two opinions about it. However, certain big powers who have geopolitical and economic interests in this region are also playing their own game.

Politics and economics go together. It will not be incorrect to say that certain powers are interested in the triangle of Kashmir, Afghanistan and Central Asian republics. From the standpoint of India, Kashmir and Afghanistan are two sides of the same coin except for the fact that India is strong enough to meet external challenges of proxy war.

Uzbekistan and Kazakhstan have misgivings about the policy of Pakistan. That appears to be the reason that they have expressed reservations about recognition of Taliban by Pakistan. Therefore, both these republics seem to be evolving a common policy. Iran too is deeply concerned about the prolonged and protracted civil war in Afghanistan.

This shows the two conflicting approaches have already developed into a civil war in Afghanistan. One approach is that of pushing the civil war in Afghanistan and bring it to the brink of a precipice.

India, Central Asian republics and Iran want that the civil war in Afghanistan should end through national consensus to protect the unity, integrity, independence and sovereignty of Afghanistan.

However, the situation in Afghanistan is fluid. No prediction should be attempted. All the countries of this region should strive for a peaceful solution of this conflict and the first pre-requisite for this is that all foreign intervention—militarily, financial and political should be stopped. The real threat to Afghanistan, which has yet to develop the concept of a modern nation state is that of its balkanisation. If this happens it will have a chain reaction on the stability of this entire region and India will be no exception to. This is clearly and objectively analysed in this study.

2

SPECIFIC FEATURE OF THE DEVELOPMENT OF FEUDALISM IN AFGHANISTAN

IGOR REISNER

Historically speaking the process of the disintegration of the primitive community system and the development of feudal relations in Afghanistan had various specific features in the different parts of the country. It developed unevenly among diverse tribes. In some regions this process was going on at a relatively rapid pace, but in others slowly. The communal-tribal system which was at an early stage of disintegration, was still comparatively stable in some regions of this country. This is a unique feature of this Asian country. No other Asian model enables us to understand the complex nature of this country.

The conditions of the disintegration of the primitive communal system and the development of feudal relations among West Afghan tribes, first and foremost the Durranis, differed considerably from those observed among the Marwats, Bannuchis, Yusufzais and other aboriginal nationalities of Eastern Afghanistan. The settling on the land here was of a much more prolonged character, nomad cattle breeding even in the nineteenth century remained the chief occupation of a considerable part of the population; transitional forms of the economy—partly cattle breeding, partly land tilling—proved extremely viable.

Back in the 1860s as a result of a drought some groups of the Ghilzais had abandoned their arable land and resumed a nomadic life. The same picture was observed somewhat earlier in 1839 in the Sohak unit of the Ghilzais in the region of Harvar. Things were by no means as simple as they seemed for pastures were far from being a 'free'—no man's land where any Afghan could tend his livestock. However, the main distinction of Western Afghans from their Eastern fellow-countrymen was that there were more shepherd tribes among the former.

A more gradual and slow transition from nomad cattle breeding to settled land cultivation (as compared with tribes on the right bank of the Indus River) going on among the Durranis and Ghilzais can be explained by the specific features of the natural and geographic environment and the concrete historical conditions of the process of the nomads' settling. Afghanistan's western regions—Seistan, Kandahar and Ghazni—had large and convenient pastures which contributed to the preservation of nomad cattle breeding economies among the Durranis and Ghilzais. Under the social conditions of production that existed in the Middle Ages these lands could be used as pastures only.

At the same time, the growth of property inequality among the nomads, the monopolisation of the basic means of production the pastures—in the hands of the tribal nobility conditioned the transition of the poorest section of cattle breeders to land tilling. More than that, a typical feature of the cattle breeding economy of the Durranis and Ghilzais in the nineteenth century, and probably even earlier, was a constant shortage of pasturage and the need to store fodder for the winter. In a number of regions in western Afghanistan cattle breeding could no longer exist as an independent branch of the economy and was more and more combined with land tilling. Durrani and Ghilzai nomads, as a rule, had small settlements.

However, the possibilities of a broad switchover of West Afghan tribes to land cultivation were limited, for three reasons. First, the arable lands area in Western Afghanistan was rather small and these land had already been developed and firmly occupied by the settlers mainly Tajik population. Secondly, this population could still put up resistance to Afghan nomads trying to seize their land. Thirdly, the foreign feudal lords ruling Western Afghanistan, the Safavids in Kandahar, the Mughals in Ghazni and Kabul, were themselves interested in exploiting the settled, mainly Tajik, peasants. Therefore, they were against the transfer of cultivated lands, first and foremost, irrigated land to the Afghans. That was why the process of the transition of the Durrani and Ghilzai tribes to a settled way of life, their seizure of cultivated land and the establishment of their domination over the Tajik peasants who tilled these lands took place gradually over a long period. The Afghan tribes inhabiting the right bank of the Indus river, captured new lands dividing it between themselves and began its exploitation, whereas the Durranis and Ghilzais were slowly "penetrating" in land cultivation oases. Settling on land there often was initiated by individual clans or even families, but not by whole tribes or their units. This had its own social consequences. Meanwhile, this slow, gradual, mixed settling by way of penetration, inevitably contributed to the undermining of the ties of relationship between the settled and nomad members of the Durrani and Ghilzai tribes and weakened their tribal organisation.

The Durranis were one of the largest Afghan tribes. According to the census conducted in 1748 by Nadir Shah's order they numbered 60,000 families. In the beginning of the nineteenth century there were 100,000 families, or about 800,000 people. The two main branches of that tribe were the Zirak and the Punjpai. However, already in the eighteenth century they ceased to be real units of a clan-tribal organisation and their names only characterised the genealogy of the Durranis. In the early nineteenth century these units had lost all meaning and only determined the origin of various clans.

The principal secondary units of the Durranis that belonged to the Zirak were the Popolzais, Barakzais, Achakzais and Alkozais. To the Panjpai branch belonged the Nurzais, Alizais, Iskakzais, Khugianis and Makus. Ahmad Shah was afraid of the power of the Barakzais who were the most numerous among the secondary units of the Durranis. In his time Barakzais numbered about 30,000 families. To weaken the Barakzais he separated the Achakzais from them, who, as a result, began to be considered an independent unit of the Zirak branch, and he appointed a special chief for the Achakzais.

These nine secondary units of the Durranis were actually rather large separate tribes. Among other Durrani tribes the most respectful and influential were the Popolzais; to them belonged the Sadozai Khan-Khel, the hereditary supplier of Popolzai chiefs, who at the same time were the supreme chiefs for all Durranis. The dynasty of the founder of the Afghan state, Ahmad Shah, had its origin among the Sadozais.

The Barakzais inhabited the region to the south of Kandahar, the Argastan valley, the banks of the Gilmend and the desert plains divided by that river. Even in the beginning of the nineteenth century the majority of the Barakzais led a nomad way of life, only a minority was settled. The Achakzais who branched off the Barakzais, were a purely cattle breeding tribe. Their winter camps were situated on the southern slopes of the Khoja-Amaran Range. The Nurzais were a little smaller numerically than the Barakzais, but in contrast to them they remained almost to the present day a cattle breeding tribe. Nurzai camps were scattered across vast desert expanses in western and south-western parts of Afghanistan, bordering on Horasan, Seistan and Baluchistan. The Alizais had settled in the vicinity of Zamindavar, and by the beginning of the nineteenth century there were no nomads among them. Their closest neighbours—the Alkozais—also completely shifted over to land cultivation. The Iskakzais lived in an area between Zamindavar and an adjacent barren plain. They were a semi-nomad and semi-settled tribe.

The majority of the nomad Durranis had their summer and winter pastures not far from each other. Roaming from place to place the Durranis usually did not go beyond the Kandahar region. Their summer camps were in the foothills of Hazarajat (north of Kandahar), on the northern slopes of the Khoja-Amaran Range and in the Toba Mountains (south of Kandahar) while their winter camps were pitched on the plains and in the foothills, not far from their summer pastures. The Nurzais were an exception. Each spring they drove their herds to summer pastures situated to the north of Herat, in the district of Badgis, and in autumn, they returned. There winter camps were scattered over an immense area from Herat to the borders of Baluchistan. This caused their inner disunity and isolation from other Durrani tribes. As for the majority of the nomad Durranis, their closeness within the bounds of a comparatively small territory where their winter camps were situated, resulted in their drawing closer together.

One can frequently come across references in literature stating that the Durranis, although they had become divided into nine independent tribes were distinguished by the realisation of their community, by the feeling of attachment to their native land which they believed to be not the territory of one individual tribe, but the whole country of the Durranis.

It should be mentioned that the impoverished Durranis who had lost land or had been deprived of cattle, never left their native parts. This could be explained by the comparatively great distance to India and the proximity of local towns Kandahar, Ghazni and others, where impoverished members of the tribe could find some means of subsistence. In the period when trade with India reached comparatively great proportions, such poverty-stricken members of the tribe could find a living by becoming drivers of pack animals or guarding trade caravans that passed Kandahar on their way to Horasan or back. As far as the Yusufzais were concerned the impoverished members of their tribe usually went to India and peasants and artisans constantly returned from India, thus reinforcing the ranks of the Hamsai, whereas there was no such emigration and immigration among the Durranis. This circumstance contributed to the development of feudal relations in Durrani society.

Due to a slow and latex transition to a settled way of life, West Afghan tribes passed through that stage in conditions when the prevailing primitive-communal system had already disintegrated to a considerable extent. It was typical for the Durranis to have a rich and influential tribal nobility, the hereditary chief of the tribe and chiefs of its big secondary units from among noble and powerful families (khan-khel).

Thus, property stratification, the division into the free and the dependent, the exploiters and the exploited in the midst of the free, which were typical features of their socio-economic system of the earlier periods, were shifting over to a settled way of life, especially in the eighteenth and nineteenth centuries. These circumstances, plus the already mentioned distinctions of the very process of settling, facilitated the further development of feudal relations among them.

Customs duties imposed on the caravans traversing the great trade route connecting India with Horasan as also plunder contributed to the growing power of the Durrani Khans. Kandahar was the main trans-shipping and commercial centre on that route. Some Durrani Khans themselves were taking part in that trade and made fortunes on it.

Finally, the Durrani Khans received from the Safavid and the Mughal rulers of Western Afghanistan in the early eighteenth century, the border between the Safavid and the Mughal India lying halfway between Kandahar and Ghazni, titles, gifts and donations in cash and grants of land, and were entrusted with the functions of tax collectors. Besides, they were obliged to supply military contingents from among their fellow-tribal people.

The "Tazkirat al-Muluk", a memorandum about the administrative structure and tax incomes of the Safavid power soon after the Afghan conquest of Iran in 1722, noted that the Afghan tribes of the Kandahar region were obliged to provide military contingents for service to the Shah. Together with Persian troops they took part in military operations against the Baluchis and Kakars. The Durrani chiefs at the end of the seventeenth and beginning of the eighteenth centuries, first Sher Khan and then Hussain Khan, were both from Safavid Shah Husain (1694-1722) investiture and they were ordered immediately to start collecting taxes and arrears which had to be transferred to the Safavid treasury. After a clash with the Safavid ruler Beghlerbek of Kandahar, Sher Khan took over service to the Mughals and received the title of Shahzade (prince) from them and the investiture of the chief of the Abdali tribe.

There is no doubt that the granting of tax collector functions to the Durrani Khans and the right to form military contingents from among their fellow-tribesmen, whom they commanded, added to the power and monetary incomes of the tribe nobility. Although we have no direct data, we may assume, on the example of the Mughals' attitude to the Hattaki Khans that the Durrani Khans also received, as an award for their service, grants of land in the form of a title or jagir, both on the territory of their own tribe and on lands inhabited by settled, mainly Tajik, peasants.

In the Durrani village community, just as in other Afghan communities, except the Waziri community, the handicraftsmen and tradesmen were not Afghans. They were mostly Tajik handicraftsmen and tradesmen, and in some cases Indian merchants and usurers, the latter predominantly in towns. From the very beginning the Durrani community lacked the inner division of labour between handicrafts and land cultivation based on hereditary. This stood as a contrast to the Afghan region on the right bank of the Indus river. In this region rural labour and artisans constituted their own entity. This was due to the influence of India. Indian community and the presence of numerous representatives of various Indian castes in those Afghan regions had their impact. In the settled community of the Durranis there were no rural servants, and the number of handicraftsmen was limited to three or four.

More than that, living among settled Tajiks, especially near big urban centres like Kandahar, the Durranis were inevitably drawn into the division of social labour that had already taken shape between town and village.

The settled Durrani community was divided into various groups. Representatives of various units of the tribe living in one and the same village settled in separate parts and had the Maliks and Mushirs of their own; but they did not experience the inner strife that was rampant among the Yusufzais; they lived peacefully with each other. In contrast to the Yusufzais and Bannuchis, as well as the Ghilzais, the Durranis were a relatively peaceful people, which could be explained by a relatively greater authority of the Khans, and also by the fact that the chief of the tribe and the chiefs of the units, together with the Jirga, not only had the right to mediate between the conflicting parties, but could also settle the matter without their consent, their decision being final and obligatory.

Blood feuds were not widespread among the Durranis. The Sadozai chiefs of that tribe repeatedly called on the Durranis never to raise the sword against one another.

In the beginning of the nineteenth century justice in especially important cases such as murder was administered by the Khans, usually together with the Jirga, and sometimes without it. In minor cases the latter passed sentences independently. The Khans and

Jirga's justice was based on customary laws. As for property disputes, the Khans referred them to the Sharia court.

The process of disintegration of the primitive-communal system among the Ghilzais took similar form to that among the Durranis, but the former had some specific features connected first and foremost, with the predominance of the family patriarchal community among the Ghilzais, with the less developed commodity-money relations, and finally with different natural and geographic environment.

Like the Durranis, the Ghilzais were a very big tribe or rather a group of tribes. In the early nineteenth century they numbered about 100,000 families. In the eighteenth and even in the nineteenth century the Ghilzais remained predominantly nomads, although the number of the Ghilzais who had already settled on land was also considerable. Many Ghilzai units combined cattle breeding with land cultivation; they were a semi-nomad people. In some districts, for example, in Tarnak, Logar and Maidan the Ghilzais had firmly switched over to land cultivation, comprising, as they did, the bulk of the settled population. The Ghilzais did not seize cultivated lands at one stroke, but steadily "penetrated", pushing aside Tajik peasants and settling among them. Taking up land cultivation Ghilzais did not begin to plant orchards immediately, although they had for a long time existed in neighbouring Tajik villages.

The Ghilzais roamed from place to place and gradually settled on a vast territory situated on the western slope of the Sulaiman Mountains. Their lands were limited by Kalat-i-Ghilzain and Poti in the south, Gul Kogh in the west, the Sulaiman Mountains in the east and Kabul-Daryev in the north. They were divided into two primary units: the Turan and the Buran. The Turan consisted of secondary units—the Hoteki and the Tohi. The secondary units of the Ghilzais were Andar and Turk-Khel. Their secondary units were like the Durranis actually individual tribes. The Hotekis were about five to six thousand families in the early nineteenth century and the Tohis, about 12,000 families, inhabited the western part of Ghilzai lands, directly bordering on the Durranis. That was the most civilised section of the Ghilzais who were engaged not only in cattle breeding and land cultivation but also in trade and economically connected with Kandahar. The political significance of the Hotekis was great, for this unit included the Khan's family (Shah-Alam-Khel) of the entire Ghilzai tribe.

The Turk-Khels occupied the district of Mukura on the Ghazni plateau. Members of the tribe roamed in winter partly to Daman, partly to the Durrani lands. The Andar tribe possessed the district of Shilagar to the south of Ghazni, which was rich agricultural land.

The biggest of the Ghilzai tribes—the Sulaiman-Khel—about 35,000 families was scattered far and wide. Two units of that tribe the Kaisar—Khels and the Ismailzais—inhabited lands south and west of Ghazni. Their winter camp sites were situated in Waziristan. The third unit of the Sulaiman-Khel—the Sultanzais—was partially cut off from the Western Ghilzais by a stretch of territory occupied by the Afghan tribe of Vardak. The Sultanzais inhabited the district of Logar and Maidan, to the north-east of Vardak territory, and they were purely land-cultivating society. They were famous for their art of building irrigation installations.

The fourth unit of the Sulaiman Khel—the Ahmadzais—were situated in the Sorhel and Safedkoh mountains, and in winter they travelled to the Kuram Valley and Terin. By the conditions of their settling—the territory occupied by the Ghilzais was a long, narrow stretch—and by the character of the location of their pastures the various units of the Ghilzais were scattered not only in summer, but in contrast to the Durranis, in winter, because their winter camp sites were mainly situated outside the boundaries of the basic territory of the tribe, namely in the district of Kandahar, in Terin, Daman, Waziristan and the Kuram valley. The Ghilzais were disunited to a much greater extent than the Durranis.

However, the principal reason for the inner disunity of the Ghilzais was predetermined by their socio-economic system and an exceptionally weak development of commodity-money relations as compared with the Durranis. Even those regions that were an exception such as Tarak, Logar, Maidan, gravitated not to one economic centre, but to different ones—Kandahar and Kabul, which were in turn disunited. As for the bulk of the Ghilzais, and above all the largest Ghilzai tribe the Sulaiman-Khel—barter predominated among them even in the middle of the nineteenth century. The main wealth of the Ghilzais was their herds. They did not engage in handicrafts except for the production of crude items. They did not understand weights and measures. Each time they had to agree between themselves about measures, they used either a definite number of handfuls, or a clay vessel into which they poured grain.

The lowest basic cell of the economic life and social organisation of the Ghilzais at least in the eighteenth and nineteenth centuries was the patriarchal family community that included about 10 small families. Either the eldest or his direct descendant was the head of the patriarchal family. Some 10 or 12 such communities usually formed a Ghilzai clan. Each patriarchal family community of the Ghilzais settled in a fortified estate (Kala). Land was the community property, but it was cultivated by individual families which had implements, cattle and personal economies of their own.

Ghilzai social life was regulated by the organs of tribal self-government and customary law. The decision of the mediating Jirga had at least in the nineteenth century a compulsory character. Its violation was punished by imposing a fine, burning the house of the culprit or driving away his cattle. A violation by the Jirga of a lower unit of a decision adopted by the Jirga of a higher kinship unit was regarded as a punishable act. Hostages were taken from the guilty unit. The most severe punishment was banishment from the tribe.

There was no powerful tribal nobility among the Ghilzais. They had their own Khan-Khel who belonged to the Hoteki unit which was a hereditary supplier of chiefs of the entire tribe. This Khan family did not enjoy any special privilege in contrast to the Sadozais in the Durrani tribe. The Ghilzai Khans did not have any established coercive power over their fellow-tribesmen. Even to impose a fine on a member of the tribe for failure to appear at an assembly of the homeguard was a prerogative of the "tsalveshti"—elected military commander, but not the Khan. The Khans received customs duties, various taxes from the Hamsai and they were also given a greater portion of military booty than ordinary tribe members.

As a result of the disintegration of the primitive-communal system inner strife and plundering attacks on neighbours became a law of the life of Ghilzai society. In this respect the Ghilzais were justly compared with the Yusufzais. In these internecine wars and attacks, the key role was played by the Khan's units and volunteer detachments.

Incomplete data about the socio-economic system of the Ghilzais in the eighteenth and early nineteenth century provide grounds to assume that the process of the development of feudalism among them was at the initial stage at that time. They had no powerful nobility. The settled Ghilzais had land belonging to separate patriarchal family communities, while the nomads pasture continued to be considered the common property of the tribe, although, probably, the right to dispose of them increasingly passed into the hands of the upper crust exploiters. The settled Ghilzais disintegrated into separate, isolate patriarchal communities. A meagre development of commodity—money relations, with the exception of several agricultural districts, such as Tarnak, Logar of Maidan to which the existence of barter testified, did not change the original, isolated life of the patriarchal community of the Ghilzais. Finally having no compact territory and disunited by the specific conditions of their nomadic life, winter camp sites of the Ghilzai cattle breeding tribes were, as a rule, situated outside the boundaries of their country and not inside it, as was the case with the Durranis. The Ghilzais did not have even the slightest degree of unity typical of their neighbours—the Durranis. For this reason, the political and military superiority of the Ghilzais in the first half of the eighteenth century was short-lived and did not leave any great imprint on the history of Afghanistan. The principality founded by the Ghilzai Khans in 1709 could not have any firm foundation and existed for only about 40 years.

Thus, the following specific features of the disinte-gration of the primitive communal system were typical of the Durranis and Ghilzais. On the one hand, their cattle breeding economy and nomad way of life were preserved for quite a long time. In the beginning of the eighteenth century the Durranis and Ghilzais remained cattle breeding tribes. At the same time property inequality was growing in their midst, and a powerful nobility especially among Durrani emerged.

On the other hand, the process of ousting the impoverished tribe members from the cattle breeding economy was going on. They partly switched over to land cultivation, partly moved to towns, first and foremost to Kandahar, in search of means of subsistence. That was how a section of the Afghan population has come into being in Kandahar and probably in Ghazni. It consisted, in the main, of pauperised tribe members thrown out of the cattle breeding economy, but it also included individual rich merchants.

The process of the Ghilzais and Durranis settling on land was proceeding slowly, gradually, rather by "penetration" than by an open and mass seizure of the irrigated lands belonging to Tajik peasants. This character of settling somewhat weakened family and tribal ties between tribe members who had shifted over to land cultivation, for representatives of various units and families mixed with each other as well as with neighbouring non-Afghan peasants.

The process of the disintegration of the primitive communal system of the Durranis and Ghilzais as largely facilitated by their interactions with the feudal surroundings. It was not only the question of granting titles and posts to Durrani and Ghilzai Khans by the Mughals and Safavids, and later by Nadir Shah, this included also the functions of tax collectors and commanders of military contingents of their fellow-tribesmen at the service of the central power. Tribe members were adopting a settled way of life and they were drawn into the already existing system of the feudal economy, which had a direct bearing on the organisational structure of Durrani community.

3

AFGHANISTAN'S INDEPENDENT DEVELOPMENT

BY AN AFGHAN SCHOLAR

Afghanistan lagged considerably behind its neighbours in socio-economic development. Democratic revolutions were brewing in Russia, Turkey, and Iran. Anti-imperialist movements were beginning in India and China in the initial years of the present century. In Afghanistan, capitalism was at that time at a rudimentary stage. Feudalism had still in a firm hold. Following the 'divide-and-rule' principle, Great Britain divided, in 1883, the ethnic majority of Afghanistan, the Pushtoons, into two isolated groups separated by the "Durand Line", including part of Afghan territory in its Indian possessions. Moreover, Great Britain established political control over the country, isolating it from the outside world.

However, despite the efforts of the British imperialists to throw a "barrier of estrangement" around the country, Afghanistan, just as the other countries of Central Asia, was being drawn into the orbit of world economy. In accordance with the general laws of economic development the new economic forms were forcing their way; commodity-monetary relations were extended; primitive accumulation of capital was underway, and the basis for the formation of the national market was developed. All this gradually changed the country's social structure, pushing into the foreground the bearers of the new economic relations—merchants and landlords of the semifeudal type with close links to the market—and the intelligentsia.

The policies of the regime of Habibullah Khan (1901-1919) preserved the feudal order and slowed down the development of productive forces. However, there was a spontaneous growth of dissatisfaction among the popular masses brought about by the tyranny of the authorities and feudals as well as by the heavy burden of taxes. The armed uprisings of 1912-13 has to be seen in this background.

Under increased socio-economic contradictions, anti-British sentiment in the country served as the background for the movement for national liberation and reforms that was called the "Young Afghan Movement." It united representatives of the emerging secular intelligentsia—the ideologists of those classes and social states that were vitally interested in the elimination of political dependence on the British Empire and in the overcoming of Afghanistan's medieval backwardness.

The Young Afghan Movement was headed by Mahmud-bek Tarzi. In 1911, he founded the newspaper *Seraj-ul-Akhbar*. This became the Young Afghan's-mouthpiece, an organ through which their ideals reached the public.

In the beginning, the Young Afghans were mostly concerned with enlightenment. Education, development of culture, national unity, and struggle against religious fanaticism were their main instruments.

As the anti-imperialist movement in the Eastern countries grew, the Young Afghans used *Seraj-ul-Akhbar* to denounce the colonial policies of British imperialism and openly called upon the people to struggle for the country's independence which in their view was inseparable from the struggle against backwardness.

The political opponents of the Young Afghans were the Old Afghans led by the highest officials with Nasrullah Khan the Amir's brother, at their head. The Old Afghans ideologists were the upper crust of the hardline clergy who insisted on the need to preserve the outdated feudal order, customs and religious traditions. The Old Afghans were also against foreign domination. They had their own ambitions and perspective. They needed national independence to completely isolate the country from the outside world and to go back to their old ways and customs. This explains their hatred of everything new and progressive, which, in their view, came from "the infidels", that is from the modern outlook.

Both these groups were in opposition to the administration for its pro-British policies. The circle that supported the Amir's policies, mostly Afghan merchants engaged in foreign trade, who were supporters of Ali Ahman Khan, the Minister for Internal Affairs, did not have any mass base. This ferment in Afghanistan was a component of world-wide upsurge.

In 1917, the situation in the country became critical. Excessive taxes and levies, frequent recruitment of soldiers and the tyranny of the authorities gave rise to discontent among the peasant masses. The actual power was concentrated in the hands of the Amir's favourite, Husein Mohammad, the Minister of Finance and a representative of the foreign-oriented merchants. He wanted to consolidate the British position. The policies of Amir Habibullah, who received large grants from Great Britain, provoked indignation among the Afghan people.

The victory of the socialist revolution in Russia and the formation of the Soviet state had its own impact on the politics of the country.

By 1919, the Afghan people's discontent at Amir Habibullah's foreign policies was stronger than ever. His inability and unwillingness to keep pace with the times created a hostile atmosphere for him.

In February, 1919 he was assassinated The Young Afghans, headed by Amir Ammanullah, came into power.

The new Amir's first major political act was an attempt to attain the country's independence by peaceful means. On March 3, 1919 he communicated to the Viceroy of India his proposals for annulling existing unfair treaties. The British authorities rejected these proposals. Armed struggle was the only way out now.

On May 3, 1919, hostilities on Afghan-India border began. The Afghan army, which was weak both in number and arms and ammunition offered stubborn resistance to the British colonialists' troops who were much stronger. The defeat of the British intervention in the trans-Caspian region, anti-British tribal uprisings all along the north-west border, and finally widespread social unrest in India, forced Great Britain to seek peace with Afghanistan. On August 8,

1919 a preliminary peace treaty with Afghanistan, which recognised Afghanistan's complete political independence was signed at Rawalpindi. This is how this war between Great Britain and Afghanistan ended the long years of British "wardship". This created objective conditions for the independent development of Afghanistan.

The new regime set before itself the task of political and economic transformation of the country. The most essential part of the political transformation was the framing and enactment of the 1923 Constitution, which affirmed the country's political independence, vested supreme power in the Amir, and proclaimed certain civil liberties.

The most important part of the reforms were the economic ones, especially tax reforms. In 1920, a law on land taxes was passed stipulating that taxes would have to be paid in money, not in kind, which helped the development of commodity-monetary relations in agriculture. In 1923, a law on animal husbandry taxation, also to be paid in monetary form was passed. This unified the taxes paid by most cattle and sheep breeders of the country. The law abolished the existing additional taxes for using roads, pastures, etc., and compulsory deliveries of goods. In 1924, the statute on the selling of estates was promulgated, which gave legal form to private ownership of land. It offered wide opportunities for land speculation and rapid growth of landowners' estates. Almost all the land was sold to major landowners, merchants, usurers, and officials.

In 1923, the law on the resettlement of the Kattaghan province was passed. That was an attempt to solve the land problem in the principal Pushtoon provinces. However, measures for resettling the nomads from the south of the country to the north proved ineffctive.The nomads always opposed any interference of the central authorities in their lives, and the necessary conditions for resettling large masses of people to the northern provinces had not been created.

Endeavouring to weaken the influence of the clergy, the Young Afghans in the first years of their administration confiscated and auctioned the *waqf* lands. However, that was not particularly successful, as most of the lands reverted to their old owners after the sales.

The Young Afghans' economic programme also included a

customs reform. The government eliminated numerous internal customs boundaries and introduced a unified five per cent tax on all commodities in all provinces. It raised considerably the taxes on many imports as well.

In 1923, a law was passed to encourage industrial development. However, attempts at stimulating industrial construction were unsuccessful, as the state had insufficient capital, while businessmen were unwilling to invest in industrial enterprises, preferring guaranteed profits from commercial operations.

The social reforms included the secularisation of education, extension of the school network, etc.

All these reforms did not have mass support. The policy of reforms stirred up acute discontent among those social groups who were in favour of preserving the old, feudal order. The peasants, who gained nothing from the reforms became the social force on which those opposing the reforms—the highest circles of the clergy, major feudal lords, and the Khans—could rely.

In the spring of 1924, an anti-government uprising began among the tribes of Ghilzai, Mangals and Jadans near Ghilzai Khost in the Southern Province, headed by the local mullahs Abdullah Lang and Abdurrashid. The rebels communicated to Kabul their demands for cutting down taxes, the return to free trade with India, and the abolition of new laws and certain reforms which they claimed was against Islam.

The British imperialism used the rebellion at Khost to weaken the new Afghan regime. They immediately gave their support to the rebels and even guided the anti-government movement through mullahs and chiefs of tribes. In August 1924, Abdul Kerim, a son of the former Amir Yakub, who had lived in India, appeared in Khost. Sent by the British to overthrow Amanullah, Abdul Kerim tried to lead the rebellion.

Unable to put down the uprising by force of arms, the government had to make a compromise. At the Loya Jirga of July 1924, a third of which consisted of the clergy, the Young Afghans had to give up a considerable number of reforms.

Late in 1927 and in the first half of 1928 King Amanullah went on a tour of several European and Asian countries. The Afghan government endeavoured to use this tour to improve the country's economic situation. Internal resources were insufficient to carry out the programme of reforms.

Throughout his foreign tour Amanullah set before himself on these two objectives. In India he openly appealled to the people that Hindus and Muslims should unite for their national independence. In Egypt too he underlined that he wanted to build an independent Afghanistan. Both in India and Egypt he was greeted by nationalist forces.

On the other hand in Italy, France and Germany he tried to explore the possibility of these countries participating in the economic development of Afghanistan. In Italy he conducted negotiations for purchase of arms and Fiat cars. In France too he evinced keen interest to purchase arms for the Afghan army. In Germany the King signed an agreement for construction and expansion of railways in Afghanistan. He also negotiated for purchase of aeroplanes. These were clear indications that he wanted to consolidate the independence of his country.

In May 1928, Amanullah arrived in Moscow. He was warmly welcomed by Soviet leaders and spent two weeks in the USSR for studying Soviet economic and cultural achievements. His negotiations with Soviet leaders covered the problems of extending economic and cultural cooperation.

Next Amanullah visited Turkey and Iran, where he signed treaties of "friendship and political unity", which according to the Iranian newspaper *Shefag-e-Sorh*, would play a great role in improving the internal and external political position of the three states with common interests.

On the whole, Amanullah's mission proved to be very fruitful. Afghanistan's prestige on the international scene had grown. The Young Afghan government re-affirmed its resolution to adhere to an independent foreign policy.

The King's foreign tour was an important element of the Young Afghans' reforms; as they understood, unless they consolidated their status on the international scene they would not be able to create a serious basis for further reforms in economic and cultural spheres. Besides, after his visit abroad Amanullah became convinced that the reforms of the first stage were not effective enough, and that new radical reforms were needed, particularly in the social sphere.

At the Loya Jirga, which was assembled on August 28, 1928, the King made a report on his tour and proposed new reforms.

Again just as in 1919-23 the principal target of the draft laws submitted to the Jirga were the feudal institutions which were an obstacle to the country's development. The major feudal lords and tribal aristocracy who formed the basis of the old feudal regime were deprived of a number of privileges.

The government also tried to weaken the political influence of reactionary clerics, who were most dangerous opponents of reform. Taking into account the ignorance of the lower classes, the Mullahs accused Amanullah and his supporters of violation of Muslim traditions.

Let us illustrate this point by one example. The attempt to change laws about marriage and the family caused acute debate. The King proposed that marriage licences should be given to boys not younger than twenty-two and girls not younger than eighteen years. This proposal met with some opposition and was rejected. Anticipating a similar reaction of the Jirga to other innovations, Amanullah and his supporters decided to relegate these questions to the sittings of Durbars—semiofficial pro-government organs. They hoped that the participation of high officials, landowners, and merchants in the Durbars would guarantee their support.

Early in October, 1928, several reform projects were put before the Durbars; on the introduction of co-education of children up to the age of eleven, on sending young Afghans, girls included, abroad for further schooling and on banning polygamy. The Durbars voted in favour of these reforms, but without much enthusiasm.

The country's economic development featured prominently among the problems on the Jirga's agenda. Amanullah informed the Jirga about the concessions he had granted to Western firms. The King emphasised the undesirability of foreign loans which he viewed as a potential threat to the country's independence. In an effort to strengthen the role of the state in regulating commercial activities, the King proposed to open a state bank. However, this project was not carried out because of the rebellion that soon broke out and opposition from private capital.

These were the principal reforms which were outlined by the government after the King's return from his foreign tour and offered for the consideration of the Jirga and the Durbars. In all, 64 reforms were proposed by Amanullah during his reign.

It has to be admitted that in the midst of these reforms two factors influenced the mood of the people. Firstly, corruption at high places and secondly, rapidly growing poverty among the masses.

Soon after, some Jirga members, particularly representatives of the Eastern province, began a vigorous compaign against the reforms. Two prominent clerics, Shur Bazar Mojaddadi and Kazi Abdurrahman, who left Kabul while the Jirga was still in session, tried to start a rebellion in the Southern province. However, the government managed to ward off hostilities by arresting both these clerics and putting them on trial. Immediately afterwards, conspiracies against the government were uncovered among the clerics of Kabul, Kuhistan, and Khost. Some of the close supporters of reforms deserted Amanullah. The situation began to change.

As Amanullah became more and more inclined to radical socio-political reforms, opposition to his policies grew. The King made frantic efforts to put together a political basis for conducting reforms. With this aim in view, an attempt was made in 1928 to found the Young Afghans' political organisation—the "Istiklal was Tajaddod" (Independence and Renovation) party, but this step met with little success. The old guard of the Young Afghans, were afraid of the King's radicalism and held more moderate views.

The support to these reforms was half-hearted because these measures were against the interest of the ruling elite. This was the main weakness of the reforms.

Subsequent developments have shown that a feudal and tribal society cannot be changed from above. The developments during the last two decades, including after the Saur Revolution have once again confirmed this conclusion. That is why various Afghan revolutions could not defeat outside interventions.

However, Amanullah's economic policy objectively speeded up the primitive accumulation of capital and contributed to the growth of the economic influence of landowners closely linked with the market and of merchants and usurers. It would appear that the classes vitally interested in the reforms would be bound to support the reformist regime. However, due to certain causes, that was not to be. This has again happened during the recent years.

What has to be clearly understood is that in a tribal and fudeal society, which has remained isolated from the world, you cannot transform the society without the support of the masses. This has been and continues to be the main weakness of the Afghan society. There was something more to it.

Things were more complicated in the case of merchants and usurers. Amanullah's government, striving to strengthen the financial position of the native merchants and weaken that of foreign capital, encouraged the setting up of joint stock companies by Afghan merchants. But the latter were not particularly eager to join these companies, as the "*shoukars*" policy signified the state's tendency to control commercial activities. The state also did not guarantee the immunity of private capital. The merchants were afraid with good reason that their independence would be restricted. In addition, the government rejected the merchants, request for a private bank, having a vested interest in a state one. Nor was the administration's economic policy supported by petty merchants and traders as they were afraid of the competition of monopolistic commercial unions in domestic and foreign trade.

The feudal chiefs of tribes suffered most from the reforms. The tribal Khans, who had earlier been the only representatives of the Amir's power in the provinces and thus handled all tax-collecting themselves, came under the control of governmental officials during the Young Afghans' administration and lost both their economic and political positions. Besides, Amanullah's government imposed taxes on some tribes that had previously been exempt from taxation or had enjoyed certain privileges.

The reforms also dealt a blow to the political influence of the clergy. Confiscation of *waqf* lands, the setting up of secular courts and adoption of new laws on legal procedure, the secularisation of education, declaration of religious equality, reforms touching on everyday life, and finally, the re-examination of the Mullahs' qualifications—all these measures of economic, social and political naturegave rise to acute discontent among clerical circles who formed, together with the feudal lords, the nucleus of opposition.

There is yet another aspect. The producing part of the population—the peasantry, the poorest cattle breeders and handicraftsmen—the Young Afghans' policies on the whole resulted in a deterioration of their economic position, although objectively the reforms weakened the feudal oppression, the abolition of a number of supertaxes, requisitions, and compulsory levies, liquidation of slavery, declaration of religious equality, etc. According to some scholars up to 45 per cent of the value of crops had been exacted from the peasants in taxes.

To pay taxes in money and not in kind, peasants had to resort to usurers and thus fell into their clutches. This accelerated the process of expropriation of peasant's lands, particularly in areas where the national minorities lived. The law concerning the sale of the state's land was actually implemented in the interests of the propertied classes, as the majority of the peasants were unable to buy land.

As a result, the Young Afghans' administration was completely isolated socially. Moreover, the Young Afghans' neglect for the vital interests of the people was responsible for a wave of peasant unrest that was used by the reactionary for its own purposes.

The Khost uprising had a shattering effect on the flimsy structure of a state undergoing reforms. The unrest in the country continued, but now it spread over the Pushtoon regions and became multinational in character. In 1925-27, a series of peasant actions shook the country with varying force. They were all directed against the administration's tax policy, abuse of power, and oppression. Brigandage and robbery became widespread. Armed groups of brigands were active in various parts of the country. This was an objective reflection of the peasants' protest, brought to the point of desperation by their local administration's extortions.

In 1926, a Tajik peasant Bacha-i Sako (water-carrier's son) became the leader of one of these bands. Bacha-i Sako's activities were confined to the area north of Kabul, where he committed acts of brigandage and killed the most hated officials. He gave part of his spoils to the peasants. Bachai-i Sako's popularity among local peasants grew. By the end of 1928, Bacha-i Sako's band began attacks on local authorities.

It was not only the Kabul province that was in a state of unrest and discontent. The same kind of armed bands appeared in other regions of the country as well.

At the end of November, 1928 a small unit under Ahmad Ali Khan, Governor of Kabul, was sent to Kuhdaman to draft recruits and suppress unrest.

Sher Agha Mojaddadi, a prominent spiritual leader, waged an intense propaganda campaign against Amanullah among the frontier tribes on Indian territory, where he lived in exile.

In mid-October 1928, a tribal uprisings broke out in the Eastern Province. The uprising was caused by pagan reforms. The social reforms and cultural innovations were one of the reasons for the uprising. However, the real cause was that the poorest sections of the tribes of the Eastern Province rose against the Young Afghan government. By the end of November the uprising assumed grave proportions.

Under these complicated circumstances, Bachai-i Sakao became the head of all rebel forces north of Kabul. Late at night on December 12, 1928 he called a conference of his supporters in his native village of Kalakan, where he declared himself Afghanistan's Amir under the name of Habibullah Ghazi. Aware of Bacha-i Sako's popularity with the masses, reactionary feudal lords and Muslim clerics decided to support him in order to take the leadership of the uprising into their own hands.

The northern part of the Kabul province became the centre of anti-reformist movement. However, other regions of Afghanistan, particularly the provinces of Kattaghan, Balkh, Maimana, and Herat were also in a state of unrest and rebellion. This was followed by the drive to capture Kabul. Thus political and economic reforms receded to the background. The political elite was either indifferent for had a share in the plunder.

The general discontent had an effect on the mood of the army, which became particularly unreliable after the rise of anti-government movement among Pushtoon tribes and Tajik peasants, who were the backbone of the army. Many of the officers as well were against the Young Afghan reforms. As a result desertion from the army and defection to the rebels became quite common.

The reactionary clerics endeavoured to make use of the mass

movement to overthrow the Young Afghan regime. On December 19, the Mullahs and Ulema of the Northern Province issued a *fatva* (a decree by a Muslim religious Judge in accordance with the canons of Islam) criticising the programme of political, social and cultural reforms. They accused the King of atheism and declared him deposed. The Mullahs proposed Bacha-i Sako as the new Amir, expressing the hope that he would rule the country according to God's will. The Mullah's opposition to Amanullah's reforms was not a manifestation of blind bigotry. There were economic and political reasons behind it.

There is one more fact which needs to be recapitualted here. Not long before the Shinwari's uprising, the famous agent of the British secret service Colonel Lawrence appeared in the Indian north-western border area. There are certain grounds for the assumption that Lawrence was carrying out the strategic plan of the makers of British foreign policy, which was intended to channel the events in Afghanistan in a certain direction.

There are other facts which give the indications of British support to the revolt. Some historians believe that Bacha-i Sako already had been connected with the British secret service when he was in India. Thus in 1926 he met Perrot, head of the frontier police, in Peshawar.

On January 9, 1929 in a situation of increasing isolation the Afghan government issued a *firman* (a royal edict) announcing the repeal of many reforms. In particular, many social reforms were abolished, including extension of women's rights; Mullahs won back their right to teach without permission from the authorities; complicated universal military service was abolished. The Senate was instituted, which was to represent the most famous Ulema, Sardars, Khans, and some other officials.

This recapitulation of historical facts about various efforts to build Afghanistan as a modern nation state and how internal and external vested interests scuttled these limited efforts speaks for itself. It needs no commands.

However, this survey has been made to bring out how in the nearly past three decades of the present century, the common people of Afghanistan are still suffering and blood is being shed to hold them back to take their destiny in their own hands.

Whatever may have been acts of omission and commission of various leaders who took over power after the Saur Revolution, one thing is certain that their energies were directed to modernise their country and build it into a modern nation state. Internally, this tribal-ridden and feudal society was confronted with landlords, tribal chiefs, religious leaders and externally, certain powers were striving through various instruments to dominate the country. The Afghanistan crisis is an extraordinary mix of internal and external factors. The geographical location of this country, which is on the crossroads of Asia has further compounded its problems.

The tragic history of Afghanistan to introduce some reforms during the last 6-7 decades, in itself is a telling indictment of those who claim to be defenders and builders of democracy and human rights. Perhaps posterity will pass its judgement and not in a too distant future the people of Afghanistan and their children will carve out a place for themselves in the world community.

4

THE TALIBAN TAKEOVER IN AFGHANISTAN

KALIM BAHADUR

The emergence of the Islamic movement 'Taliban' (students of religion) in Afghanistan in 1994 and later their takeover of two-thirds of the country within a short span of time has changed the entire scenario of the region. About 25,000 people were killed and much of Kabul was destroyed by the Taliban. Ever since the withdrawal of the Soviet forces and later the fall of Najibullah regime the various Mujahideen factions had carried on an endless bloody internecine war. Most of these groups were almost evenly matched and there appeared no likelihood of any one of them decisively defeating the others. All attempts by Pakistan, which had played host to these Mujahideen factions during the years of Soviet intervention, to bring about an agreement on the formation of a consensus regime in Kabul had been foiled by the ego of one or the other leader. It was in this background that there appeared, as if from nowhere, a powerful, well organised and well armed forced which defeated every warlord one after the other and later captured Kabul in an almost peaceful coup d'etat in September 1996.

Various interpretations have been given by observers of the Afghan scene for the genesis of the Taliban. One description of their origin traces their roots to the uprising in Kandahar by a group of young men, formerly students of religious schools set up by the Jamiat-ul Ulema-i-Islam led by Maulana Fazlur Rahman for Afghan refugees in various parts of the North-West Frontier Province in Pakistan. The students drove away the local Mujahideen boss and established a 'pure Islamic rule' led by one Mulla Umar. He was a veteran of the fighting against the Soviet army. Later the Pakistani intelligence agency the Inter Services Intelligence (ISI) took over their organisation. Pakistani army personnel were inducted to train young men, supplied with sophisticated weapons and even commanded by Pakistani officers. This was how Taliban came on the scene.

The other interpretation rejects the spontaneous origins of the Taliban. The ISI mobilised the students from the Madarsa of the schools, trained and armed them and inducted them into Afghanistan. The military skills of the Taliban, their training in the use of sophisticated weapons and their fighting tactics rule out spontaneous emergence of the force and points to greater contribution by the ISI to Taliban's strength and victories.

There cannot be much controversy about the political-strategic objectives of the Taliban-Pakistan coordination. The first and the foremost is the setting up of a pro-Pakistan regime in Kabul. Successive Pakistani regimes earlier had put their stakes on Gulbuddin Hikmatyar, Rasul Sayyaf and Rabbani. But each of these had his own ambitions and showed no inclination to subserve Pakistani interests. Under President Rabbani Afghan-Pak relations had been continually deteriorating with Rabbani vociferously protesting against Pakistani interference in Afghanistan's internal affairs. He had become a major hurdle in the way of Pakistan's strategic goals in Afghanistan. Another strategic objective in Pakistan's creation of the Talibans was to provide Pakistan free access to Central Asian States. Pakistan also shared this objective with the United States. The vast markets of the Central Asian states and their strategic importance was of great significance to Washington. The only easy route to this region was through Afghanistan. The northern route via the Black Sea was long and dependent on the uncertain political climate of Russia and the other access through Iran was ruled out given the hostility of the U.S. with Tehran. Some Pakistani analysts have ascribed Pakistani desire to have control over Afghanistan to give strategic depth to Pakistani defence. Taliban control over Afghanistan has caused anxiety in

Iran as its eastern flank has now gone under hostile control. This explains the U.S. indulgence for all religious and human rights' excesses of the Talibans and Iranian unease at their appearance in the neighbourhood.

What has caused widespread consternation about the Taliban takeover of Kabul was the so-called rigid Islamic Code that is being forced upon the people in their occupied part of the country. In the name of implementing the Shariat the Taliban closed down girl's schools, colleges and other institutions, prohibited women from doing jobs, and forced them to observe *purdah* (maintaining a veil) and any violation of these Codes has been harshly punished. The male citizens have been compelled to grow beards and are driven to mosques to offer prayers at the point of the gun. These coercive measures have been denounced throughout the world as violations of human rights. The Ulema have condemned these measures as contrary to Islam. What has caused concern has been the soft-pedalling of these excesses by the United States and also by Pakistani official circles which points to their links with these diehard elements.

These developments could be understood better in the context of the history of Afghanistan. The Afghan State is of recent origin. It came into existence in 1747 in a *Jirga* evolving out of a confederation of tribes which grew into a monarchy with the accession to the throne by Ahmed Shah Abdali. The State, however, remained on the periphery of an Afghan's daily existence which has been free from its intrusion. Afghan tribals never had any concept of a nation with a definite territory. It was the British and the Russians during the nineteenth century which gave it a boundary through imposing various treaties on the Afghan monarchs, viz.. Gandamak, Durand Line, treaties of 1885, 1895, etc. Ordinary Afghans identified Afghanistan's territory with what was ruled by their king.

Islam in Afghanistan has existed at three levels. The legalist Islam of the Ulema which meant the *Quran*, *the Hadis*, the texts provided by the various schools of throught during the centuries since the advent of Islam. Another level of Islam is that of the Mulla who is not much educated, knows only few prayers to suit births, deaths and other occasions of the daily life of a citizen. The third level of Islam is that of intellectuals. This Islam came to

Afghanistan through the writings of the fundamentalists, the modernists and the liberal intellectuals of the Muslim world. It is no wonder that many Mujahideen leaders were deeply influenced by the interpretations of the Jamaat-i-Islami of Pakistan and the Muslim brethren of Egypt and elsewhere. Ulema have always enjoyed high prestige in Afghan society. Monarchs have generally sought Ulema's support to legitimise their rule and the latter have sought privileges and status from those in power. As against this, a Mulla stands in a very low position in the village hierarchy. His low economic status but his commitment to Islam mixed with the tribal traditions of the tribe he belongs to make his vision narrow and his conduct harsh. The Taliban represent the world view of the Mulla.

There are three categories of norms in Afghan society. First has been the *Shariat*; second, traditional laws and third, the tribal laws. The force of tradition has always held sway over the other two norms. When there is conflict between *Shariat* and traditional law the latter usually takes precedence.

It is in the background that the Taliban phenomenon has to be analysed. Taliban Islam is not the Islam of the Shariat or of the intellectuals but of the Mulla who is mixing Islam with the worst of the tribal traditions. The Pakistani decision to chose the Talibans was motivated by the following factors. The Mujahid leaders were mostly followers of fundamentalist Islam and were divided on account of personality clashes, sub-tribal prejudices and foreign linkages. They could not be united to set up a stable regime in Kabul. Their foreign links would prevent them from following Pakistani dictats. Therefore, Pakistani agencies chose from among the religious circles most amenable to their interests. The Taliban being lower middle class had no international connections. They were not well-educated and therefore would be under the firm control of the ISI. There are no big names among them and no personal ego clashes. They are nameless and faceless entities. They are all Pakhtuns and Sunnis. The Taliban phenomenon could be compared to Bacha saga of the late twenties. He rose from an ordinary background as a leader of peasant revolt and took up the banner of Islam against King Amanullah's radical reforms. Once he had captured Kabul he also rigidly applied Islam against women's education and their jobs, and forced them to observe *purdah*, etc.

He also forced prayers and beards. Once he declared himself as Amir he was overthrown and later hanged by the new King Nadir Khan.

The contribution of Pakistani agencies in planning the Taliban project in Afghanistan has been well documented. There have been reports about the conflicts of interest among various Pakistani institutions in the formation of the Talibans. The genius of the former home minister in Benazir Bhutto's government Maj. Gen. (Retd.) Nasirullah Babar has also been given credit for conceiving the Taliban campaign. No great wisdom was needed to realise that given the tribal equations only a Pushtoon force could mobilise a powerful militant group to overcome the non-Pushtoon factions. Such a force would belong to Sunni sect which is the majority sect in the country. The young men who would comprise this force initially came from the Madarsas set up by the Jamiat-ul Ulema-i-Islam led by Maulana Fazlur Rahman. His father, the late Mufti Mahmood had been the Chief Minister of the NWFP in the early seventies. The late Mufti's popularity could be gauged from the fact that in 1970 the late Zulfikar Ali Bhutto who had contested five seats for the National Assembly's general election won four of them. He had lost the one seat against Mufti Mahmood. Both the late Mufti and his son Maulana Fazlur Rahman had wide contacts in Saudi Arabia and other Gulf countries and their organisation was aflush with funds. However, the Pakistani agencies which organised the Talibans had given them only minimal military training. The local people in Afghanistan who joined up with the Talibans and those who came from Pakistan did not make up a very well organised fighting force. During the three years of their exist Taliban had fought no sustained battles. Their major tractics had been to buy up opposite commanders and thus weaken the enemy before the final assault. Wherever they had to fight a major battle they did very poorly. This explains their long siege of Kabul lasting about a year. They moved into Kabul only when they were assured that President Rabbani and Ahmed Shah Masood's forces had withdrawn from the capital.

Once the Talibans had captured Kabul they had some legitimacy to claim to rule entire Afghanistan. Traditionally anyone who captured Kabul had been accepted as the ruler of Afghanistan though no ruler could ever claim unchallenged control of the entire country. After the fall of Kabul to Taliban Pakistan made relentless efforts on behalf of Taliban on the one hand to bring about some agreement between Kabul and Dostam who still controlled Mazar Sharif and Rabbani and Masood who controlled the Panjsher Valley and on the other hand to gain international acceptance for Taliban including their representation in the United Nations.

The Pakistani mediatory efforts to persuade recalcitrant Dostam and Masood to yield failed because neither the Taliban were ready to make any concessions for their opponents nor the others were ready to accept Taliban as the rulers of Afghanistan. Taliban succeeded in toppling Dostam and taking over Mazar Sharif albeit for a few days by their familiar method of purchasing Gen. Rasul Malik and his brother Gen. Abdul Malik. It was reported that 200 million US dollars had been paid to them for toppling Dostam. However, it was mainly because of the rigid policies of Talibans of imposing their religious ideas on the population under their control which led to the uprising against them in Mazar Sharif. The Uzbek militia and the Hizb Wahdat of Karim Khalili inflicted a devastating blow on the Talibans. It was the first time since their emergence that Taliban had suffered such a shattering defeat and humiliation. Very soon both Abdullah Malik and Ahmed Shah Masood had driven the Talibans to the outskirts of Kabul.

The defeat of the Talibans in Mazar Sharif marked a turning-point in their fortunes. It also marked an abject failure of Pakistan's policy in Afghanistan. Once the Taliban marched into Mazar Sharif Pakistan believed that the Taliban now had won the last battle and their control over entire Afghanistan was complete. Pakistan recognised Taliban government and attempted to persuade others to follow suit. Within a few days the Taliban were in disorderly retreat. Pakistan's recognition of Taliban regime prematurely killed whatever credibility it had to act as a go-between the various Afghan factions. Pakistan's claim of neutrality in the Afghan imbroglio was exposed.

Talibans have aroused worldwide disapproval for their social and political policies which they have sought to impose on areas they have captured. Recently they have shown some moderation in these policies. How far this softening up is or just only to mollify international opinion or is just a ploy to gain international recognition is yet to be seen. They know it very well that they will have to live in a world which is economically, socially and politically interdependent and they cannot defy world opinion for long.

The complexity of Afghan society is such that Taliban even if backed by Islamic ideology will not be able to integrate the diverse people and mobilise them behind their regime. The people of Afghanistan cannot be insulated from the information revolution that is reaching the darkest corners of the most backward sections of the world. The younger generation of the Afghan society will eventually come in conflict with the conservative tribal Islamic ideology of the Taliban. They have also strong Pushtoon dominant nation prejudice in their dealings with the smaller ethnic communities of the country. This signals that even if the Taliban gain control of the entire country there is little likelihood of the end of ethnic and sectarian bloodshed and conflicts in the country.

There is already evidence that the Taliban ideology is spreading into the neighbouring Muslim countries. Pakistan has paid a heavy price for the Afghanistan policy of Gen. Zia-ul-Haq which the Pakistani establishment has continued since then. The spread of drugs, Kalashnikov culture and sectarian strife have been tearing the country apart. Though the Taliban political culture is yet to have its full impact on Pakistan, political circles in Pakistan are already giving warning signals about the dangers of Taliban ideology spreading into Pakistan.

Given the history, social and political traditions of Afghanistan the Talibans cannot remain for long a cohesive force. Already there have been uprisings in the Taliban ruled territories. Any attempt by the Taliban to centralise and expand state control from Kabul in the name of Islam will lead to resistance and disintegration of the force, in spite of the Pakistani backing. Talibans failure to solve the economic problems of the people is likely to lead to local revolts and weaken their hold. In any event Taliban will be one more ephemeral event in the troubled history of Afghanistan.

5

THE RUSSIAN AND CENTRAL ASIAN RESPONSE TO TALIBAN TAKEOVER OF KABUL

DEVENDRA KAUSHIK

The seizure of Kabul in late September, 1996 by the Taliban forces met with a prompt response from Russia. The Russian Ministry of Foreign Affairs in its statement circulated through the RIA-Novosti on 27 September, 1996 expressed concern over enlargement of the scope and intensiveness of the armed confrontation in Afghanistan. It described the Taliban takeover of Kabul as a threat to international peace and referred to its destabilising effect on the situation in the region. The Russian Foreign Ministry's statement laid emphasis on ceasefire by the warring groups and ruling out any interference from outside in the internal affairs of Afghanistan, called upon the world community "to intensify its peace efforts, making utmost use of the UN deplomacy." Moscow urged the United Nations to turn its peace initiative to the Afghan conflict and reaffirmed its support to the efforts of the UN Security Council and the General Assembly towards helping the Afghan sides in reaching a peaceful settlement of the conflict.

On 30 September, 1996 the Speaker of the State Duma, Gennady Seleznyov, expressed shock at the execution of the former Afghan President Najibullah and his brother without any charge or trial. The same day the Press Secretary of the President of Tajikistan, Emamali Rekhmanov, in a statement issued on behalf of the Tajik President condemned the escalation of hostilities in Afghanistan by the seizure of Kabul by the Taliban forces which in the opinion of the Tajik President was fraught with the danger of an immediate negative effect on the Tajik-Afghan border. The Tajik leadership called upon resolution of the conflict through peaceful means and confirmed its readiness to participate in a conference on a peaceful Afghanistan. The Kazakhstan Foreign Ministry in a statement issued in Alma-Ata expressed concern over the situation in Afghanistan which according to it might lead to "disintegration of the country and the destabilisation of the situation in the region." Kazakhstan called for an immediate meeting of the UN Security Council to work out urgent measures to end the bloodshed and render assistance to civilians and refugees.

Not only the Foreign Affairs Ministry of Russia but the Defence Ministry also strongly reacted to what it perceived as a "threat to Russian national security as well as to that of other CIS nations" in the light of the situation obtaining in Afghanistan. The Defence Ministry's Analytical Department Chief told the RIA on 2 October, 1996 that the Taliban were quite likely to choose the south of the CIS to materialise the long-standing dream of the Islamic fundamentalists of "conquering the unfaithful." He informed the press of the Russian President's proposal on an urgent meeting of the CIS leaders to discuss the situation and also referred to the National Security Council Secretary Alexander Lebed's support for rendering financial aid material aid to the forces fighting the Taliban. The Defence Ministry analyst called for stopping the Taliban from crossing the Salang Pass. In Dushanbe the Commander of the United Peace-Making Forces of the CIS states briefed the press on 2 October, 1996 about the formation of the second line manned by his forces in addition to the 201 motorised infantry division of Russian Army guarding the Tajik-Afghan border.

Thus in contrast with the vacillating and delayed Russian response to the fundamentalist Islamic threat in Tajikistan in the autumn of 1992, the Russian response to the threat posed by Islamic fundamentalist forces represented by the Talibans in Afghanistan in 1996 was quite prompt and forthright. In 1992 the Russian Foreign

Ministry was headed by the pro-Atlanticist Foreign Minister Andrei Kozyrev who had to be bluntly reminded about the Russian national interests by Tajik leader of the Popular Front, Sangaka Safarov. A reluctant Kozyrev was presented with a *fait accompli* by the Russian Army stationed in Tajikistan which taking advantage of the long distance from the centre acted on its own in an extremely turbulent situation in 1992 to save the civilian population including the Russian minority from being massacred by the Islamic extremists. The Foreign Ministry of Russia in 1996 under the stewardship of Yevgeny Primakov was more responsive to national interests of Russia. Thanks to the increasing Eurasian tilt in public opinion as manifested in the significant gains of the left-patriotic opposition in the 1995 Parliamentary elections and the high percentage of votes (42 per cent) polled by its candidate in the Presidential elections in 1996, it was difficult to openly ignore a serious threat to the country's territorial integrity and the strategic and geo-political interests of Russia in the neighbouring Central Asian republics. These republics with the sole exception of Turkmenistan are bound with Moscow through the Treaty on Collective Security signed on 15 May, 1992. The responsibility for guarding the international borders of Tajikistan as also of neutral Turkmenistan rests with Russia in accordance with the terms of multilateral and bilateral treaties between the countries concerned.

Russia took initiative to convene a meeting of the leaders of the Republics of Kazakhstan, Kyrgyzstan, Tajikistan and Uzbekistan and of the Russian Federation on 4 October, 1996 in Alma-Ata. The joint statement issued after the meeting expressed serious concern over the escalation of the armed conflict in Afghanistan. Noting that the "flame of the war is moving closer to the borders of the member countries of the CIS" which poses a "direct threat to the national interests and security of these states and the commonwealth as a whole" and "destabilises regional and international situation." The leaders of Russia and the four Central Asian republics declared that "any activity destroying stability on the borders of Afghanistan with the CIS countries is unacceptable." The Alam-Ata Joint Statement warned that such activities would be regarded a threat to their common interests and treated on the basis of Article 4 of the treaty on Collective Security signed in Tashkent on 15 May, 1992 and would receive an adequate response from the participants of the Alma-Ata summit. The CIS leaders in Alma-Ata laid emphasis on non-interference in internal affairs of Afghanistan from outside as also on the territorial integrity of that country. They proposed a special meeting of the UN Security Council with a view to ending the military activities and achieving comprehensive political settlement of the Afghan conflict and also for providing assistance to civilians and refugees.

Besides taking initiative to coordinate with Russia the response of the Central Asian republics to the Taliban's northward advance, Moscow was reported to have sent covert assistance to Masood's forces fighting against the Taliban. An alliance among the Uzbek General Abdul Rashid Dostum, Tajik leader Ahmed Shah Masood and the Shiite leader Karim Khalili was also forged with the active diplomatic assistance of Russia. The *Guardian* (London) reported that the Russian Vice-Consul in Mazar-i-Sharif (the headquarters of General Dostum) was present at a meeting between the anti-Taliban Afghan leaders. According to a report published in *Asia Times* at a meeting held in Moscow during the first week of October, 1996 among the then Defence Minister Igor Rodionov, Chief of Foreign Intelligence, General Vyacheslav Trubnikov, Chief of General Staff Gen. Mikhail Kolesnikov and some senior representatives from the Security Council of Russia it was agreed to send covert supply to Masood's forces. High-ranking officials of the Defence and Security ministeries are believed to be convinced that the American action in supporting Taliban through Pakistan is aimed at squeezing out Russia both politically and commercially from Central Asia which is considered to be their natural sphere of influence. Incidentally, it is also aimed at excluding India from developing relations with Central Asia by making that region dependent upon Pakistan for access to the Indian Ocean port of Karachi through roads and pipelines laid across Afghanistan controlled by the Taliban. The Russian objective behind supporting the anti-Taliban Northern Alliance is to draw a line against the northward extension of Taliban influence which threatens Central Asia regarded as its soft underbelly by Moscow. The American gameplan in Central Asia was revealed by Zbigniew Brzezinski on 21 October, 1996 while inaugurating the Central Asian Institute at John Hopkins University. Brzezinski stated that the creation of the Institute was an acknowledgement of the new strategic importance of Central Asia where all efforts should be directed to stop the Russian influence from growing.

The military situation in Afghanistan which for a short while seemed to be in favour of the Taliban in the wake of Dostum's flight from Mazar-i-Sharif following the revolt of his deputy, General Malik, changed with the sudden somersault of the latter in May 1997. With about ten thousand of Taliban fighters including a hundred of their best commanders and several hundred Pakistani soldiers killed or taken prisoner in Mazar-i-Sharif and with Masood's troops now just 20 kilometres from Kabul, Pakistan launched an intensive campaign for a peace accord to bail out its protege-the Taliban. Pakistan's proposal for a conference in Islamabad has been rejected by the leaders of the three Central Asian states—Kazakhstan, Uzbekistan and Kyrgyzstan. At the 10th Inter-State Council Session of the Central Asian Union held in Cholpon-Ata on 25 July, 1997 on the bank of lake Issyk-Kul in Kyrgyzstan, the three leaders warned the Afghan warring factions to give up a military solution of the issue and seek peaceful settlement by establishing a coalition government with extensive representation of all ethnic, religious and political forces currently fighting each other. They approved an initiative by President Askar Akayev for a UN-sponsored Afghan Peace Conference to be convened in Bishkek, the capital of Kyrgyzstan. President Akayev thanked Russia, China and the UN Secretary General for their support of this initiative. The Central Asian leaders also confirmed the status of the Central Asian Peacekeeping Battalion under the UN aegis. The battalion including the Kazakh, Kyrgyz and Uzbek units will be based in Kazakhstan.

For the conclusion of the peace accord in Afghanistan under the UN aegis it is necessary that the Taliban are made to realise the futility of their efforts to forcibly establish their domination over the entire Afghanistan. This can only be done by holding them at bay under the sustained pressure of the forces of Masood and Malik which are not averse to a UN-brokered peace settlement and which also represent the lawful government in Afghanistan headed by President Rabbani.

Closer cooperation among Russia, India and Iran is necessary to stall the game of using a Pakistan controlled Afghanistan for destabilising the newly independent states of Central Asia. It has to be clearly understood that there can be no stability in Central Asia if Afghanistan remains a stronghold of terrorism, drug export and Tajik opposition. The break-up of Afghanistan might become a source for destabilisation within and outside the region. There are about 4 million Tajiks in Afghanistan, 1.7 million Uzbeks and 0.5 million Turkmens. While there are 8-9 million Pushtoons in Afghanistan, some 13-14 million of them are settled in Pakistan. There are 170 thousand Baluchs in Afghanistan and 3.1 million in Pakistan and 1 million in Iran.

For the present the active Russian response to the Taliban threat to its "soft underbelly" in Central Asia has worked remarkably well. But the question is about the long-term prospects of its success given the continuous decline in Russia's military and economic power. Against the backdrop of President Yeltsin's health problems, an acute succession struggle is already on in Moscow. The key figures involved in this struggle have at times shown their total disregard for national state interests of Russia. The agreement on Chechnya is a case in point. A strong lobby has appeared in the Russian media which is trying to make out a case for total withdrawal of Russia from the Central Asian region.

A series of articles published in the *Nezavisimaya Gazeta* on the situation in Afghanistan, Tajikistan and the threat from Islamic fundamentalism particularly, by Alexander Umnov, a former senior faculty member of the Moscow Institute of World Economy and International Relations presently working for the Institute for Studies on Middle East and Israel, have strongly argued for a withdrawal of Russia from the borders of Tajikistan and Turkmenistan. Similar articles are also being published in military newspapers like Soldat *Rossii* (Soldier of Russia) an organ of the 201 Motorised Division guarding the frontier of Tajikistan with Afghanistan. The main thrust of Umnov's articles is that the extension of Russia's strategic frontiers to include the Central Asian republics represents the legacy of the Russian empire.

Even communist newspapers like *Pravda* have carried articles raising serious doubts about the present Russian military capability to cope with the threat by the Pakistan-backed Taliban. Thus in its issue of 19 June, 1997 *Pravda* published a long article "The Southern

Sector of Threats" by Anatoly Baranov. The Russian commentator expresses doubts about the capability of the forces of Masood to withhold the Taliban tide in a long drawn-out struggle because of the sparse population and other scant resources in the Punjshir valley—his main stronghold. The Talibans's success is, in his view, likely to result in a large exodus of population to neighbouring Central Asian republics throwing their fragile economy out of gear and creating new challenges to the present regimes largely dependent on support from a particular regional and clanish elite. The Russian military strength of some 25,000 men (20,000 Border Guards and 5,000 soldiers of the 201 Motorised Infantry Division) is not adequate enough to meet the sustained onslaught of a large Taliban force from the side of Afghanistan. According to Baranov two additional divisions of reserve Russian force are needed in Tajikistan to deal with the situation created by the Taliban threat which Russia is financially not in a position to raise. Tajik opposition is also believed to be in two minds viz-a-vis the Taliban. While the headquarters of Commander Masood, himself a Tajik, is in the zone controlled by Tajik opposition, the radicalism of the Taliban is attractive for a majority of the Tajik Islamic opposition. The Russian weekly *Moskovskie Novosti* of October 6-13, 1996 quoted the Tajik opposition leader Said Abdullo Nuri as favouring "neutrality with all the Afghan factions." Tajik opposition leader Davlat Usmon is reported to have met the Taliban leaders. At his press conference in Moscow on 28 June, 1997 following the signing of the inter-Tajik peace accord on 27 June, the Deputy Leader of Tajik Islamic opposition Akbor Turajonzoda, clarified that the "armed groups of the Tajik opposition staying in Afghanistan have not taken anybody's side in the conflict and maintain good relations with all." (*News From Russia*, Vol. VI, No. 27, July 4, 1997, pp. 18-19).

Russia may or may not be in a position to sustain militarily for long the extension of its strategic frontiers to Tajikistan, it has not panicked so far and shown any inclination to retreat. Moscow did not show any nervousness in May 1997 in the wake of deposition of General Dostum. A statement of the Russian leadership issued on 25 May, 1997 warned that "if CIS frontiers are violated the treaty on collective security of CIS members will be immediately brought into force." It also added that the "corresponding agencies are instructed accordingly." (*News From Russia*, Vol. VI, No. 22, 30 May, 1997, pp. 23-24). A high-ranking official at the Airborne Forces Headquarters told the RIA-Novosti on 4 June, 1997 that a week ago orders were issued to the commanders of airborne divisions to prepare a fully staffed detachment each for possible operations on the Tajik-Afghan border. About 4500 Russian airborne troops have been put on high alert and are prepared to fly to Tajikistan any moment to render support to the Russian frontier troops and units of the 201 Motorised Infantry Division deployed in that republic. (*News From Russia*, Vol. VI, No. 23, 6 June, 1997, pp. 20-21).

India needs to take an active interest in Russia and UN-backed Central Asian republics' initiative for a peace settlement in Afghanistan even though it was ill-advised to keep aloof from the inter-Tajik peace process. Transborder terrorism and proxy war financed by drug money, has already reached the Indian state of Jammu and Kashmir. Afghanistan is not only geographically the bridge to landlocked Central Asia but also the gateway to the South Asian subcontinent. What Frederick Engels wrote about Afghanistan for the American Encyclopaedia is quite relevant even today. He wrote: "Afghans are brave, energetic and freedom-loving people. Only their innate contempt for state power and love for personal freedom prevents them from becoming a powerful nation... . This spontaneity and inconsistency of conduct transforms them into dangerous neighbours given to overriding influence of momentary passions and vulnerable to outside political intrigues which easily fire their passions. Their character and isolation brought about by geographical situation has created in Afghanistan a platform for destabilisation of the region."

6

RUSSIAN PERCEPTION OF THE AFGHANISTAN CRISIS

O.N. MEHROTRA

Afghanistan has been an enigma for most of the countries who have chanced to deal with its internal affairs as well as made efforts to command its government's policy. Perhaps it is easier for a foreign country to involve in its state affairs than to control them or leave the country with desirable successes. Its internal political developments are generally unpredictable because it has been divided into various factions ruled by heterogeneous ethnic or tribal leaders in their respective regions. However, Afghanistan remains a strategically important country ever since the Great Game between the two world powers Britain and Russia in the nineteenth century.

Since Moscow has bitter memories of its military adventure in Afghanistan, therefore, it distastes an idea of direct intervention in Afghan affairs. But at the same time Moscow would always welcome a friendly government in Kabul. The Burhanuddin Rabbani regime was deposed by the Taliban at a time when Moscow could hardly establish linkage with Kabul to ease the situation at the Tajik-Afghan border. In the last week of August, 1996 Russia and Afghanistan signed a protocol according to which the Afghan side would create an exclusion zone of 140 km long and 25 km wide on its territory, into which Tajik opposition fighters would not be allowed. Incidentally the peacekeeping forces of CIS have been maintaining peace in Tajikistan as well as guarding its 1200-kilometre border with Afghanistan. There are approximately 25,000 peacekeeping forces drawn from Uzbekistan, Kazakhstan, Kyrgyzstan and Russia, including the 21st Motor Rifle Division of Russia, have been deployed in Tajikistan.

The capture of Kabul by the radical Islamic forces was a discomforting development for Moscow because the Russian leadership generally believes that "the spread of radical Islam from the Muslim states from the south was a threat to Russia."[1] Somehow Russia could contain the radical Islamic forces in Tajikistan but with the Taliban's seizure of Kabul, Tajikistan was believed to be again threatened by the Islamic fundamentalist forces. That would not only destabilise the secular regime of President Emonali Rakhmonov in Dushanbe but also strengthen the radical Islamic forces in other Central Asian countries as well as in some Russian republics Moscow apparently perceived. Russia was already engaged in controlling the bloody civil war in Chechnya where secessionist forces launched a war against Moscow. It may be noted that Moscow had already expressed its aversion to its involvement in another Chechnya type conflict in Russia or any former Soviet republic with whom it had signed multilateral or bilateral collective security agreements.

For Russia, its borders can be secured only by defending the CIS borders rather than the Russian one. In November, 1993 President Boris Yeltsin announced the Russian military doctrine which amply demonstrated Russian military's commitment to defend the "near abroad," referring to the former Soviet republics. In other words, Moscow made its defence policy sufficiently clear that it considers entire former Soviet Union as its area of security concern. It also made explicit that it would not allow other countries to interfere in any part of the former Soviet Union. The pronouncement of this policy by Russia is also called its own version of "Monroe Doctrine." Since then this policy has been reaffirmed by Russian leaders time and again.

Apparently Moscow never anticipated that the Talibans would depose the Rabbani regime without encountering much resistance in Kabul and summarily execute Afghanistan's former communist President Najibullah who was in safe custody of United Nations since his removal by the Mujahideen in 1992. While the former

Soviet President Mikhail Gorbachev immediately condemned the Taliban for brutally killing Najibullah, the Kremlin was restrained in issuing an immediate official statement on the violence in Kabul. No doubt it is not an unusual practice in international diplomacy to wait for stabilisation of situation in a country where the government was overthrown by unconstitutional or violent means. But the Russian leadership failed to react to the developments in Afghanistan because of lack of unanimity in the Kremlin on various crucial foreign policy issues, including that of Afghanistan. In fact the Russian government was almost rudderless at the time of fall of Kabul because President Yeltsin was waiting for his impending operation and Foreign Minister Yevgeny Primakov was out of the country. Keeping in view of Russian tradition, Prime Minister Victor Chernomyrdin should have issued a statement on the Afghanistan crisis in such a situation. Instead the Russian foreign ministry issued a critical statement on the Afghan imbroglio.

Since the Central Asia is considered as a soft belly of Russia because that may easily be destabilised by foreign forces of neighbouring countries as they have religious and ethnic affinity with them therefore the seizure of Kabul by the Taliban was a serious development for Moscow. It might open the floodgates for the radical Islamic forces to influence Muslims who constitute the majority in Central Asian countries. Afghanistan has common borders with Tajikistan, Uzbekistan and Turkmenistan. The Russian government did not have a clear policy to deal with such a critical situation in Afghanistan and the political decision-making process was in abeyance, therefore, the then controversial secretary of the Security Council, Alexander Lebed made a valiant effort to take over the foreign policy direction from the foreign ministry on the ground that the issue was basically concerned with the national security of the country.

Apparently without seeking clearance from Yeltsin, Lebed advocated that Russia should immediately extend moral and material aid to the deposed Rabbani government, including Gulbuddin Hekmatyar, Abdul Rashid Dostum and Ahmad Shah Masood in order to prevent the whole of Afghanistan being seized by the Taliban movement. He also presented a distressing scenario that the north-advancing Taliban militia reportedly carrying an ulterior design to unite part of territories of Uzbekistan and Tajikistan, including Bukhara, with their Islamic state. Though Primakov did not concur with Lebed yet he expressed his concern on a great danger posed by the Taliban in the region. Agreeing with the possibility of the Taliban's effort to export Islamic revolution to other countries, Primakov advocated the policy of wait and see before rushing to any hasty policy decision on extending assistance to a particular person or faction engaged in a bloody civil war.

Be that as it may, the Russian leadership was not inclined to bear the burden of facing the challenge posed by the Taliban to the CIS. Thus President Yeltsin instructed Prime Minister Victor Chernomyrdin to contact heads of concerned countries of CIS and hold a conference with them on the recent developments in the region as a result of seizure of Kabul by the Taliban. No doubt Russian wanted to check the influence of radical Islam in the neighbouring CIS but it also wished that other CIS states should also make their contribution to guard the CIS borders from the sway of Islamic extremist forces. The Duma (lower house of the Russian Parliament) Communist faction expressed its deep concern over the consolidation of Islamic fundamentalism in Afghanistan which would not only be influencing Tajikistan and other CIS countries but also disturb stability in the region.[2] The leader of Liberal Democratic Party of Russia, Vladimir Zhirinovski, felt that the Central Asian countries wished to push Russia into a second Afghan war.[3]

The CIS summit meeting was held in Almaty (formerly Alma-Ata) capital of Kazakhstan on 4 October, 1996. As expected the leaders of Russia, Kazakhstan, Tajikistan, Kyrgyzstan and Uzbekistan attended the summit meeting but the leader of Turkmenistan did not take part in it because he declared that his country would like to be a neutral in the Afghan crisis. The participating leaders of the summit meeting called on the UN Security Council to take urgent measures to end the military activity in Afghanistan. They also proposed for an urgent sitting of the UN Security Council to be held with the participation of all interested/concerned countries.

Though the summit meeting did not accept the proposal of extending military aid to the northern Afghan warlord, Dostum as suggested in certain quarters, yet they declared that they would jointly face the challenge on the Afghan border because any disturbance there would be regarded as a threat to their common interests and in accordance with Article 4 of the Collective Security Treaty signed by them in Tashkent on 15 May, 1992. They also agreed to take "commensurate measures" if the Afghan crisis spills over on to their territory.[4]

The purpose of such agreement was to warn the Taliban and their collaborators to desist from encroaching into the borders of the CIS.

The immediate reaction of Taliban to the CIS[4] warning was to assure CIS that there was no cause of concern for their activities. It was announced that Taliban's envoys would soon visit the Central Asian countries to clear their position in the region.[5] But at the same time, the Taliban acting Foreign Minister Mola Mohammed Ghaws warned the CIS of the consequences of any interference in Afghan affairs and warned Dostum against inciting such actions. "We do not want the Russians to forget the lesson they were taught here and we ask the UN to prevent their interference in Afghan affairs," said Ghaws.[6] The Taliban leadership is believed to be apprehensive of a Russian hostile reaction to radical Islamic forces in Afghanistan and its offensive against any influence of these forces in Tajikistan and Uzbekistan as well as their brethren in Afghanistan. But the Taliban tried their best to keep their strong command in the country and not display any sign of lassitude.

Apart from the rise of radical Islamic forces in Afghanistan and their likely adverse impact on neighbouring Central Asian countries and Russian republics, Moscow was also upset by the foreign interference in the Afghan internal affairs. The involvement of Pakistan in raising theTaliban militia was evident but there were also reports about support to their cause by some Islamic countries as well as the United States of America. In spite of direct or indirect entanglement of some foreign countries in Afghan domestic affairs, Russia was not in a position to blame them explicitly like the Soviet Union during the Cold War era. Instead Primakov sent his counterparts, in the US, Britain, Germany, Italy and other countries, a message regarding the latest development in Afghanistan. He proposed for convening a special session of the UN Security Council, to find a political solution through an inter-Afghan dialogue which needs to be comprehensively contributed to and holding a peace conference on Afghanistan. He called for stopping with immediate effect the Civil War in Afghanistan before making any move towards establishing durable peace there. He also expressed his country's willingness to involve Talibans in a dialogue in spite of their hostility towards Russia and the brutal execution of Najibullah by them as well as forceibly imposing their diktats.

The Afghan crisis raised the strategic importance of Central Asian countries, which emerged independent countries as a result of disintegration of the Soviet Union in 1991 but until then remained minor players in the international arena. Thus, the interested neighbouring countries, which wanted to influence the policy of Central Asian countries on Afghanistan, sent their political leaders to persuade them to adopt a particular policy on Afghanistan in line with their own policy. Pakistan President Farooq Leghari and Iranian Foreign Minister Velayati paid visits to Central Asian countries with that objective. At the same time the Taliban Acting Foreign Minister Ghaws also met leaders of Central Asian countries during his visit to those countries. While Turkmenistan adopted a neutral policy on the Afghan crisis, Uzbekistan distanced itself from Iran which took initiative to hold an international conference on the crisis.

Russia wanted to involve regional countries as well as international organisations to defuse the Afghan crisis without its adverse impact on Central Asian countries as well as its own republics. The Afghan crisis brought the concerned countries of CIS together to meet the challenge posed by radical Islamic forces at the sensitive Tajik-Afghan border. They formulated a common security and diplomatic policy in dealing with the Afghan problem, when the Talibans were gaining abundant successes, economic interests of many countries in the region surfaced which were considered a serious concern for Russia. Moscow looked with suspicion and apprehension at the growing economic interests of Washington and Riyadh in Central Asia. The UNOCAL, the American Petroleum giant, and its business partners-Saudi Arabia's Delta Oil Company—were reported to have made efforts to establish links with Turkmenistan and lay a pipeline through Afghanistan to Pakistan for supply of Central Asian gas and oil as an alternative to schemes involving links through Iran to the Persian Gulf. Russia has been opposed to such projects because it wants to retain control of the flow of oil and gas from the old Soviet fields in Kazakistan, Turkmenistan and Uzbekistan. In fact Russia has shown its concern on American economic linkages with Central Asian countries on sensitive trade and military affairs. Incidentally, Iran has offered its transport facilities to India for establishing trade links with Turkmenistan. Such a proposal has not been countered by Russia so far.

Though the Taliban movement captured a large area of Afghanistan, they encountered strong resistance in the northern area. Consequently Moscow is believed to be relaxed and perhaps contemplated that there was no imminent danger of radical Islamic forces intruding into its southern flank. But its relaxation was short-lived because of the Taliban's sudden onslaught towards north and capturing of Mazar-i-Sharif on 24 May, 1997. The Uzbek warlord Dostum lost his leadership and was replaced by Abdul Malik who reportedly entered into a secret deal with the Taliban. The Afghan crisis again assumed significance and thus diplomatic activities were resumed in Central Asian states. Russia began consultations on Afghan crisis with its collective security partners in Central Asia.

In connection with the worsening situation in Afghanistan, Moscow issued a statement on the crisis warning the Taliban not to intrude into the CIS. In fact it felt that there was a threat to the security of CIS especially in Uzbekistan and Tajikistan because of the Taliban's unexpected successes in northern Afghanistan. Moscow made it clear that in the event of a violation of the CIS border, the mechanism of the treaty on the collective security of CIS members would immediately be brought into effect.[7]

Moscow's concern on the Afghanistan development was expressed by Russia's First Deputy Foreign Minister Igor Ivanov who said that there was an evident threat of the Afghan conflict overflowing into Tajikistan in the form of the penetration of Islamic extremism, possible inflow of refugees and streams of arms from Afghanistan into the neighbouring Central Asian republics. He said that if the peace process in Tajikistan failed, the wave of instability would hit other Central Asian countries located near the Russian border. In such a situation the Russian peacekeeping would be a necessary condition for preventing a domino effect throughout Central Asia, he perceived. At the same time, "extreme concern" was also expressed by the State Duma Security Committee chairman, Victor Ilyukhin who did not rule out the possibility that the Taliban movement might direct its aspirations to neighbouring Tajikistan. For defusing the Afghan crisis he called on Russian foreign ministry to hold urgent consultations with both the UN Security Council and the US congress "because it is the Americans who offer military and financial aid to the Taliban and have influence over it."[8]

At the same time Moscow and its Central Asian partner's representatives in the CIS collective Security jointly expressed their grave concern about the potential threat to the Southern borders of the CIS from the Afghan Taliban movement and declared that they would take action if these frontiers were violated. Russian Foreign Ministry's spokesman declared on 27 May, 1997 that although Moscow considered the development in Afghanistan to be primarily that country's internal affairs, "if CIS borders are violated the mechanism of the CIS collective security treaty will be put into action." He also pointed out that the military authorities in Uzbekistan, Tajikistan and Kyrgyzstan, as well as the command of the Russian border troops and the 201st Motor Rifle Division, which forms the core of the CIS peacekeeping force in Tajikistan, had tightened security measures.[9] Subsequently, commanders of CIS border troops discussed the situation on Afghan border. According to Army General Andrei Nikolayev, the director of the Russian Federal Border Service, who chaired their meeting, present threats relating to the state border of the commonwealth's member countries were entirely of a non-military nature, such as illegal immigration, transportation of contraband and illegal drug trafficking.[10] Later he visited Turkmenistan, Uzbekistan and Kazakhstan where he discussed the Afghan issue with concerned officials of those countries.[11] Incidentally, about a month later he observed that no longer the situation in Afghanistan disturbed Russia, though "this issue has not been removed from the agenda."[12]

As far as diplomatic initiative was concerned, Russian Deputy Foreign Minister, Victor Posuvalyuk went to Islamabad and Tehran to discuss the Afghan issue there. In Islamabad he held consultations with the Pakistani Foreign Ministry leadership and met a Taliban representative. He strongly urged the Taliban movement to give up attempts to resolve Afghanistan's internal problems by force. He claimed that he had been in touch with the Taliban leadership.[13] Later, the Pakistan Foreign Minister Gohar Ayub Khan visited all the Central Asian states and Russia for taking initiative in preparing full-scale negotiations to involve all warring sides of Afghanistan in talks to be held under the UN's aegis and in the presence of Russia and the United States as guarantor countries. He also called for the involvement of all border states, including India, China and Iran, in the negotiation. In fact, he included India as a participant in the negotiations on resolving Afghan crisis, reportedly only during his meeting with Russian Foreign Minister Primakov but he dropped India's name while discussing the proposal with his counterparts in other Central Asian countries.[14] Apparently he failed to secure approval of his proposal in the countries he visited, except in Turkmenistan and Azerbaijan as reported by Radio Pakistan on 18 July, 1997.[15] Until early August, 1997 the proposed international negotiations on resolving the Afghan crisis could not commence. In the meantime the Taliban suffered setbacks and its opponents gained advantages against the Taliban.

The emergence of organised and committed forces in the form of Taliban in Afghanistan was a unique phenomenon. Their military successes in Afghanistan against the Rabbani regime were known to Moscow but apparently the Russian leadership was not accepting the fall of Kabul without much resistance. The abundant success of Taliban sent a warning signal to Moscow because radical Islamic forces in the former Soviet Union were likely to raise their heads against the secular governments in Central Asian countries as well as Russian republics where Muslims constitute the majority. This problem was further accentuated because the US, Saudi Arabia and Pakistan were supporting Taliban, directly or indirectly to achieve their own objectives in the region against Russian strategic, political and economic interests. Russia wanted to reduce their influence on Taliban as well as not allowing radical Islamic forces to prosper in the former Soviet Union as a result of Taliban's growing strength in Afghanistan.

Russia seems to be disinclined to interfere in the Afghan internal affairs or become a competitor in the gameplan. But at the same time it would be vehemently opposed to any foreign interference in Afghanistan that would be inimical to the Russian economic, political and strategic interests. The Afghan crisis has not unfolded as perceived by Russia immediately after the seizure of Kabul by the Taliban. They have not destabilised regimes in neighbouring Central Asian countries as suspected in certain quarters in Russia. Nonetheless, the Afghanistan imbroglio will remain an uncertain problem for Central Asian countries and Russia in the near future

References

1. Renee do Nevers, ***Russia's Strategic Renovation: Russian Security Strategies and Foreign Policy in the post-imperial Era.*** Adelphi Paper 289, (London: Brassey's for the IISS, 1994), p. 44.
2. British Broadcasting Corporation, ***Summary of World Broadcast***, Part 1, SU/2732, 2 October, 1996, P.B./10.
3. *Ibid.*, SU/2734, 4 October, 1996, P.B./15.
4. *Ibid.*, SU/2736, 7 October, 1996, pp. G/1-2.
5. *Ibid.*, p. G/2.
6. *Ibid.*, SU/2738, 9 October, 1996, p. G/1.
7. *Ibid.*, SU/2928, 26 May, 1997, p. B/8.
8. *Ibid.*, SU/2929, 27 May, 1997, p. G/1. According to Radio Russia report on 7 April, 1997, quoting an unspecified report as saying the Taliban were receiving arms from other countries via Turkmenistan territory "from a third country, in particular Ukraine." See *Ibid.*, SU/2889, 10 April, 1997, p. G/3. On the other hand, informed Afghan and diplomatic sources told "Al-Hayat", London, on 21 April 1997 that Ahmad Shah Masood, the former commander of the Afghan Presidential Force, received 12 fighter planes from Moscow to boost his military capabilities against the Taliban movement. Masood's official spokesman confirmed the reports of the presence of Afghan planes at Kulob airport but said they were Afghan civilian aircraft. However the Taliban accused Tajikistan and Russia of supporting the opposition. See *Ibid.*, SU/2908, 26 April 1997, p. B/12.
9. *Ibid.*, SU/2930, 28 May, 1997, p. B/6.
10. *Ibid.*, SU/2938, 6 June, 1997, p. B/8.
11. *Ibid.*, SU/2941, 10 June, 1997, pp. G/2-3.
12. *Ibid.*, SU/2963, 5 July, 1997, p. G/2. In fact on 21 July, 1997. President Yeltsin and Russian Defence Minister Igor Sergeyev discussed the current situation in Afghanistan. See *Ibid.*, SU/2977, 22 July 1997, p. B/6.
13. Ibid., SU/2942, 11 June, 1997, pp. B/6-7 and *Ibid.*, SU/2951, 21 June, 1997, p. B/10.
14. *Ibid.*, SU/2967, 10 July, 1997, p. B/10; SU/2953, 24 June, 1997, p. G/2 and SU/2973, 17 July, 1997, p. G/2.
15. *Ibid.*, SU/2975, 19 July, 1997, p. G/1.

7

AMERICAN ROLE IN AFGHANISTAN

CHINTAMANI MAHAPATRA

The United States of America since the end of World War II has been a global power whose role and influence reaches almost all the four corners of the world. During the prolonged Cold War between the United States and the former Soviet Union, any area or country that received any kind of attention from the former Soviet Union automatically brought in the US factor into it. Areas outside the Cold War playground were relatively more peaceful. And Afghanistan was one such country that received scant attention from either Washington or Moscow until the late 1970s when the former Soviet leadership sent military troops to that country in order to affect, among other things, even the domestic political set-up in Kabul.

Although the internal Afghan political trouble actually started since a coup d'etat in July, 1973 when Sardar Mohammad Daud overthrew the monarchy of King Zahir Shah and declared Afghanistan a republic, headed by himself with the help of military. The event had drawn little attention of the US administration. Around this time, the United States was terribly preoccupied with its efforts to extricate itself from Indochina and had little incentive to focus its energy on an internal political development in the remote Afghanistan. However, the Soviet military intervention in December 1979 in the backdrop of American reverses in Indochina, Iran and

Nicaragua sparked off the second round of intense Cold War between the US and the former USSR. Afghanistan loomed large in the American radar screen, as Washington began to perceive a larger than life threat in the Soviet military advance into an area which was "within striking distance of the Indian Ocean and even the Persian Gulf... an area of vital strategic and economic significance to the survival of Western Europe, the Far East, and ultimately the United States.[1] The US policy-makers soon decided to bleed the Soviets in Afghanistan, interestingly with the help of the Afghan Islamic groups, known as the Mujahideen.[2] The Western liberal democracies, led by the US, which were very critical of the Islamic Revolution in Iran in 1979, joined hands with the Afghan Mujahideen to fight back the Soviet Communist expansionism by making the Soviet presence in Afghanistan expensive in terms of money, material and human lives. According to Abdus Sattar, a former Pakistani Foreign Secretary, the US "raised covert allocations for supply of arms to the Mujahideens, from 250 million US dollars in 1985, to 470 million US dollars in 1986 and 630 million US dollars in 1987. The American contribution was reportedly matched by Saudi Arabia.... Pakistan calibrated the flow of assistance to the Mujahideen cautiously so as to minimise the risk of expansion of the conflict, but it became bolder with time and experience."[3] In the words of Robert McNamara, former US Secretary of Defence, "As a response to the Soviet incursion, the Carter Administration postponed the Senate vote on ratification of the SALT Treaty, blocked 2 billion US dollars in grain sales to the USSR, prevented American athletes from participating in the 1980 Moscow Olympics, halted sales of advanced technology to the Soviet Union, increased military aid to Pakistan after earlier refusing to do so, and accelerated contacts with the People's Republic of China. US-Soviet relations never recovered from the effects of Afghanistan until the tenure in Moscow of Mikhail Gorbachev."[4]

Once Ronald Reagan came to power, he acted as Super Cold Warrior. The main application of Reagan's Doctrine outside Central America was in Afghanistan. Both the Reagan and the Bush Administrations considered the US war efforts against the Soviet military presence in Afghanistan so vital that the so-called US crusade against the proliferation of weapons of mass destruction also took a back seat in their foreign policy priority lists. The US congress, which is quite often critical of the foreign policy initiatives of the White House, generally went along with the Reagan and Bush policy approach towards Afghanistan, "despite the virtually unaccountable manner with which the CIA managed" the US assistance to Afghan Mujahideens.[5]

The American war efforts in Afghanistan, both covert and overt, finally brought them victory when the former Soviet Union decided to withdraw its troops from Afghanistan in 1989. The rise of the Gorbachev phenomenon in the Soviet Union in the second half of the 1980s, the internal economic problems and the intractable Afghan imbroglio were responsible for the Soviet decision. What would happen to American role in Afghanistan after it would cease to be a Cold War battleground? It was almost inevitable that the US would no longer make it a priority area of its national security policy. The conflict in Afghanistan, which hit the headlines around the world for about a decade during the second round of intense Cold War between the United States and the former Soviet Union, in fact, failed to receive the amount of international attention it used to during the Cold War period. For about three years after the Soviet troops left, the Afghan conflict continued and was largely marked by fighting between the Communist regime headed by Najibullah and the various factions of Afghan Mujahideens. The Najibullah Government fell in 1992 and soon after that armed conflict within Afghanistan took another turn, as various Mujahideen factions began fighting each other.

All these years of political and social unrest and widespread violence in Afghanistan were overshadowed by momentous changes in Eastern Europe and the former Soviet Union marked by the collapse of communism and emergence of new independent states. And even the eruption of conflicts in the former Yugoslavia and a few African countries dominated the international agenda so much that Afghanistan appeared to have been buried in oblivion. With the lacklustre performance of the United Nations in resolving the Afghan conflict by persuading the Afghans factions to conduct peaceful negotiations among themselves, no other big power, including the United States came forward to take active interest in the affairs of that country. The Afghan question had become more or less a sub-regional issue.

There is no doubt that for a while after the Soviet withdrawal, the Bush Administration in the US kept its interest alive in Afghanistan in view of the continuation of the Najibullah Government with Soviet support. But such interests grew more and more faint, as unprecedented improvement in US-USSR relations, including the Soviet cooperation in the Gulf War, induced the Bush Administration to look for an alternative to wind up its operation in Afghanistan. Consequently, an agreement was signed by Washington, DC and Moscow in September, 1991 to discontinue military assistance to the rebels and the Government forces respectively. The collapse of the Soviet Union in late 1991 was the last straw. Ever since, the US State Department lost all direct interest and contact with the Afghan affairs except, as will be discussed subsequently, extending financial assistance for humanitarian purposes.

It would be a sad commentary in world affairs that the United States which later boasted of winning the Cold War against the Soviet Union so much, little appreciated the contribution made by the Afghan Mujahideens to the American effort. The minimum that was expected of the USA was a continuing endeavour to put an end to the factional fights in Afghanistan and working towards re-building of that war-torn country. On the contrary, the Afghan Mujahideens and other warring factions in Afghanistan were blamed for their failure to arrive at a national consensus to end the prolonged instability and focus on national reconstruction. In the past, the US policy-makers after winding up their role in a foreign country have always sought to put the blame on the locals for failure, while keeping for themselves all the credit for the successes. In China's civil war in the late 1940s, for instance, the US after its diplomatic failure in that country put the blame on the nationalist forces. Similar stories have been cooked up or disproportionately highlighted in the case of the Vietnam War.

If the former President Bush ignored Afghanistan, what did his successor do? Like his predecessor, the first post-Cold War US President Bill Clinton evinced little interest in resolving the Afghanistan conflict. Clinton's foreign policy agenda simply did not have any space for Afghanistan. For more than two years after assuming office, Clinton sent no envoy to Afghanistan even to take stock of the situation in a country that was pivotal to America's Cold War strategy for more than a decade. It was in November, 1995 that the US Assistant Secretary of State for this region cared to visit Afghanistan. As the strategic planners in the Pentagon no longer considered Afghanistan strategically important in the post-Cold War environment, the Clinton Administration appeared content with a policy of supporting the UN efforts in Afghanistan in principle and providing political blessings to Pakistani activities in Afghanistan. The US congress which conducted innumerable hearings on the Afghan situation throughout the 1980s too showed little or no interest in what was happening in Afghanistan. For more than five years after the Soviet withdrawal from Afghanistan, there was no congressional hearing on the Afghan situation. It is significant to note that the US congress held the first discussion over Afghanistan in May, 1996 after six years.[6]

Even this discussion would not have taken place, had Senator Hank Brown and Assistant Secretary of State Robin Raphel not visited that country in the previous month. While these visits sparked off speculation in the Asian diplomatic circles about a renewed US interest in the affairs of Afghanistan, the fact remained that this "renewed interest" was still confined to low level of American foreign policy bureaucracy. The higher-up in the US State Department, Pentagon, media and the influential in the US congress hardly paid any sustained interest in the events in Afghanistan.

It would, however, be wrong to conclude that there was absolutely no American role in the Afghan development in the post-Soviet withdrawal period. In fact, the lack of a sustained high-level attention in the US on the Afghan developments in a way camouflaged the low-level US role in that country which was not always positive and helpful towards resolving the Afghan chaos. To cite an example, one may refer to the present Secretary of State Madeline Albright's remark at the Overseas Writers' Club soon after Taliban's victory over the Rabbani's forces in September, 1996 and the fall of Kabul. On 3 October, 1996, days after the fall of Kabul, the then US Ambassadress to the United Nations Albright spoke at the Overseas Writers's Club on a large range of international issues and the role of the United Nations. While discussing "limits" and "flaws" of the United Nations, she touched upon issues such as Cambodia, Cyprus, El Salvador, Haiti, Iraq, Libya, Mozambique, Myanmar, Nigeria, Rwanda, Somalia, South Africa, former Yugoslavia, etc. There was absolutely no mention about Afghanistan, despite the fact that Senator Hank Brown had suggested the resignation of the UN envoy in Afghanistan in his letter to President Bill Clinton on the ground of his inability to bring various warring Afghan factions to the negotiating table.[7] Significantly, Afghanistan did not even figure during the question-answer session.

While it indicated that the US did not bother at all about the developments in Afghanistan, it camouflaged the US role of supporting the Pakistani involvement in the Afghan internal power struggle, particularly the Pakistani hand in training and equipping the Taliban. The word "Taliban" is a Pushtu word meaning "student." While theories abound on the origin of Taliban, there is little doubt that it was a Pakistani creation. It was in the backdrop of rise of power of the political forces in Kabul friendly to Russia, India and Iran that Pakistan, with American blessings, began to train the Taliban as a militia and political force. By September, 1995, when the civil war conditions in Kabul were beginning to look normal, the Taliban was already a rising force.

In a year's time, the so-called religious Afghan students succeeded in overthrowing the Rabbani regime in Kabul. Would it have been possible for these students to win a spectacular military victory over the highly experienced and battle-hardened Afghan fighters without the backing of the external forces? There is a belief that the US gave not only political blessings to the Taliban but also the necessary inputs in strategic planning to this force.[8] The *Jane's Intelligence Review*, in fact, questioned the capability of the Taliban in the following words: "That semi-literate Afghan Mullahs could have been capable of such planning and execution defies belief... circumstantial evidence points strongly towards Pakistani involvement at the planning level, and reliable reports of cross-border logistics support this. Pushtu-speaking ex-Pakistani military personnel operating on the ground suggest Islamabad's backing was not confined to the map room."[9]

It would perhaps be appropriate to quote a Pakistani source

to indicate the US involvement in the training and equipping of the Taliban. According to a Pakistani commentator, "The Taliban occupied Jalalabad and Kabul by the force of superior arms said to have been supplied by the USA.... One of the distinguished representatives of the Organisation of European Security and Cooperation is also on record to have accused the USA of supporting the Taliban in their sweeping victory in Afghanistan. The American spokesman has publicly disclosed that "the USA had been carefully courting the Taliban for last two years for countering Iran and Russia and that it had been regularly holding meetings with them."[10]

During all these years of consolidation of power by groups unfriendly to the US and Pakistan, Washington kept funneling a modicum of humanitarian assistance to Kabul, but carefully resorted to reducing the amount of aid to that country. Such a policy enabled Assistant Secretary of State Robin Raphel to claim that the US never abandoned Afghanistan after the Soviet withdrawal and to cite the example of 700 million US dollars of US humanitarian assistance to given to Afghanistan since 1989. This statistics, however, concealed the fact that both the US bilateral and multilateral assistance to that country had consistently declined since 1989. While the US multilateral assistance to Afghanistan in 1989 was 74 million US dollars it came down to 44 million US dollars in 1995. The bilateral assistance, on the other hand, declined from 102 million US dollars in 1989 to 1 million US dollars in 1995.[11]

Several important factors appeared to have induced the US policy-makers to review their attitude towards Afghanistan and begin support to the Taliban. One was the oil factor. As the US oil production began to decline and the American oil companies began to plan for replenishing reserves by investing in friendly countries, the Central Asian republics looked very lucrative as an area where the US could explore the possibility of investing in the region's energy sector. In 1993, the American oil company Chevron had concluded a deal worth 40 billion US dollars to develop Tengiz oil field on the north-eastern shore of the Caspian. However, the deal required construction of oil pipelines which in turn depended on regional stability. Peace and stability in Afghanistan was regarded as a prerequisite to the construction of pipelines through alternative routes other than through Iran and Russia. Subsequently, when the

Central Asian republics themselves began to perceive a need for alternative oil routes to reduce their dependence on Russia, several international oil companies, including the American companies stood in the queue. One of the US companies, UNOCAL planned for the construction of an oil pipeline through Afghanistan at a cost of about 8 billion US dollars. The Clinton Administration without any hesitation gave its blessings to UNOCAL and applauded its project "as an alternative to schemes involving links through America's old nemesis Iran to the Arabian Sea."[12]

The oil factor made it easy for the US to implement its policy of "dual containment" in the Persian Gulf. Iran and Iraq have been the targets of this post-Cold War American containment policy. While Iraq has been suffering from the UN imposed sanctions and has been successfully contained, it was not easy for the United States successfully to contain Iran. The European, Japanese, Russian and even the Chinese attitude towards Iran had made it difficult for Washington to provide enough teeth to the policy of containment. The growing Iranian influence in Afghan affairs was bound to negate the UNOCAL project of laying gas pipelines. Iran's offer of its territory for laying gas pipelines would not only enable Tehran to have greater say in the affairs of Central Asian republics but also could particularly render the American containment policy redundant and ineffective. Under such circumstances, it was logical to believe that Washington supported the Pakistani gameplan in Afghanistan.

Furthermore, the US desire to deny the Russians a monopoly of control and influence over Central Asia and to establish an American presence in this region which carries in its bosom the potential of unexplored energy resources also motivated Washington's policy-makers to redesign the country's Afghan policy. The US belief that the Taliban forces would support the US goals of fighting terrorism and drugs trafficking provided additional thrust to the US attitude towards the rise of the Taliban in Afghanistan. It is significant to note that Washington's decision to renew ties with Pakistan by amending the Pressler Amendment was based on the new look given to America's Afghan policy.

During a Senatorial hearing on "Conventional Weapons and Foreign Policy in South Asia" in September 1995, Robin Raphel stated: "Pakistan has strategic and cultural reasons for wanting to play a constructive role in Central Asia, an area with which it has ties dating back to centuries. As a moderate Islamic state, Pakistan is often seen as an alternative model to Iran in Central Asia. Pakistan has contributed to Central Asian stability in Tajikistan, using its ties to Tajik opposition to promote an end to the conflict... The Government of Pakistan has also played an important, if sometimes controversial role in Afghan affairs. The Bhutto Government has also sought to build closer ties with the Central Asian republics through the recently revived Economic Cooperation Organistaion.... It also has sought to build a gas pipeline from Turkmenistan across Afghanistan to Pakistan to supply its growing energy needs. Neither of these efforts have yet borne fruit, however. Ultimately, a stable, peaceful Afghanistan is a prerequisite for prosperous and stable Central Asia."[13] It was with this understanding that the US policy towards Afghanistan began to evolve. While giving tacit support to the Pakistani activities, the US State Department did not want to put all the eggs in the Taliban basket, particularly since the future power configuration in the domestic political scene in Afghanistan was uncertain. It sought to keep a line of communication with the Rabbani regime too.

Raphel paid her second visit to Kabul on 19 April, 1996 and as expected, intimated President Rabbani of the US interest in a "peaceful solution in Afghanistan" and in improvement of relations between the Afghan and the Pakistani Government. Although it was the second visit by Raphel in six months, quiet diplomatic moves were undertaken earlier to give a proper shape to the evolving US strategy. Raphel's second visit, in fact, took place after Afghan Deputy Foreign Minister Abdur Rahim Ghafoorzai and Civil Aviation Minister Abdul Rahman's trip to Washington.

Soon after her return to Washington, Robin Raphel reappeared in the Subcommittee on Near Eastern and South Asian affairs. Her statement in the subcommittee indicated that she was hopeful of a desired political change in Kabul. Accordingly, she outlined the need for a political change in Afghanistan which was increasingly becoming a place for international terrorist activities and drugs trade. However, uncertainty in the Taliban's success induced her to refrain from supporting any particular group in Afghanistan. She stated that "Afghanistan has become a conduit for drugs, crime and terrorism that can undermine Pakistan, the neighbouring Central Asian states and have an impact beyond to Europe and Russia." She also maintained that terrorist incidents in the Middle East and elsewhere had been linked to individuals in Afghan camps and that Ramzi Ahmad Yousef, indicted in World Trade Centre bombing in New York, also had Afghan links. In a Senatorial hearing the following month, Robin Raphel explained in detail the State Department's views on the Afghan problem. She said: "... The conflict in Afghanistan prevents the new Central Asian states from establishing trade and oil and gas outlets to the south: it provides another venue for Pakistan-India competition: It feeds Iranian fears of being surrounded by unfriendly regimes; and finally it promotes a dangerous fragmentation of Afghanistan. The stability of this region is important to the USA... The proliferation of militant training camps and increased narcotics production and trafficking can only be reversed by cooperation between those inside and outside Afghanistan.... Afghanistan is the second largest producer of opium in the world after Myanmar.... Opium processed into heroin finds its way into Pakistan, Central Asia, Russia, Europe and the USA.... The human suffering in Afghanistan must be addressed to if the country is to rebuild and rejoin the world country... *We remain convinced that the only solution to this impasse (in Afghan civil war) is a negotiated settlement that leads to a representative, broadly supported central government. Steps along the way must include a ceasefire, a neutral security force, demilitarising Kabul, agreement on an interim government arrangement and planning for a permanent form of government.... The USA does not favour one faction over another nor does it support any group or individual. We believe that the Afghan people have the right to a government of their own choosing free from outside interference....*" (Emphasis added).[14]

Five months after Raphel's trip to Afghanistan, a military miracle occurred in Kabul. Rabbani regime fell as Taliban forces achieved a spectacular military victory and entered Kabul. The UNOCAL executives could not hide their happiness at the Afghan development. The president of the company's Pakistan operations, Richard Keller, expressed his hope that the Taliban would bring stability to Afghanistan and clear the way for the construction of the gas pipeline.[15] Washington, on the other hand, gave a "cautious welcome" to the Taliban advance, taking the view that a unified country would at least be at peace after 17 years."[16]

However, Washington's hopes and UNOCAL's happiness were belied within days, as the Taliban militia turned out to be hardcore fundamentalists and ultra reactionaries, who ordered prayers, forbade cigarettes, told men to grow beards, banned music and movies and, worst of all, closed down the girls' schools and forbade women from working. Even the Iranian clerics branded the Taliban as "narrow minded."[17] Washington quickly distanced itself from the Taliban. Raphel announced: "We do not support any individual or any group in Afghanistan.... We've supported very much the UN effort to bring the parties to the table" in Afghanistan in search of a lasting solution to the issue.[18]

As days passed by, it was realised that the Taliban neither cooperated with the US in tracking down terrorists nor in controlling narcotics trafficking. Nor was it capable of extending its power and influence all over the country. Washington, as a result, could neither accept nor reject the Taliban. It merely reiterated its support to the UN effort in Afghanistan. The Afghan civil war of late has been a story of shifting alliances. The reverses suffered by the Taliban in the northern provinces, particularly in Mazar-e-Sharif and the renewed effort by the anti-Taliban forces to regain the lost territories all indicate that the Afghan conflict is nowhere near any solution. Several peace efforts are going on but the US is conspicuous by its absence in major efforts and initiatives for resolving the Afghan conflict.

References

1. *American Foreign Policy: Basic Documents, 1977-80*, Quoted in Abdus Sattar, "Afghanistan: Jihad to Civil War," *Regional Studies*, 1996.
2. *Ibid.*
3. *Ibid.*, pp. 13-14. Also see *Time*, 24 June 97.
4. Robert McNamara, *Out of the Cold: New Thinking for American Foreign and Defense Policy in the 21st Century* (London, Bloomsbury Publishing Ltd., 1990), pp. 82-83.
5. George Shultz, the former US Secretary of State has gone on record saying that the "CIA was running the war" in Afghanistan. See, John Dumbrell, *American Foreign Policy: Carter to Clinton* (London, McMillan, 1997), p. 100.
6. *Far Eastern Economic Review*, 13 June 1996.

7. "Albright to Overseas Writers Club," Transcript, *Wireless file*, USIS, New Delhi, 9 October 1996.
8. For a detailed account on the Taliban factor see, Sreedhar, ed., *Taliban and the Afghan Turmoil* (New Delhi, Himalaya, 1997).
9. *Jane's Defence Review*, December, 1996.
10. *Dawn*, 4 July 97, POT, Afghanistan, 1 August, 1997.
11. *Fact Sheet*, USIS, New Delhi, 16 October, 1996.
12. *Newsweek*, 4 November, 1996.
13. "Conventional Weapons and Foreign Policy in South Asia," Hearing, Subcommittee on Near Eastern and South Asian Affairs of the Committee on Foreign Relations, 104th Congress' First Session, 14 September, 1996 (Washington, D.C., Government Printing Press, 1996), p. 47.
14. Robin Raphel's statement during the Senatorial hearing was reproduced in *Nation*, 8 June, 1996, POT, 13 June, 1996.
15. *Newsweek*, 5 November, 1996.
16. *Ibid.*
17. *US News and World Report*, 11 November, 1996.
18. *Official Text*, USIS, New Delhi, 12 October, 1996.

8

THE US RENEWED INTEREST IN AFGHANISTAN

P. STOBDAN

The US renewed interest and involvement in the Afghan conflict is closely linked to its past policies, when it poured in more than 6 billion US dollars to defeat the rival superpower, the USSR. There have been widespread articulation in the American strategic community in the recent years that the US has undoubtedly been the single most import country responsible for the current state of affairs in Afghanistan. The way the USA cynically used Afghanistan as a strategic pawn in its struggle against the Soviets had produced disastrous consequences, the impact of which is expected to be felt for very long time to come. Afghanistan's importance for American foreign policy during the last phase of the Cold War has been described in the words of Simes as:

"Afghanistan was perceived as a blessing of sorts... In the United States, an influential school of thought clearly felt that if the Soviets 'fraternal' aggression against Afghanistan had not happened, it would have had to be invented.[1]

Although the US policy of arming the Afghan Mujahideen was hailed as an unqualified success and moral triumph, nobody in the US ever envisaged that there would be a post-Soviet Afghanistan. The post mortem analysis of the US involvement in Afghanistan tends to suggest America's too much confidence in Pakistani assessment of Afghan development. Whatever might have been the US compulsion to meet Pakistan's price, America's acquiescence, according to Ted Galen Carpenter, "led inexorably to developments that served the interests of Pakistan's growing elite while creating a long-term tragedy for the people of Afghanistan".[2] The American ignorance about the Afghan situation tended Washington to be misled by the Pakistanis who were pursuing their own interest based on General Zia's concept of achieving a strategic depth vis-a-vis India rather than looking for peace in Afghanistan. For Zia, it was the most opportunate time, and in fact, he saw to it that the Soviet forces remain bogged down in Afghanistan for a longer period, the ultimate objective being to draw the spectre of Cold War closer to the South Asian situation, which in turn would internationalise if not helpresolve the Kashmir issue. There has been a corresponding relationship between the withdrawal of Soviet troops from Afghanistan and the heightening of Pakistani inspired terrorist acts in the Kashmir valley.[3]

The American inability to gauge the political reality and the Pakistani action of overly supporting the fundamentalist contingent of Afghan resistance group has been largely responsible for the present political mess in Afghanistan. According to some analysts, ISI's selective distribution of almost 50 per cent of the US aid to the fundamentalist Hekmatyar group, while ignoring the importance of moderate "Peshawar Seven" has greatly strengthened Islamic fundamentalism as an Afghan political force. For the ISI, Hekmatyar qualified as the most suitable candidate, who would fulfil Pakistani multiple goal of integrating Afghan territory within the strategic fold of Pakistan. For Pakistan the concept of "strategic depth" was not just acquiring military space, but a wider political canvas of diluting and undermining of "Afghan nationalism" that threatened to exacerbate the demand for Pushtoonistan. The close historical and emotional proximity of Afghan nationalism with those of Indian nationalism acted as the biggest impediment for Pakistani regional policy, which is seeking to expand influence in Central Asia in the post-Cold War era. Islamabad was aware of the fact that whichever Afghan regime comes to control Kabul, it ultimately gets closer to New Delhi, not only for the consideration of gaining political legitimacy, but also due to the perception in Kabul, perhaps dictated by strategic logic which tends to make Pakistan a greater hegemone for Afghanistan. The Pakistani objective in Afghanistan can be vividly gauged from Zia's comments in an interview with Salig Harrison.

"We have earned the right to have a very friendly government in Kabul. We won't permit it to be like it was before, with Indian and Soviet influence there and claim on our territory. It will be areal Islamic state, part of a pan-Islam revival, that will one day win over the Moslems in the Soviet Union, you will see."[4]

Although Pakistan started cultivating Hekmatyar and others in 1974, before Zia came into power and before the Soviet intervention in Afghanistan, the General's vision and the American and Saudi largesse complemented Islamabad's drive at Islamisation of Afghan politics as an anti-dote to a resurgent Afghan nationalism.

Throughout the war in Afghanistan, the US normally chose to defer major decisions to the policy preference of the Pakistani government, many of the operational matters including, the distribution of aid to the Mujahideen, were, however, made in consultation with the CIA and Saudi intelligence service[5]. It was only in late 1989, the US appeared to have shown some reservation about American aid being given directly to the Hekmatyar group, amidst congressional and public outcry at reports of Hekmatyar's assassination plots and other human rights violations[6].

Following the end of the war against the Soviets, it however, became more apparent that Pakistanis and Saudis allies continued to provide funds for Afghan war veterans to recruit and train Muslim volunteers from other Islamic countries in various terrorist training camps opened in several towns of Pakistan-Afghanistan frontier. Much to the disbelief and dismay of the Americans, those recruits estimating 30,000 during 1990, belonged to Egypt, Algeria, West Bank, Indonesia, Morocco and Sudan[7]. What came to known as the "Afghanis," many of these zealots were later implicated in anti-Western terrorist incidents. In fact, since the summer of 1992, the terrorist actions of the radical Islamic groups in Algeria, India, Egypt and other countries sharply increased. Several countries, including Egypt, Algeria, Jordan, Tunisia, Malaysia and others protested to the US as also to the United Nations about Pakistan having emerged as a training ground for the fundamentalist militant outfits from their countries. It was at that stage the US seriously thought of including Pakistan in the list of terrorist countries.

Perhaps the most shocking and disturbing of all was the news of sophisticated Stinger anti-aircraft missiles, supplied by the US to the Mujahideens, turning up in the hands of Islamic fundamentalist activists in other parts of the world, including the Iranians and Libyans[9]. Even a tiny country like Qatar managed to buy Stingers through underground trade. It was more unsettling for Washington, when it's request to the new regime in Kabul, run by its old allies, refused to return the left over Stingers. So much was the implications of the US-Afghan policy that in the words of T.G. Carpenter :

> *"... the United States, together with its Pakistani and Saudi allies, has helped bring to power in Afghanistan political forces that are nearly as odious as the communists they overthrew. Today the people of Afghanistan are ruled by a collection of authoritarian warlords and sectarian fanatics. A Soviet puppet regime has been replaced by an assortment of Pakistani and Saudi puppets, and Afghanistan has the become breeding ground for terrorists. If that outcome is a US policy triumph, one shudders to contemplate what a policy failure would look like...the United States was not merely a relatively passive accomplice in the destructive agendas pursued by Islamabad and Riyadh—it was an active collaborator in foisting an oppressive political system on the people of Afghanistan, the result of that policy is a damning enough indictment of American actions."* (Emphasis added)

The policy implications of such a magnitude compelled many congressmen as well as other vocal people to question Washington's policy that tended to ignore the tragic aftermath of the US-Afghan policy. In the meeting of the Sub-Committee on Asia and Pacific of the House Foreign Affairs Committee, to hear the testimony, Afghanistan always dominated the hearing with members expressing concerns not only about narco-terrorism and Stinger missiles but also contended that the US bore considerable responsibility for the current introglio and should assume moral responsibility to rectify the situation.[10] It appears to be in that context of rectifying the US past policies that have begun to boomerang, Washington has sought to involve itself in the current phase of civil war in Afghanistan.

The evolution of the new Afghan guerrilla force, the Taliban, is closely linked to the US commitment to combat the international terrorist networks. Since 1993 the menace of terrorist attacks had increased. The killing of two CIA officials, outside of CIA headquarters in Langley, Virginia, on January 25, 1993 was followed by the bombing of New York's World Trade Centre. The FBI has found the involvement of Pakistani holy warriors like Mir Aimal Kansi, Ramzi Ahmed Yousef, and an Egyptian Sheikh Omar Abdel Rahman in the above terrorist acts. In both the incidents of November, 1995 and June, 1996 bombings of US military facilities in Saudi Arabia that killed twenty-four US soldiers, the FBI once again uncovered links to the Afghanis. Earlier in 1993, the assassination of Egyptian President Anwar Sadat was also carried out by the Afghan trained terrorists. In Sudan the source of fundamentalist activities were linked to Pakistani origin. On a number of occasion, Egypt and other countries blamed America and Pakistan for creating a terrorist network. According to Benjamin Netanyahu, leader of Israel's Likud Party and a known expert on global terrorism noted in his new book *Fighting Terrorism: How Democracies can Defeat Domestic and International Terrorism*, "In Afghanistan an international Sunni terrorist network has sprung into being, composed mainly of Islamic veterans and their religious leaders. It has built a sympathetic relationship with the government of Sudan and has excellent ties with the fundamentalist side in the simmering civil war in Algeria, the militant Islamists in Tunisia, Pakistan and Indonesia."[11] The spectre of pipe bombs explosions and Olympic Games in Atlanta, the loss of 230 lives on board TWA Flight 800 in 1996, the bomb explosion at Egyptian Embassy in Islamabad, the killing of two CIA officials in Karachi, the hostage taking of six Europeans by Al-Faran in Kashmir sent shock waves in the Western world to do something about putting an end to the growing menace of terrorism across the world. These developments led to the Group of Seven Anti-Terrorism Conference, held in July, 1996 in Paris to initiate a global, coordinated effort to identify and locate thousands of veterans of the US-backed, 1979-89 Afghan war against the Soviet.[12]

Over the years the Americans have been waging an unrelenting war to hunt and punish the perpetrators. The findings of the antiterrorist planners firstly suggested that most of the convicts are being sheltered in Afghanistan. These includes the renegade Saudi construction tycoon and one of the most significant financial sponsors of Islamic extremist activities in the world Usama bin Muhammad bin Awad Bin Ladin.[13] Secondly, the Americans desperately tried to prove an Iranian hand in many of these terrorist bombings. The growing closer relationship between Tehran with Hekmatyar as well as with the Rabbani regime in Kabul added to Washington's suspicion. The Benazir's government showed willingness to abandon Pakistan's old protege Hekmatyar on the condition that the US would give help through other channels. Thus, there has been a clear-cut American incentive for the introduction of the Taliban movement, that emerged on the Afghan political scene in October, 1994, which took over one-third of Afghan territory within a few months.

The US took a favourable attitude towards the Taliban, which promised to put an end to the growing of opium in Afghanistan, disarm the gunmen guerrillas and reunite the country under a single stable government, fight against Islamic fundamentalism and finally drive out international terrorists who had taken shelter in Afghanistan. The mood in the Western world at the time was that there would be nothing wrong in supporting the Taliban so long as it brings peace in Afghanistan, without realising the blunder that they are merely replacing the old monsters with the new ones.

The renewed American interest in Afghanistan after a period of relative disengagement was also not unrelated to the growing active Iranian regional policies not only in Afghanistan but also in Central Asia. For the US, stability and restoring peace is not the key issue—it is the regional dimension of Afghanistan that makes the American involvement important, especially vis-a-vis its containment of Iranian influence in the region. Washington has been strongly opposed to the increasing Iranian political and economic penetration into Central Asia, specially after the opening up of the latter's ports facilities to the Central Asian region where 55 million Muslims inhabit. In Afghanistan, the US interest increased when it became clear that the Rabbani regime had drawn close to Tehran, following the execution of Iranian backed Shia leader Hizb-i-Wahdat Abdul Ali Mazari by Taliban, after a brief alliance between the two in early 1995. It was Tehran's diplomacy which brought Rabbani and Hekmatyar together to an agreement in June, 1996. On the other hand, right from the start, Tehran perceived the Taliban as an outfit aduocating Sunni Islam backed by its opponents Saudi Arabia and the US. In the recent years the US intelligence has been trying hard to destroy the extremist camps in the Persian Gulf area which had associated with Iran. Analysts also drew linkage of the US supporting the "Afghan operation" with the CIA's debacle in northern Iraq.[14]

A possible Iranian-Taliban nexus also caused American anxiety. Following the much speculated meeting between the Taliban and Tehran, US Senator Hank Brown and Assistant Secretary, Robin Raphel made back to back visits to Afghanistan in 1995, and met with the Taliban leaders. Brown was the first elected US representative to visit Afghanistan in 16 years. On the eve of Raphel's visit to Afghanistan and Pakistan in April 1996, the Uzbek warlord, General Dostum visited Washington via Islamabad and Tashkent. The US also organised an international conference on Afghanistan in Washington in early 1996, wherein every important faction was invited including the ex-king Zahir Shah but excluded Hekmatyar and Shia leader Kalim Khalili. The US Ambassador in Pakistan is reported to have toured the Taliban bases with the Pakistani Interior Minister Naseerullah Khan Babar. Interestingly, in the recent years, the US had especially sought to encourage the biggest Central Asian republic, Uzbekistan to act as a regional anchor. In several ways the US helped arouse Uzbek sense of geo-political responsibility in the region. Tashkent too took a discordant perspective and made a shift in its orientation towards West to safeguard vital national/regional interests. Throughout 1995 and till October 1996 Islamabad-Washington and Tashkent took a common approach towards the Afghan situation. Both Pakistan and US had tried to push the Uzbek proposal of a UN sponsored "Arms Embargo" on Afghanistan. Pakistan earlier pledged to support the idea in return of Uzbek position for a UN sponsored talk on Kashmir.

Both the US and Pakistan were also seen perturbed by India's response to the new political changes in Kabul. Not only New Delhi welcomed the new arrangement, while the then Indian Prime Minister Dev Gowda sent congratulatory message to Gulbuddin

Hekmatyar for assuming the Prime Ministership, but the Indian charged' affaires also invited the new Afghan Prime Minister to India's Independence Day reception at the Embassy in Kabul on August 15, 1996. Washington and Islamabad's concerns were also borne out of the successful completion of the railway project sponsored through Iran-India-Turkmenistan trilateral agreement. Some of these developments were sufficient enough for the US to prevail upon the UN to sack the UN negotiator Mehmoud Mistiri.

It was in this backdrop, that the first flush of the Taliban victory in Kabul was a welcoming sign for the US. Washington talked about its plans to dispatch its diplomats to Kabul to confer with the Taliban, as well as expressed an interest in reopening its embassy. The State Department spokesman Glyn Davies expressed the hope that the Taliban "will move quickly to restore order and security and to form a representative interim government that can begin the process of reconciliation nationwide." While the US only expressed "regret" at the execution of Najibullah, it was only after the United Nations had deplored the brutal execution, that Washington decided on 30th, September to condemn the summary execution. The US also wanted to defer the decision on whether the representativs of Rabbani government should continue or not. The State Department spokesman Nicholas Burns acknowledged that the US had contacts with the Taliban "regularly in the past years but also this year."[15] He also said that the US has national interests in Afghanistan, and added that "we may not like every thing that they are doing, but that does not mean we should just cut off all their contacts with the United States." In general the Americans welcomed the militia as a moderate force for peace and stability. The editorial comment of the *New York Times* said, "the Islamic fundamentalist movement that gained control over much of Afghanistan with a recent string of military victories has brought a measure of stability to the country for the first time in years." Similarly, a former State Department official who dealt with the US Afghan policy, Zalmay Khalilzad has said, that "the US should actively assist the Taliban because even though it is fundamentalist, it does not practise the anti-US style fundamentalism of Iran."[16] The Americans have described the Taliban as "anti-modernism" rather than "anti-Western," and also noted that it is keen in restoring a "traditional society" rather than "exporting Islam."[17]

Within less than a month of Taliban's takeover of Kabul, the US made a shift in its position, when the State Department official Lee Coldren said that the US does not support the student-led Taliban militia in Afghanistan. It also abandoned the plan to send an envoy to Kabul to set up a working arrangement with the militia government. Such a decision came amidst mounting international criticism against Taliban's appalling policies, its savagery and arbitrary medieval rules while imposing strict Islamic social code, banning women from working and shutting down girls' schools turned off the international community, drawing condemnation even from the orthodox Iranian clergy.

Washington's denouncement of the Taliban action also came in the backdrop of the Presidential election in the US, as supporting such a regime that held contempt for human rights would have negatively effected Clinton's position. On November 4, the US State Department official admitted that the Taliban militia will not be able to establish a stable government in Afghanistan and the civil war is likely to continue indefinitely. Robin Raphel said that the "US had little influence in Afghanistan, and supports none of the warring factions, and has no plan for bringing the conflict to an end." Another senior official of the US administration denied that the US had assisted the Taliban to capture Kabul. The official asserted that "as far as US policy is concerned, we have always maintained that peace and security in Afghanistan can only be achieved through the establishment of a broad coalition government."[18] However, in the aftermath of the election, the State Department soften its position on Taliban. Robin Raphel said that "it will not be in the interest of Afghanistan that the Taliban be isolated." "If we want to moderate their policies, we should all engage with them," she said at the UN meeting on Afghanistan.

However, in general, it was too late for the US to persuade the Taliban to change their style of functioning. Its policymakers were rattled not only with the ISI's ill-conceived plan but also horrified and ashamed with Taliban's defiance. Many of the American assessment of Taliban proved to be naive and misleading, which had evoked mounting criticism for being too dependent on

Pakistani inputs and analyses. As one of the US officials is reported to have noted that "the US's initial embrace of the Taliban, which proved to be an embarrassment, was prompted by Pakistan, which had misled Washington into thinking that the Taliban could stem narcotics-trafficking from Afghanistan and close down all the terrorist exporting camps in that country." "We soon realised the Taliban could do neither and more so we found that they were to a large extent funding their own operations with the profits from drug-trafficking." Ironically, the US repeated the mistake despite bitter experience with its favourite Mujahideen leader Gulbuddin Hekmatyar, who proved much to American disgust to be a source terrorist threat. The recent tactical blunder on the part of Americans inevitably raises the question, whether the ISI had scrupulously carried out the assigned operation. Knowing from ISI's past track record, when it held on to a substantial portion of weapons supplied for Mujahideens, a good portion out of the estimated 2.5 billion US dollars, sponsored for Taliban operation this time may have been pocketed by the ISI commanders.

Any move at repeating the Reagan type military option would have failed since the remote controls moderating Afghan affairs this time no longer lie in Moscow, Washington and Islamabad but in Cairo, Riyadh and Jeddah. In other words, confrontation is no longer between Islam and communism but among various Afghan factions to gain political supremacy, sanctified through religious legitimacy. Therefore, an astute and subtle diplomacy moderated by the Mullahs rather than any military manoeuvres was what had actually determined the Afghan scene after the Soviet withdrawal. Had there been no *fatwa* by the Ulema Shura, Dostum would have militarily taken control of Kabul long before the Taliban. Rabbani's biggest strength so far lies not so much in Masood's military muscle but the support he enjoys from Sibghatullah Mojaddedi (Naqshabadiyya's Hazrat of Shor Bazar), Pakhtoon's Wahhabi Chief Professor Rab Rasool Sayyaf, and other senior Mullahs of former Nangrahar Shura, including Mullah Abdul Qadir. They sanctified Rabbani with the title of Amir-ul-Momineen, when he became the President.

Consequently, the US was also worried about the way Taliban's action prompted the Central Asian states, with the exception of Turkmenistan, to look back at Moscow. While agreeing for a strong military bulwark against Taliban's threat, the Almaty summit decisively altered the Taliban's gameplan. Not only the high-pitched tone of the State Department, but also the euphoria among officials of UNOCAL and Delta Oil Company, for Taliban's success as a positive devolopment for trans-Afghan gas and oil pipeline projects too has died down amid uncertainty over peace in the war-torn country. The Taliban's venture has not just ruined the future prospects for peace but instead evoked fresh interests among other countries like Britain and Germany to lay claims on Central Asian resources and markets. Regardless of American political interest, the European business companies may act independently to secure markets in the region considered by them as their own backyard. The latest European sale of radio-communication sets and their help in fixing up the radio frequency for Rabbani signify growing conflict of interests in this resource rich region.

Moreover, to the American disbelief, who had earlier hoped of Taliban cracking down on drug-trafficking, the latest UN report confirmed the increase in opium output as well as Taliban's control over 80 per cent of narcotic trade in the Golden Crescent (Afghanistan, Pakistan and Iran). In fact, as the original source of funding dried up, it has been widely reported that the ISI and Taliban have been relying on the 17 major drug-barons of NWFP, in exchange of major business concessions offered to them in Afghanistan. Around the end of 1996, the Taliban controlled areas producing about 95 per cent of Afghanistan's opium crop.[19] The UN Drugs Control Programme estimated Afghanistan's total production of raw opium to about 2248 tonnes in 1996.[20] In the recent years, drug related studies have shown that the gravity of the drug trade has shifted from the Golden Triangle (Thailand, Myanmar and Laos) to the Golden Crescent (Afghanistan, Pakistan and Iran), primarily due to the Afghan guerrialla war. In the current illicit world market, the opium derivatives such as morphine and heroin account for around 500 tonnes of which 200 tonnes alone comes from Afghanistan. According to one estimate heroin exported from Afghanistan accounts for 75 to 80 billion US dollars profit which is laundered through financial markets. Instead of banning the opium cultivation, the Taliban seemed to have found the revenue and profit from opium hard to resist. Although there have been confirmed reports of Taliban's success in destroying over 30,000 hectares of fields used for hemp (hashish) cultivation, but the ruling Mullahs have turned a blind eye to the growing of poppy, which yields opium. The Taliban's rationale behind banning hashish and not poppy is that former is consumed primarily by Afghans themselves and is therefore anti-Islamic, whereas opium which fetches 100 per cent more than hashish is only exported to the West. The Mullahs justify opium production and exports as it does not contradict with Islam nor such activities, according to them are banned by the Koran. Apart from the profit motives, poppy cultivation has become a necessary means to hold sway over the territories the militia conquered. Any harsh crack down on such activities would mean losing sympathy for the Mullahs among the rural population. In a way, the coming of Taliban regime has further facilitated the growth of opium in rural Afghanistan, as recently reported by Ahmed Rashid in Far Eastern Economic Review, "poppy farmers are benefiting from the relative peace and security that the Taliban militia have brought to the two-thirds of the country they currently control."[21] Another dimension of the opium production is Taliban's intention to use it as a bargaining chip to gain international recognition for itself, as one of the Taliban official reported to have remakred, "If the West support the Islamic demands of the Taliban and recognise our government then we can stop those cultivating opium poppy."[22] Such kind of narcotic-blackmail would become a major factor in shaping Western policy towards Afghanistan. As a junior British Minister has accused the Taliban of profiteering from the flourishing drugs trade in Afghanistan and noted that most of the heroin that reaches the UK comes largely from Afghanistan.

Again, contrary to Taliban's pledge to fight against terrorism as well as promise to drive out international terrorists, the Americans were horrified to see the new rulers providing sanctuaries to hundreds of Arab "Afghanis" who were on the FBI's list for attacking American establishments. At the initial stage Taliban seriously chased off many of these Arab veterans including Bin Laden and his people as they had drawn towards Jalalabad in September, 1996. In fact, it was a part of Taliban's puritanical pronouncement that it will come heavily on drug-trafficking, as was clear by militia's

Information Minister Mullah Amir Khan Mutaqi that, "we don't want subversive actions to be launched from here against any other countries." He promised that there will be no terrorists in Taliban controlled areas.[23] However, as the time passed, the Taliban leadership found that Bin Laden was not a terrorist but a fellow "Islamic brother-in-arms", who is like Taliban fighting for the cause of Islam. A senior Taliban member Mullah Mohammad Sadiq has reported to have told *Time* that "until we are sure that he committed crimes, how can we proceed against him. All we know is that Bin Laden is a good Muslim and has taken part in the Afghan *jihad* (holy war) against the Soviets." It is a well-known fact that many of these convicts are still closely linked with the Pakistani ISI. Many of the Pakistani top military and intelligence officers continue to sympathise with these Afghan war veterans. Recently, the former ISI Chief General Hameed Gul had challenged the Pakistani government for allowing FBI agents to arrest Mir Aimal Kansi, responsible for killing two CIA official in 1994. Moreover, Taliban forces had reopened some of the old terrorist camps at Khost, in the foothills of the Hindukush. The two training camps Al Badr 1 and Al Badr 2 were earlier used to be run by Hizb-i-Islam of Gulbuddin Hekmatyar.[24] It must be particularly noted that Aimal Kansi's handover to the US agencies on June 15, 1997 came only after the Taliban's military setback against the northern alliance. Seeing the American cold response to the militia's taking over of Mazar-i-Sharif, Taliban leadership and the ISI were compelled to oblige the US or at least sought to fulfil some of their commitments for American strategic interest. One is by turning over of FBI's much wanted fugitive, on whose search the US spent 3.5 million US dollars, and had offered 2 million US dollars award as bounty for information on him. Secondly, the Taliban's decision to close down the Iranian embassy on June 2, 1997 too must be seen in the context of winning American sympathy. The Taliban received diplomatic recognition only from Pakistan, Saudi Arabia and the United Arab Emirates following its victory over Dostum on May 24, 1997.

The American hope of Taliban doing away with large unexploded land-mines in Afghanistan, has also got shattered as they proved useful for sustaining Taliban's own warfare. Despite the expertise and help offered by countries like India, no serious effort was made by Taliban to de-mine the world's worst mine affected country. More than 20 million mines were buried in Afghanistan during the 14 years of fighting. The worst victims of these land-mines have been women and children. Prior to Taliban capture of Kabul, international agencies like Halo Trust helped clear thousands of mines in and around Kabul.[25]

Although Pakistan and Saudi Arabia quickly recognised the Taliban government following the militia's brief victory over Mazar-i-Sharif, Washington did not show much interest following the footsteps of its ally Pakistan and Saudi Arabia. Washington called all factions to avoid violence, repression or reprisals in the aftermath of Dostum's flight. The State Department official John Dinger said that "the issue of recognition is not actually germane since the US only recognises states and not governments."[26] In fact in the changed circumstances, the US reasserted for a broad-based government in Kabul, and noted that there simply cannot be a military solution to the problem. The US cold response to Taliban victory in Mazar-i-Sharif was to be seen the context of the Iranian Presidential election which was due in June. Washington avoided strong action in Afghanistan which would have spoiled the prospect of moderate leader Khatami's chances. Obviously, Central Asian states would not have welcomed such an action by Washington either.

Though a belated realisation, Washington is unlikely to insist for a Pakistani solution to the complex Afghan issue. The Taliban may have temporarily helped containing international terrorism, it is unlikely that the US will risk experimenting with yet another monster Islamic group. Amid speculation about the US revamping its Afghan policy, including a positive dialogue with Iran, besides adopting a broader framework may prove to be a major breakthrough to resolve the intra-Afghan conflict. The world community in general and the Afghans in particular would expect the American leadership to demonstrate wisdom and take a balanced view of the situation, if it has any genuine interest for restoring a durable peace in Afghanistan.

References

1. Simes, Dimitri, "The Death of Detente," *International Security*, No. 5, 1980, pp. 1-19.
2. Ted Galen Carpenter, "The Unintended Consequences of Afghanistan," *World Policy Journal*, September, 1993.
3. P. Stobdan, "Kashmir: The Key Issues," Strategic Analysis, April, 1996.
4. Quoted in "What Now in Afghanistan?" editorial, *Washington Post*, April 3, 1989.
5. Statement of Barnett Rubin, Hearing, March 7, 1990, p. 27.
6. John F. Burns, "US Cuts off Arms to Afghan Factions," *New York Times*, November 19, 1989, p. 11.
7. Marvin G. Weinbaum, "Pakistan and Afghanistan: The Strategic Relationship," Asian Survey, June 1991, pp. 507-7.
8. Tim Weiner, "U.S. Will Try to Buy Anti-aircraft Missiles Back from Afghans," *New York Times*, July 24, 1993.
9. Carpenter, No. 2, p. 84.
10. Ludwina A. Joseph, "Afghanistan Dominates Congressional Hearing," *The Pioneer*, August 15, 1994.
11. Quoted by Rammish Chandran, "Islamic Militancy is Terror of the 90s," *The Times of India*, November 2, 1995.
12. John K. Cooley, "Counterterrorism assignment: Keep Track of the Afghanis," *International Herald Tribune*, July 1996.
13. "State Department Factsheet on Bin Ladin" Wireless File, USIS, New Delhi, August 15, 1996.
14. "America's Link to the Taliban," Nael Mokhayber, *Al-Watan al-Arabi*, (Arabic Weekly), Paris, October 11, 1996, as reproduced in the World Press Review, January 1997, pp. 22-23.
15. *The Hindustan Times*, October 10, 1996.
16. *The Times of India*, October 12, 1996.
17. As cited in the *World Press Review*, January 1997, p. 23.
18. "US claims it was misled on Taliban," as reported by IANS, *The Pioneer*, November 23, 1996.
19. "Opium-poppy production in Afghanistan : High but Stabilised, New UN Survey Finds," UN Information Service, Vienna, September 1996.
20. According to the Annual Report of the Vienna based International Narcotics Control Board (INCB), released in the worldwide tele press conference, on March 10, 1997.
21. Ahmed Rashid, "Drug: The Infidels," FEER, May 1, 1997, pp. 25-26, also see Robert Fisk, "Afghan farmers reap lethal crop", *The Independent*, London, as reproduced by *The Hindustan Times*, New Delhi, July 21, 1997.
22. Ahmed Rashid, No. 21.
23. *Time*, December 16, 1996, p. 12.

24. ANI, PTI quoted *London Daily* of November 20, 1996, "Guerrilla training camps reopened in Afghanistan," *The Hindustan Times*, November 22, 1997.

25. Jennifer Griffin, "Afghanistan: The New War Against Mines," The Pioneer, June 6, 1995.

26. "US Treading Warily on Afghanistan," *The Hindu*, May 29, 1997.

9

THE AFGHANISTAN CRISIS AND ITS IMPACT ON SOUTH AND SOUTH-WEST ASIA

UMA SINGH

It is rather unfortunate that Afghanistan is in turmoil for the last two decades. More so, because even the end of the Cold War has not brought any peace to the war-ravaged state and it has not yet resolved its international contradictions. The ongoing struggle for power in Afghanistan is an indisputable manifestation of a proxy war of attrition being fuelled by regional powers in pursuance of their political strategies and economic agenda in violation of the UN charter. It is indeed tragic that the international community remains indifferent and ambivalent towards the civil war and the resultant human tragedy in Afghanistan. The inability of the special UN mission to resolve the crisis and to broker a political settlement is equally regrettable. UN Secretary General Kofi Annan while explaining the inability of the UN special mission in his most recent remarks blamed mainly the warring Afghanistan while condoning the unbridled nature of foreign interference which, undoubtedly, is equally responsible for the ongoing massacre and religious fanaticism in Afghanistan. The resolution of Afghan conflict lies only in genuine intra-Afghanistan dialogue without foreign interference. The Taliban in their ideological delusion and their strategic patrons in their ambition to emerge as major regional powers have ignored Afghanistan's most heterogenous ground realities and the stakes of the adjoining states deeply involved in the conflict.

The Afghan civil war and the overt and covert support of neighbouring countries and trans-regional governments to warring groups in Afghanistan has only resulted in devastation of that country. The age-old differences among the Tajiks, Uzbeks and the Pushtoons have now become the main hurdle in implementing and maintenance of peace in Afghanistan. The crux of the problem in Afghanistan is the strife between the regional and the trans-regional governments that are determined to damage Afghanistan. The control of the Taliban over the northern Afghanistan has collapsed despite the support lent by Pakistan and the Arab countries (particularly Saudi Arabia) along with the USA.

What makes Afghanistan geopolitically significant is that historically the great powers have converged here. It has provided and continues to provide access to avenues leading to Iran, Central Asia, China and India. What happens in Afghanistan therefore could easily spill over to some of these countries. Any strategic agenda towards this region would require the fastening of the high plateau of Afghanistan to which Pakistan is the stairway. This gives Pakistan a crucial role in the 'New Great Game' being unfolded in Central Asia. Pakistan's agenda in Afghanistan is related to its desire for being the main trade route, especially for evacuating the hydrocarbon reserves of the countries of this region. It wants to build a corridor to Central Asia through Afghanistan which would be an alternative to the trade route through Iran. The puppet regime in Afghanistan would also provide a strategic depth to Pakistan vis-a-vis India. The India factor has been critical to Pakistan's gameplan in Afghanistan. Pakistan's military and strategic interest in Central Asia is determined by its rivalry with India. In fact Pakistan is using its relationship with the Central Asian countries within the framework of ECO as a counterweight against India at the regional level. It has been particularly wary of growing influence of Iran, India and Turkey in Central Asia. Thereafter, Pakistan is pursuing diplomatic efforts to keep Afghanistan within its sphere of influence. Within days of the Taliban capturing Kabul, a special envoy of the former Prime Minister of Pakistan Benazir Bhutto visited Tajikistan, Turkmenistan, Uzbekistan and Iran. But the significance of the war in Afghanistan, many political observers believe, goes beyond the boundaries of that country as other powers seek to fill the vacuum created by the collapse of the Soviet power. They argue that the developments made in Afghanistan represent many distinct geopolitical agendas—one up to the Oxus and others beyond it. Up to the Oxus, the question is of consolidating control over Afghanistan. Such has been the eagerness of the western media to legitimise the Taliban that no one has bothered to ask how the students of theology came out of Madrasas one day and then were going on bombing sorties, driving tanks and using sophisticated arms and ammunition the next day. The Taliban force has ostensibly been engineered by Pakistan. But it is increasingly clear that Pakistan is being used by the bigger powers with their own agenda for the region, especially one of containing Russia, Iran and China and exercising an overwhelming control over the relatively unexplored reserves of Central Asia. By drawing neighbouring countries into the Afghan conflict, by invoking the ethnic and sectarian cards, the possibility of peace and security in the South Asian region has been further eroded.

However, the fact remains that Taliban have been created by invoking two mutually ungovernable forces—Islamic fundamentalism especially in the form of Wahabiism and sub-nationalism. Islamic fundamentalism has been quite alien to Afghan culture and history. But as far the forces of sub-nationalism are concerned, Afghanistan is the microcosm for entire Central Asia with its Tajiks, Uzbeks, Turkman, Aimaqs Ismailies, Shias and Sunnis. With the Taliban takeover of Kabul and prolonged instability in Afghanistan both the south and south-west Asian region have been threatened with instability. As has been mentioned earlier, Taliban is largely a creation of Pakistan and its military successes as are clearly attributed to the generous help it has been receiving from Pakistan mainly in weapons and experienced military guidance in battle. There is understandable jubilation in Pakistan particularly within its army. The ISI ran the Afghan operations with full autonomy during Benazir Bhutto's regime and supported the Hizb-e-Islami under Hekmatyar. The Interior Ministry under Major General (retd.) Naseerulla Babar then assumed the conduct of Pakistan's Afghan policy despite stiff opposition from the ISI. Officially Pakistan favoured peace efforts by the UN, OIC and other regional actors because most of the Mujahideen groups maintained bases inside Pakistan.

The Central Asian republics are landlocked countries and

therefore an access to the sea for their growing trade, commerce and industry can easily be provided by Pakistan. In fact the major communications routes from Pakistan to the Central Asian republics lie through Afghanistan.

A Pakistan backed government in Kabul would give Pakistan the strategic depth it was longing for ever since it came into being. It would make Pakistan an even more valuable ally for America as the keeper of a corridor for America to reach the resource-rich and strategically located Central Asian states. It would also serve the shared interest America and Pakistan have in further reducing the importance of Iran as an outlet for the Control Asian States to the outside world through the Persian Gulf and India would thus get further isolated from an area of great interest and concern to it.

Two important factors have weighed with the US to review its attitude towards Afghanistan. As has been earlier mentioned, apart from the Iranian factor, US oil companies found Central Asian republics more lucrative than even the Middle Eastern allies due to their refusal to "countenance foreigners running their oil industries." In 1993 the American oil company Chevron concluded a deal worth 540 billion to develop Tengiz oilfield on the north-eastern shore of the Caspian. Peace and stability in Afghanistan is a prerequisite to the construction of pipeline through alternative routes other than Iran. One of the US companies UNOCAL had planned for the construction of an oil pipeline through Afghanistan at a cost of 8 billion US dollars. The Clinton administration had openly supported the UNOCAL project "as an alternative to schemes involving links through America's old nemesis Iran to the Arabian Sea." One of the reasons why the Clinton administration changed its approach towards Pakistan and sought to renew its ties by enacting the Hank Brown Amendment was due to the developments in Afghanistan and Central Asia. In September, 1995 Robin Raphel made a statement that "Pakistan has strategic and cultural reasons for wanting to play a constructive role in Central Asia, an area with which it has ties dating back centuries. As a moderate Islamic state, Pakistan is often seen as an alternative model to Iran in Central Asia.

Islamabad has also played an important (if sometimes controversial) role in Afghan affairs. Under the present circumstances, Washington does not seem to have any option except keep reiterating its support to the UN effort in Afghanistan. It was on US insistence that a new UN envoy has been sent to that country. The way the US has provided cautious support to the Taliban and managed to distance clearly from them in the wake of international outcry against their fundamentalist policies indicates that it desires to open the line of communication to various Afghan factions. After his defeat by the Taliban Hekmatyar accused the Taliban of being patronised by ISI and US. This view was also corroborated by the retired Chief of Pakistani Army General Mirza Aslam Beg who said that the US was fully supporting the Taliban in Afghanistan to contain Iran's influence. In early 1996 the US organised an internal conference on Afghanistan in Washington. The renewed American interest after a gap of seven years is directly related to its strategic and economic interests in Central Asia. Of late, the US has pursued a policy aimed at changing the political matrix in Central Asia which cannot be accomplished without pushing the Russians further north, curbing the spread of Iranian influence and undermining the importance of India in the Central Asian region. In their pursuit, the US has especially sought the support of Uzbekistan with an aim to establish its own sphere of influence in Central Asia. Islamabad, Washington, Riyadh and Tashkent have formed a political and strategic nexus towards the Central Asia. For quite some time Pakistani and American quest for a direct trade route to Central Asia has been frustrated by the civil war in Afghanistan.

Pakistan was the first country to recognise the Taliban government and the Benazir's government despatched officials to Kabul to have a liaison with the new government. Apart from the regime, the fundamental parties which have sponsored the Taliban effort since 1994 have been too pleased with the turn of events. The Jamiat-e-Ulema Islam (JUI) led by Maulana Fazlur Rahman has been the principal supporter of the Taliban and sent experts to Kabul to help the new regime to draft Islamic laws. Pakistan had understandably, more than one motive for creating the Taliban. Its leaders claim that the Taliban represent Afghanistan's best hope for a return to peace. Without this, the remaining two million refugees will never go back. But the desire for peace does not explain Pakistan's opposition to the various UN sponsored attempts to bring back peace. The fact is that Pakistan has always had a second more important goal to bring Afghanistan under its control and extend both its "defence in depth" and its influence in the region.

The question that arises is defence against whom? The obvious answer is—India. Pakistan's strategists have been clamouring for a defence in depth against India ever since the emergence of Bangladesh. These strategists will hardly fail to claim that with the Taliban victory, they have at last, obtained what they had so long sought. The immediate end to which the newly found accretion of strategic muscle will be put is to renew the bid to annex Kashmir. That was one of the reasons why Sikh and Kashmiri militants began to be given training in the Mujahideen camps when the Afghan war began to wind. It was why the Harkat-ul-Ansar was created (according to the US State Department by merging two organistions, the Harkat-ul-Jehad-i-Islam and Harkat-ul-Mujahideen in 1993). There was also a third reason why successive Pakistan governments sought to turn first the highly bloated ISI, then the residual Mujahideen towards an external enemy. This was to shield its own society from the further encroachment of fundamentalism.The November, 1995 bombing of the Egyptian embassy in Islamabad and internecine violence in Karachi has shown how easily Pakistan can be driven by fundamentalist violence. That it should also seek to turn the Taliban's attention towards Kashmir is inevitable.

The right-wing of Pakistani elite which is most attached to the concept of 'defence in depth' is also opposed to fundamentalist Jamaat-Islam and other related parties within the country. It wishes to portray itself to quote the US President as 'modern and moderate' a stabilising force in the region. But to change this goal it will have to deal with the Taliban. The Taliban however is a product of Jamaat's Madrasas and like the Harkat-ul Ansari has close links with it. No matter how the realignment of forces works out, it will leave the fundamentalist forces stronger and the democratic forces weaker. Pakistan's persistence in its present policies with or without American blessings cannot but prolong the increasing bloody civil war in Afghanistan. The Tehran meeting made a fervent plea for a cessation of hostilities. It has also created apprehension among the G15 and Moscow' in particular the meeting of CIS in Almaty.

Thoughtful people in Pakistan are themselves worried that the supremacy of the Taliban would cause enormous problems for Pakistan itself because this fanatical group promotes the kind of sectarian fundamentalism which is already tormenting Pakistan. At the same time, the Taliban leadership's determination to improve the Shariat which is acceptable to Sunni denomination compounds the problem because of large Shia population in the area.

Instability in Afghanistan has always spilled over into Pakistan, spreading through the body politik—the triple poison of ethnic strife, gun-culture and drug traffic. The Taliban 'fattened by the soaring profits from heroin trade has' contributed to the pool of international terrorism. And in alliance with ISI it has fostered narco-terrorism. It has turned Kandahar airport into a heroin and arms centre. Best poppy fields are under its control. Baluchistan and Sindh, the two western provinces of Pakistan have always been vulnerable to these dangers as Punjab and NWFP are to strife between Shia and Sunni Muslims which also can be further ignited by the fallout of developments in Afghanistan.

Another possibility which looms large and could be damaging to Pakistan rests as a quandary which Pakistan had always faced: how to promote Pushtoon ascendancy in Afghanistan, which alone can produce a pro-Pakistan regime in Kabul and douse Pushtoon ambition in Pakistan's own NWFP for a great Pushtoonistan—the creation of which would be disastrous for the integrity of Pakistan.

The glorification of fundamentalism by them in Kabul can rouse the same sentiments in Pakistan and other Muslim countries. There is a clear and immediate danger in Kashmir—the Taliban victory boosted the morale of militants. One Pakistani leader named Rashid has publicly announced that he is opening two transit points in Pakistan to facilitate the movement of Afghan Mujahideen to the valley and he would like to know who in Islamabad would try to stop him. Recently a new irritant has emerged in Sino-Pakistan ties. A report in Bangkok-based newspaper as well as a western news agency despatch has reported that Tabligh: Jamaat—an Islamic outfit with headquarters near Lahore had been sending copies of religious works—into Xinjing—a Muslim majority province of China with a view to incite the Muslim population there. Pakistan's relations with Iran have also been going through a strained patch over its wholehearted backing of the Taliban forces. Its absence from the Tehran meeting riled the Iranians. A meeting of 'Friends of

Afghanistan' was held in Tehran in October, 1996. Iran has been trying to wrest the initiative from Pakistan which is the main supporter of Taliban militia. Shia Iran is worried about the unrest to its western flank from the Sunni Taliban. Iran is also apprehensive of the US and Saudi Arabia support to any Afghan group that may contain Iran's regional clout. The Tehran meeting was attended by the representatives of Russia, Tajikistan, Turkmenistan, Kyrgyzstan, China, India, Turkey and the United Nations, the Organisation for Security in Europe and the Organistation of Islamic Conference. Among those who did not participate were Pakistan, Saudi Arabia and Uzbekistan. On Benazir's dismissal from government, the Iranian state radio commented that the Taliban had harmed Pakistan's political prestige especially that of Bhutto.

Incidentally, the Taliban leadership had refused to comment on the change of guard in Islamabad in November, 1996 but the changes did have an impact in Afghanistan. Nasrullah Babar who was to meet Afghanistan warlord Rashid Dostam, abruptly cancelled the meeting.

Both sides of Afghanistan faction face major political and military differences within their own ranks making it difficult for either of the two to assert enough strength to either initiate peace process or implement the military option effectively. The division within the northern allies and the Taliban have been further fuelled by the disaster in Mazar-e-Sharif some months ago, when the Taliban's traditional leadership and military muscle drawn from southern Afghanistan was shattered. The northen alliances had to deal with the double betrayal by general Malik Pehalwan and increasing operation of tensions among the Uzbeks, Tajiks and Hazaras.

Afghan travellers from Mazar-e-Sharif and workers and western officials say "differences within the Uzbek High Command have increased in recent weeks and General Malik is far from having control of all the forces and territory under his command." General Malik is still not trusted by many of his own Uzbeks while his betrayal of General Dostam and his willingness to handover Ismile Khan, the former Governor of Herat to the Taliban along with 700 fighters has earned him the bitterness of Persian-speaking westerners. General Malik is treated as a pariah by many and seems to be straddling two stools, wanting to strengthen his alliance with General Masood and the Hazaras but also keep the door open to the Taliban.

Likewise General Masood is suspicious of Malik and there seems to be very little military cooperation between the two. Significantly, in the heavy fighting and the wide front that he controls North of Kabul, General Masood had not solicited General Malik's help.

The Hazaras are more unhappy with General Malik for inviting the Taliban to Mazar-e-Sharif. The Hazaras of Hezbe Wahadat under Karim Khalili have emerged as a major fighting force after breaking the siege of the Hazarajat by the Taliban immediately after the Mazar debacle. They have also been helped by a large influx of Iranian weapons aid. They were the first to rebel against the Taliban presence in Mazar-e-Sharif forcing General Malik to break with the Taliban. They also broke the nine-month Taliban siege of Hazarajat and Taliban attempts to capture their capital Bomiyanin in central Afghanistan. They pushed the Taliban out of the Shibar Pass inflicting heavy casualties, moved east along the Ghorband Valley forcing Pakhtoons to leave the area and then swept southwards along the western line of Kabul.

The Taliban also face increasing internal problems. The majority of Taliban's main Kandhar Shoora, the Kabul Shoora, the Government in Kabul, its military commanders and its most loyal and experienced fighters were drawn from the Duwan tribes in the south. The majority of Taliban leadership is drawn from the southern provinces of Kandhar, Urozgu and Helmand. But recently after having lost 10 of its leaders captured in Mazar-e-Sharif, over 3600 troops captured and thousands more killed and wounded in the fighting, the Taliban have been forced to draw upon new recruits from the Ghilzar tribes of eastern Afghanistan, the Afghan refugee camps in Pakistan, where the majority is also Ghilzar and are inexperienced. The Taliban ability to offer negotiation to the opposition is also hampered by a clear declaration of what will be the nature of government they want for the country in the future. The Taliban are willing to negotiate with the opposition but on one condition that no political party can take part in the discussion. Islam is against all political parties, said one Taliban cabinet minister. "The constitution is shariat and we do not need a constitution, People love Islam, and that is why they all support the Taliban, "commented another Taliban minister. Apart from Pakistan support the Taliban are now effectively isolated in the region. Iran has closed its borders with Afghanistan after the Iranian embassy was asked to leave. The border closure has put a serious strain on the Taliban's administration in Herat as Iranian sources of fuel, wheat and other supplies dried up. In the month of July 1997, Taliban carried out provocative military manoeuvres just seven miles from the Afghan border.

The Taliban are furious with the role of Iran but there is no attempt to either initiate a dialogue or a compromise with either Iran or Hazaras. "Iran and Russia are interfering and supporting the opposition and they do not want the refugees to return. India is also encouraging the opposition and as Pakistan has good relations with us, so India is trying to destabilise that "said Maulvi Jililullah, the Taliban Attorney General.

Likewise Uzbekistan has virtually closed its borders with northern Afghanistan. Displeased with General Malik's coup against General Dostam and unwilling to trust him as an ally while also publicly critical of Taliban and Pakistan, Uzbekistan border closure has put an equally severe strain on food and fuel supplies, into both the north and the south. Meanwhile, Turkmenistan which faced a sudden influx of some 9000 Turkman refugees from western Afghanistan who have now returned home is extremely nervous of the Taliban. Also Turkmenistan is coming under increasing pressure from Russia and Uzbekistan to take a tougher line against the Taliban and close their border with Taliban administered west. All these actions illustrate the apprehensions of Afghanistan's neighbours about a possible Taliban victory and conquest of the north. None of their neighbours is prepared to accept a permanent Taliban government or further expansion by Taliban.

With the Taliban reluctance to broaden the ethnic base of its own movement, it will find it increasingly difficult to govern the cities and earn the loyalty of the non-Pashtoons in the north. And given the rivalries, mistrust and lack of unity within the northern alliances, its ability to offer a real solution to the problems of forming an interim government is limited. At the heart of this crisis is the ever increasing ethnic strifes and the sudden turn of sectarianism in the country with the battlelines between the Pushtoons and the non-Pushtoons becoming sharper and less accommodating everyday.

A perusal of some Pakistani newspapers of the last few months indicate that the losses in northern Afghanistan have "tamed the rigid Talbans" Having exhausted the military options to find a settlement of the Afghan issues, the foreign officer in Pakistan is trying to evolve a political settlemet to the intricate issue. It is a settled fact now that Taliban and the opposition forces have failed to militarily resolve the problem. War does not solve problems but only complicates the issues and prolongs them. Prime Minister Nawaz Sharif called for the convening of a regional conference in which all parties concerned with the Afghan issue are invited Interestingly the decision has been well received by the regional players including Iran, Central Asian republics, Russia, US and the United Nations. As a result the foreign minister Gohr Ayub Khan started a shuttle diplomacy and went to Central Asian Republics and the Russian Federation. The Foreign office is also co-ordinating the Chief of UN special mission to Pakistan Norbert Hall to promote peace settlement on the basis of governing a broad-based government.

Evidently by trying to impose a military solution to the Afghan issue the vested interest have done the maximum damage to the national interests of both Pakistan and Afghanistan and yet the Taliban reversal is a greater rebuff for them and their militaristic approach. More importantly the recent ignominous reversal suffered by the ultra radical student militia in Mazar-e-Sharif at the hands of Shiate Hezb-e-Wahadat and General Malik's forces points to the Taliban's overambitions and counter-productive agenda. As the situation exists Taliban credibility in areas under their control seems to be eroding due to combination of factors *inter alia* strict interpretation and enforcement of Islamic Shariat, pattern of brutality, their contemptuous disregard for the time-tested Afghan traditions, lust for power and unmistakable presence of non-Afghan combatants within their ranks as well as ascendancy of those hailing from the Kandahar province. Compelled with the Talibans's repeatedly growing influence in the frontier, the recent skirmishes at the Pakistan-Afghanistan border are an ominous sign that the students militia may well take its *jihad* across the borders. Over the last three months the Taliban have established contacts with the religious groups based in the frontiers Peshawar, Charasadha, Swabi and Mardan as well as in the northern and southern districts of frontiers. The results of the elections in PATA show that religious leaders have a decisive influence in the border regions as overtly pro-Taliban candidates with strong religious Madrasa links in their respective areas were returned by PATA voters in the area's first adults elections. In early April, 1997 a contingent of the Taliban border guards posted at Naava Kandas, a creek on the Kunnar Mohammed Agency border crossed over to a patch of disputed territory and ordered the Pakistsani paramilitary officials stationed there to evacuate the area. Frontier corps officials posted at Nawagai Bajaur told *Herald* in the first week of June, 1997 that in spite of several representations by Pakistan authorities the Taliban were adamant about holding on to the area as also to its cemented bunkers and a packed helipad. Meanwhile as the main Torkham crossing down the Khyber Pass, border tension has been simmering since the Taliban takeover of Kabul. The tension has brought into focus an old dispute involving a strategic Pakistan oil port located well inside Afghanistan territory

Recent border incidents show that if the Taliban are able to seize full control of Afghanistan, they are likely to use to the maximum their clout in the tribal areas where they have ethno-religious allies in the form of TIUQ, the TNSM and the JUI backed leadership of the two Warizstan agency. The situation may worsen, however, if the Taliban fail in Afghanistan believes Abdul Khattak, an Afghan journalist. "The Taliban's reversals in the north will Pakhtoonise them and send them back over the borders with a vengeance. This may well mean a resurgence of Pakistan-run nationalism in the frontier province and Baluchistan."

The Taliban perception of Pakistan as a friendly country underwent a radical transformation when the former governor of Nangarhar Haji Abdul Qadeer launched an anti-Taliban drive in Kunar province in early 1997. The Taliban responded by re-activating the long redundant ministry of border affairs and establishing contacts with religious groups deep inside the Pakistani territory. The question arises, how potent is this threat? "Pakistan, particularly the less urbanised region of the frontier and Baluchistan are fast descending into a state of economic anarchy" says Amal Khan, a journalist who covers Afghanistan affairs for a Lahore based daily. This threat is more directly by the officials responsible for implementing the country's border policy with Afghanistan.

That the Afghan Taliban tangle has a multifaceted dimension

is beyond doubt. The Taliban movement into northern Afghanistan has had a serious impact on the security and stability of the region. Because of the threat perceptions, the Taliban's military operations, Russia and four Central Asian states threatened to use force against them if it crossed into the former Soviet Union territory during the CIS summit held at Almaty in the month of October, 1996. The fall of Kabul has also brought a de-stabilising Islamic fundamentalist regime to the doorsteps of most of the Central Asian states. Two of the Central Asian republics Tajikistan and Uzbekistan have ethnic population that straddle their border with Afghanistan and are vulnerable to the profound change in the ethnic power balance in Afghanistan.

The recognition by Pakistan of the Taliban government in Afghanistan even though they were not the de facto rulers of most of Afghanistan but also because their ultra conservative mindset is unacceptable. There are also fears among Afghanistan's neighbours about their alleged agenda of exporting their own brand of Islam. Such fears have also been strengthened by the statement about their goals being the capture of Samarkand and Bukhara. Pakistan's decision to turn a de facto situation to a de jure recognition of Afghanistan is not surprising either. Pakistan may not agree with the Taliban brand of fundamentalism but Pakistan's commercial interest with the CAR and friendly government in Kabul is a must. Billions of dollars worth of projects in gas and oil pipeline would be at stake if civil war in Afghanistan continues. Being perceived as a major backer of Taliban Islamabad has exacerbated the fears of Central Asian allies as well as Iran about its own role in the Afghanistan imbroglio.

Although Hekmatyar himself is a Pushtoon he has revealed secrets about the Taliban groups. He has mentioned that those few heading the Taliban group have made secret deals with the US and will try to get the country out of the hands of Jihadi group.

In its latest official statement on June 11, 1997 the Pakistan government announced that it does not recognise the government established by the Taliban as the legitimate government of Afghanistan. The statement also said that Pakistan is in favour of government in Afghanistan which comprises of all factions and groups. In fact a faction within the Taliban has recently reached some agreements with the US on the return of the deposed Afghan King Zahir Shah.

Taliban are openly violating the human rights in Afghanistan but the western countries particularly the US which claim to advocate the cause of democracy and human rights do not object to such violations. The former Pakistani Prime Minister Benazir Bhutto in an interview with BBC was asked to comment on the reason for her country's support to the Taliban. She said, "We are not alone. This is a plan headed by the US and impaired by some Persian Gulf countries. We just train the Taliban." Nawaz Sharif during the initial days after his victory announced that he is going to review the country's policy on Afghanistan.

Ultimately the Afghanistan issue will be settled through peaceful means as no group in that country can ensure its intervention through fighting. The Tehran meeting of the Afghan leaders and the representatives of different political groups were a political move and the different Afghan factions agreed on a provisional government through negotiations.

India has not played a very active role in the Afghanistan crisis. Unlike other powers India never supported either covertly or overtly any group or faction in Afghanistan but recognised the ruling regime in Kabul. India's assistance to Afghanistan has been humanitarian and for development purposes. Although India failed to react quickly to the Taliban's capture of Kabul, it favoured the deposed President Rabbani's government as the legitimate ruler of Afghanistan. India positively responded to the Iranian initiative by sending a high-level delegation to Tehran. India was also among the 19 countries to participate in the UN conference on Afghanistan held in New York in November, 1996.

Since the 1950's Pakistan has aligned its strategic interests with the US and the congruence of interests between the two has resulted in escalation of the Afghan civil war and a continuous confrontation between Islamabad on one side and Tehran, a majority of CAR and Russia on the other side. It has become clear to all the regional actors that Afghanistan cannot return to normalcy so easily and like Hekmatyar, the Taliban's leadership is not acceptable to other factional leaders. In fact, the new alliance that emerged between General Dostam and Ahmed Shah Masood after Taliban's capture of Kabul and their successful efforts in repulsing Taliban's attack on Panjsheer Valley has made Taliban's position (though they occupy 24 provinces in Afghanistan) untenable and failure of Pakistan's efforts to make Taliban a legitimate force. Even after so many years, the objectives of Pakistan's Afghanistan policy have remained inconclusive. It still remains unclear as to how its perceived objectives are going to be achieved in the complex situation that has emerged in Afghanistan. Within weeks of taking over as United Nation's Secretary-General Kofi Annan's special envoy to Afghanistan Lakhdar Brahimi is assisting him to prepare a report on Afghanistan that he has to submit to the 52nd session of the UN General Assembly to be held October, 1997. He has met all the rival factions battling for control of Kabul and discussed peace prospects with the regional powers that are actively involved in Afghanistan. He is also trying to put pressure on Islamabad to coax the Taliban into agreeing to unconditional talks. Both the Taliban and the Northern Alliance have put forward some pre-conditions. The Taliban are demanding the release of prisoners while the Northern Alliance has made the demilitarisation of Kabul a pre-condition for talks. There is no doubt now that without a broad-based representative government in Kabul the idea of a peace conference or restoration of normal peace will remain elusive.

provinces in Afghanistan untenable and failure of Pakistan's efforts to make Taliban a legitimate force. Even after so many years, the objectives of Pakistan's Afghanistan policy have remained unfulfilled. It still remains unclear as to how its perceived objectives are going to be achieved in the complex situation that has emerged in Afghanistan. Within weeks of taking over as United Nations Secretary-General Kofi Annan's special envoy to Afghanistan Lakhdar Brahimi is assisting him to prepare a report on Afghanistan that he has to submit to the 52nd Session of the UN General Assembly to be held October, 1997. He has met all the rival factions battling for control of Kabul and discussed peace prospects with the regional powers that are actively involved in Afghanistan. He is also trying to put pressure on Islamabad to coax the Taliban into agreeing to unconditional talks. Both the Taliban and the Northern Alliance have put forward some pre-conditions. The Taliban are demanding the release of prisoners while the Northern Alliance has made the demilitarisation of Kabul a pre-condition for talks. There is no doubt now that without a broad-based representative government in Kabul the idea of a peace conference or restoration of normal peace will remain elusive.

10

TALIBAN POSES A DILEMMA TO MUSLIM WORLD

JAGDISH P. SHARMA

It is unfortunate that Afghanistan consistently in turmoil. No nation has been left more ravaged than Afghanistan and none has suffered as much from direct foreign intervention and fundamentalist genocide as this single country. The Afghans are in agony, caught up in a spiral of militant and fanatic violence that has almost brought the state to its knees. The emergence and capture of power by Taliban, a politico-military, radical Islamic force in the latter half of (on 27 September), 1996, supported by Pakistan, in the shrdded fabric of the war-torn Afghanistan, has confused the already complicated struggle for power in Kabul. Since the Taliban tookover, tyranny has ruled the roost in most parts of Afghanistan followed by military dictates, religious fanaticism, that is, imposing restrictions on women, forbidding them from appearing in public unless covered from head to toe and forcing men to grow beards and pray at mosques. Replacing communism with an Islamic ideology has not helped in healing the division.

Afghanistan has been the focus of worldwide attention for more than two decades now. It was the last staging post for the Cold War confrontation, and the withdrawal of the Soviet troops from Afghanistan signified the end of the Cold War. While the end of the Cold War brought relative peace at the global level, peace and stability have eluded Afghanistan like a mirage. Of late signals from the US indicate that American policy-making is reverting to Cold War policies in South Asian region which it seemed to have abandoned after withdrawal of Soviet forces from Afghanistan. Pakistan is again being armed discreetly to play the role which it had played during Cold War years, this time aimed at the oil reserves of Central Asian States adjacent to Afghanistan and also for cornering the Iranian regime which has been Washington's ***brete noir*** since 1979 when the pro-US Reza Shah Pehlavi was overthrown. The US administration has not taken kindly to the efforts of Tehran to establish close regional trade linkage between the Central Asian republics and India.

Landlocked Afghanistan, known originally as Ariana and then as Khorasan (the land of the rising Sun), was formed as a separate state by Ahmed Shah Durrani in 1747. Modern Afghanistan emerged between 1884 and 1919. Historically it had owed its existence to its geographical location. Its strategic position had saved it from absorption by Britain or Russia.[1] Afghanistan is situated in South-West Asia and occupies an area of approximately 652,090 square kilometres. Afghanistan shares a border with the former Soviet Union. (2,384 kilometres long) in the north with the People's Republic of China (75 kilometres), India (120 kilometres) in north-east with Pakistan (2,180 kilometres) in the east and south and with Iran (820 kilometres in the west). Even in the past Afghanistan's strategic importance was so crucial that Abul Fazal (1551-1602), Persian scholar and famous writer patronised by Akbar, recorded that Kabul and Kandahar were two gates of India: "The custody of these highways secured India from foreign invaders and they are likewise the appropriate portals to foreign travel."[2]

The Simon Commission in its report of 1929 also recognised the strategic importance of Afghanistan. "North-West Frontier of India is not only the frontier of India, it is an international frontier of the first importance."[3]

Afghanistan is a highly traditional and tribal-oriented state. It was only around the latter part of 1940s and 1950s that the superpowers aid began to make perceptible inroads in the form of setting up schools.

The US military designs and the subsequent closure of the Pak-Afghan border over the issue of the future of the Pushtoon tribe forced Afghanistan to re-route its trade through the Soviet Union and seek assistance to modernise its army. The eventual outcome of this move was Soviet intervention in Afghanistan.

Afghanistan passed through a period of uncertainty during the regime of Lt. Gen Muhammad Daud, who came to power after overthrowing King Zahir Shah in a bloodless coup on July 17, 1973. Daud, who became the head of state on August 23, 1973, seemed in full control of the situation and on good terms with the neighbouring country (the USSR). In the act of crushing the left-wing opposition, Daud was himself overthrown in a military coup (April 1978) which was led by army and air force officers who released the imprisoned Leftist leaders to form a new government. The Soviet Union recognised the new regime.

The new government was dominated by civilians of the People's Democratic Party of Aghanistan (PDPA) founded in 1965 and its Secretary-General Nur Muhammad Taraki succeeded as Prime Minister. Taraki's hopes of building a new society floundered quickly as his party split into two rival factions and the country drifted into civil war. In quick succession the chief figures of PDPA became presidented each after the murder of his predecessor—Taraki replacing Daud (as mentioned), Hafiz-ullah Amin replacing Taraki and after the Soviet intervention in December 1979, Babrak Karmal stepping into the shoes of Amin and Maj. Gen. Najibullah replacing Karmal in May, 1986.

Since 1979, there has been an almost complete breakdown of the Central government administration over its 28 provinces. The Soviet intervention in Afghanistan since December 1979 was defended on the basis of November 1978 Treaty of Friendship and Article 51 of the UN Charter. It was claimed that Amin, who was accused of plotting to partition Afghanistan with foreign imperialist powers had been overthrown by an internal revolution and that military support from the Soviet Union had been requested by the new regime. World opinion, however, was sceptical of such claims and a Soviet withdrawal was demanded by the UN General Assembly, the Islamic Conference Organisation (ICO), the Association of South-East Asian Nations (ASEAN), the Non-Aligned Movement (NAM) as well as by Western powers.

Since the spring of 1979 the Soviet Union began to play a

greater role in Afghanistan. Evidently alarmed at the extent of the hostility to the regime and the prospect of being drawn into a protracted civil war and concerned about the possible international complications of Afghan disputes with her neighbouring countries, Islamic Republics of Pakistan and Iran respectively, it began to argue for less radical policies, conciliation of the opposition and the formation of a broad-based government. But at the same time a steady built-up of Soviet military presence in Afghanistan had been felt. The US State Department has issued a series of diplomatic warnings and protests since then.

However, for the first time since the Soviets have intervened in Afghanistan in December, 1979, they have made determined diplomatic efforts to try and bring about a peaceful settlement there. The year 1987 also saw widespread intensification of the war between the Soviet troops and the Afghan Islamic guerrillas (operating from Pakistan and Islamic Iran). The war and unrest in Afghanistan both have largely wiped out three decades of development progress there. Schools, medical clinics and farmers' access to fertiliser and improved seed from the state agencies have suffered in the general destruction. Besides the costs to the Soviet Union of this war were considerable and mounted rapidly both in casualties suffered and losses incurred in military hardware.

Moreover, foreign interference in the region took a serious turn with the US's espousal of the theory of an "arc of crisis", in the wake of the fall of the Shah of Iran. The developments in Afghanistan came as a blessing in disquise for the then Pakistan President, General Zia-ul-Haq, who used the pretext of a "Soviet threat" to obtain enormous US military and economic aid. The Soviet Union and the Babrak Karmal and Najibullah regimes in Kabul repeatedly expressed their readiness to pull out the Soviet troops the moment an international agreement was concluded on cessation of foreign interference in the internal affairs of Afghanistan. India supported this position.

Accordingly, the Great Geneva Agreement reached on April 14, 1988, the Soviet troops started pulling out from Afghanistan and completed the same on February 15, 1989, after eight turbulent years of undeclared war there.

Internationally, the Geneva Accord gave the US first time an equation with the Soviet Union in the region. The Soviets lost even if they had everything in their favour in Afghanistan. They could not afford to continue as they realised the cost was higher in terms of international goodwill.[4]

After Soviet troops were withdrawn from Afghanistan in February 1989, the Islamic Mujahideen, who had waged nearly a decade-long war of resistance, turned their guns on the Soviet installed regime of President Najibullah. But it was not until the fall of communists in the USSR in August, 1991 and the end of Soviet aid that they were able to deal a decisive blow to the Najibullah regime in Kabul. The interim Mujahideen government under President Burhanuddin Rabbani was sworn in 1992. Many were hopeful that with the fall of Kabul work would begin on the reconstruction of Afghanistan, the repatriation of refugees, and the installation of an elected government. This proved wishful thinking. With the fall of communist regime in Kabul the last thread that had united the Mujahiddeen was gone. Cold political divisions that had been suppressed in the name of *Jihad* reemerged. The war had dramatically shifted the balance of power among the different Afghan ethnic groups. Meanwhile, a new force emerged in the South. In late 1994, a group of Pushtoon Islamic radical students and their leaders, allegedly trained in Pakistan, began to seize power from local Afghan warlords. By March, 1995 they were at the gates of Kabul. Since then, the fighting in Afghanistan has marginalised the country. Afghanistan no longer exists as a single country but is divided into separate areas controlled by different Militias.

However, a continuous conflict in Afghanistan affects regional stability in Russia, Central Asia, Iran and India. Russia has warned the Taliban that should they succeed in getting their conflict to northern Afghanistan bordering Russia's southern neighbouring states of Uzbekistan, Tajikistan and Turkmenistan, Russia's role in the region would become inevitable. The Taliban occupation of Kabul made the leaders of Russia, Kazakhstan, Kyrgyzstan, Uzbekistan and Tajikistan come together in Alma Ata. However, the leaders of the CIS states "concerned" found it possible not to enter into war against fundamentalism immediately. The Russian advocates of a strong state see the execution of the former Afghan President Najibullah and fall of Kabul to Taliban militia as a fresh geopolitical defeat for Moscow after the decision of NATO's expansion to the East and the withdrawal of Russian federal forces from Chechnya.[5]

The ultra-conservative Taliban Islamic militia has taken almost total control of Afghanistan in a matter of months, with former President Burhanuddin Rabbani and his key military commander Abdul-Rashid Dostam being forced to flee the country. Pakistan, followed by Saudi Arabia and the UAE, is the first country to recognise the new Taliban government losing no time in extending its support. This was to be expected considering the deep interest Pakistan has been taking in the activities of the Taliban. A counter-offensive by the Tajik guerrilla commander Ahmad Shah Masood and other supporters of the Rabbani regime, however, drove back the Taliban from Mazar-e-Sharif and some north areas of Kabul. India is concerned about Pakistan's growing involvement in the Afghan region which is seen as a threat to its national security. This is the reason which has brought India and Iran, closer to each other. Iran has an ancient rivalry with the Pushtoon Afghanistan from which the Taliban is drawn and is concerned that Sunni Taliban may dilute Iranian Shia influence in the region. The other reason for concern is the oil, gas and mineral resources in the Central Asian states. Pakistan wants a route through Taliban-controlled Afghanistan to Turkmenistan and other Central Asian states, which would be independent of Russia. Iran has a direct link to Turkmenistan and Turkey has a planned one. Incidentally one more consequence of the Taliban's victorious advance on Kabul apparently was upsetting the peace-making plans for Afghan settlement which were initiated at Iran's foreign ministry. Not long ago Mr Vayazi, Deputy Minister of Foreign Affairs of Iran, made a tour of the Central Asian capitals and invited their representatives to Tehran where an international conference was held in October 1996. Here both Russia and India were also invited.

The October, 1996 Tehran conference criticised the recent flagrant violations of human rights in Afghanistan, particularly the rights of women. It called for an immediate end to such practices in conformity with the relevant provisions of the UN Charter. Iranian Foreign Minister Ali Akbar Velayati announced that Iran would continue to stress a regional initiative to resolve the Afghanistan dispute. But he also made it clear that it could not be an isolated effort. "It has to be reinforced by active international efforts and should be connected to them", he said.[6]

Compared with other neighbouring nations, the Iranians have greater affinity with Afghans. A common religion, history, culture, and especially language tie these two nations together so that the slightest sociocultural or even political development in either of these countries makes an inevitable impact on the other. Since Soviet invasion and occupation of Afghanistan in 1979, Iran denounced the occupation of the Afghan territory and called for the unconditional withdrawal of the Russian forces. After Soviet withdrawal (April 1988-Feb. 1989), Iran was among the first countries to recognise the Mujahideen government there. Along with Turkey, Iran, Pakistan and the six Central Asian states, Afghanistan was included in the Economic Cooperation Organisation in 1993. Drug trafficking is another major factor that has affected Iran as a result of Afghanistan's instability, inflicting serious economic and psychological concerns to the Iranian nation. Iran is seriously committed to her policy of non-intervention in the internal affairs of Afghanistan. Afghanistan's various warring factions ought to facilitate Afghanistan's integrity and unification. The neighbouring countries, in turn, must prevent the intervention of outside powers. The persistence of the status quo, Iran feels, would drive Afghanistan towards disintegration and heavy damage to the Afghan national resources. It is in this context that Iran feels seriously threatened.[7] Hence, Iranian President Ali Akbar Hashemi Rafsanjani's keenness to promote close economic, political and strategic alliance with India goads the Indian foreign and defence policy planners to give a thought to the above arrangement.

India and Iran need to intensify coordination to get the warring factions in Afghanistan to the negotiating table, the Speaker of the Iranian Parliament, Mr. Nateq Noori opined in his last visit to India. The visiting leader praised India for its contribution and participation at last October's (1996) conference on Afghanistan held at Tehran. Both India and Iran were also present at the subsequent UN sponsored conference on Afghanistan at New York. Mr. Noori, who held wide ranging discussions with former Indian Prime Minister, Mr. H.D.Deve Gowda, the External Affairs Minister, and new Prime Minister Mr. I.K.Gujral, and other leaders, said India and Iran are coordinating to bring the warring factions together in Afghanistan to end the hostilities which would help usher an era of peace in that country.[8] "Wherever there is crisis it does affect the neighbouring areas. Any unsettled condition in Afghanistan is bound to affect Iran, India, Pakistan and Central Asian republics. If the crisis drags on, it will harm Pakistan more than anything else in terms of political stability and economic development," says Nasser Saghafi-Ameri, Deputy Chief of Mission, Embassy of the Islamic Republic of Iran, New Delhi. In the opinion of the Iranian ambassador to India, Mr Ali Reza Sheikh Attar, "Afghanistan is a sensitive and vital issue for both India and Iran. India is a major player in Asian affairs. Hence it has the potential to establish peace in Afghanistan."[9]

Current developments in Afghanistan are of considerable long-term relevance to India. The Taliban militia has threatened neighbouring countries with severe consequences if they attempt to help the embattled alliance fighting them. Iran, Russia, Tajikistan, Uzbekistan and India have been accused of providing aid to northern-based rival forces led by General Abdul Rashid Dostam, the ousted Rabbani government of Kabul and Shiite faction. More fighting in Afghanistan would continue to pose a risk not only to Afghanistan but it has a potential of spreading out to the whole South-West Asian and Central Asian region. It is likely to affect Indo-Pak relationship quite adversely. It has become one more source of discord because what worries India is the possible impact of the Afghan conflict on Kashmir. India has expressed concern over reports that terrorist training camps are being run in the Khost area of Afghanistan. Without naming Pakistan, Indian ambassador to UN Prakash Shah warned that the "consequences of imparting training to terrorists would only recoil on the societies which promote such activities." Afghanistan was the focus of attention in India's External Affairs Minister I.K. Gujral's recent talks with the Iranian leaders, especially the role of the Taliban militia. India has also told Iran that the elements backing the Taliban militia in Afghanistan are the same which have been trying to destabilise Kashmir through terrorism. Mr Gujral said that India and Iran had common perceptions on the necessity to maintain the unity, independence, sovereignty and territorial integrity of Afghanistan. "We believe that peace and stability in Afghanistan is essential for peace and stability in the region", Mr Gujral asserted.[10]

According to Mrs Gillane Allam, Egyptian ambassadress to India, there is fall out of the Afghan crisis on the Arab world, Iran, Pakistan and South Asia. Arab countries, Mrs Allam feels, are basically supportive of President Rabbani's government. It is only the Pakistani government which has got direct links with the Taliban militia. The assessment at Cairo now is that both the Rabbani and Taliban factions are losers in grasping power in Afghanistan. There is no winner and no loser in that country except the innocent Afghans. The crisis there, led Afghanistan to be the centre for the export of terrorism and fanaticism directed towards Kashmir, Central Asian republics, Egypt, Algeria and neighbouring Gulf. The Taliban projection of Islam seems to be very negative. It hurts Islam in terms of its image, in terms of Hindu, Christian and other world religions. The Indian, Egyptian and Algerian intelligence services are also uncovering evidence that a large number of skilled Muslim guerrillas waging bloody campaigns in Algeria, Egypt, Tunisia and other North African states were trained in Afghanistan. Since 1980s, hundred of Arabs went to Afghanistan to fight alongside the Islamic guerrillas against the Soviet Union.

For nearly two decades, the frontier city of Pakistan, Peshawar became the home and gateway to Afghanistan for thousands of fervent Islamic militants from Libya, Algeria, Iraq, Egypt and Sudan. "*The Afghan Jihad*" (holy war), became the international projection of the Muslim world, according to Hamid Gul, a retired ISI Pakistani general. It became an ideological obsession among Islamic youth who were studying in the United States and Europe. They had liberal ideas, but they saw that the western liberalism was not the answer for what they were looking for. They tried to re-discover themselves. The instrument for re-discovery was the *Jihad*. Twice in May, 1992, Egyptian intelligence and military officials came to Peshawar looking for Islambouli and other Egyptian fundamentalists. On both visits, although they interviewed many Egyptians living in Peshawar, they were unsuccessful in their search. Indeed, Afghans living there have said that Islambouli had moved across the border to Jalalabad.[11] "All these fundamentalists have been trained in Afghanistan and Pakistan," says Mr Abdelhamid J. Bereksi, Algerian Ambassador to India. He adds, "They have a great network serving in the Arab world. The link of Afghanistan with what is happening in Europe and Arab world is direct. Many youths have been brain-washed, trained, armed and financed. The implications of the Afghan crisis on Algeria are very much direct. Our people were trained and used in Afghan drama. I see no difference between the Algerian GIA (Armed Islamic Group), Jamaite Islami in Egypt or Taliban in Afghanistan. What is happening in the name of religion in Afghanistan will open the eyes of Muslim nations. Taliban is using the religion of Islam as a political and military weapon. In a Muslim country one must have the courage to say that this is religion and this is politics. Islamists represent only the past which is totally dead."

To Dr Khalid el-Sheikh, Palestinian Ambassador to India, "the Afghan people are victims of international conspiracy. Their territory is an important transit point for Central Asia, West Asia and South-West Asia. The US wants to control the resources of the region to protect its economic interests. The Taliban militia is there to stay as it may be used by the US as a base against Iran." On Pakistani role, Dr Khalid said, "Pakistan has its own interest in building bridges with Central Asia. Everybody is trying to extract his own bit in order to exploit this region. There won't be much scope for stability in the region. The Taliban's fanatic impositions are un-Islamic prejudiced and backward. The religion of Islam has a humanist appeal. It is against oppression in the name of religion. The primitive approach of Taliban is distorting the picture of Islam. It is very sad and tragic to learn about the uncivilised execution of President Najibullah. India has reasons to express its concern." The Palestine Liberation Organisation, (PLO) was among those which played an important role in working out a peace plan for Afghanistan. It mediated between the different Mujahiddeen factions, the late Najibullah regime and Pakistani government. Mr Abu Khalid, a special representative of PLO chief Yasser Arafat, met the then Pakistani Prime Minister Benazir Bhutto and Afghan Mujahiddeen leaders in Islamabad during the days of Soviet withdrawal from Aghanistan in 1989.

To the Jordanians, the Afghan crisis is complicated. The main issue one time was the presence of foreign troops there. But now the main issue is the intervention of foreign powers directly or indirectly. It's time for the Afghan factions to find out national consensus. This can be possible only by restricting intervention of foreign powers like Pakistan, Tajikistan, Saudi Arabia and others. All warlords in

Afghanistan are controlled by different powers. Once again, the use of religion as an instrument of power is unacceptable. "Leave the language of guns and tanks. Who pays the price? It's the people's development that suffers. People also suffer. It is disastrous. A valid regime with Afghan people's mandate should take control of Afghanistan. We still recognise the legitimate government of President Rabbani. When the Afghan problem started in 1979 with Soviet intervention it encouraged young Arab people including from Jordan to join the holy war against foreign intervention. The US role in promoting Islamic military camps is also deplorable. The superpowers, particularly the US, have their own strategy and interests in promoting arms, drugs, money and all other issues," says Dr Mazen I. El Tal, counsellor of Jordanian embassy in India.

The financing of the Islamic militant movements has played a significant part in their success. In Egypt, Algeria, Sudan and Afghanistan, large amounts of external money, especially from Saudi Arabia, contributed to the strength of these groups. Money has been regularly and lavishly distributed by Saudi Arabia to world-wide Islamic movements for many decades, especially after 1980, in an effort to influence and strengthen them against "Iranian pretensions to the leadership of Islam." Some 2,000 Algerians were recruited by the Saudi-based World Muslim League and transited Jeddah on their way to training camps in Sudan and in Pakistan before taking on Soviet occupation forces in Afghanistan. By 1992, most of them had been repatriated to Algeria.[12] A Dhaka-based Bengali daily *Janakanta* (voice of the people) has claimed that about 3,500 Bangladeshis were fighting in Afghanistan alongside the Taliban. The daily also claimed that Bangladeshi Mujahiddeen, who were earlier motivated to fight against Indian forces in Kashmir were taken to Afghanistan where they joined the Taliban.

Neither the Organisation of Islamic Conference (OIC) nor Syria recognise the present Taliban militia in Kabul. It does not want the religious conservatives to take Afghanistan five hundred year's back into history. "We are all for the peaceful settlement of the Afghan crisis. The only solution to the turmoil in Afghanistan is to have all factions come and sit together rationally to think about a situation of peace. If there is any justification for the forces to counter during Soviet occupation of Afghanistan, this is history now. They are killing themselves and their brethren. There is no justification for such killing of brothers, children and women in the name of Islam," says Mr Ali Mansour, Syrian representative in India.

"The Taliban is the most extremist Islamic movement in the world. Their success to overthrow Kabul's Islamic government has reduced the country to rubble. Afghans of all persuasion find it difficult to understand why their country has been forgotten by the world. It was once a piece on the international chessboard, and now the game has been changed. All the geopolitical rhetoric about being at the crossroads of Asia, and the praise that was heaped on them by their western friends has gone. Asia, however, has found other crossroads and the world has found other crises to worry about. What happens in Afghanistan is no longer relevant. Afghanistan served its purpose in the 1980s, as far as the West is concerned. It helped to bring down communism in the Soviet Union and eastern Europe. Now it does not matter. It can be abandoned to cynical warlords, to the agents of outside powers, to ultra extremists who hang human beings at their sweet will."[13]

Reacting to the response of the Arab world, Mr Masood Khalili, Afghan ambassador to India says, "the Arab world helped us during the war against Soviet occupation. Now they have passively reacted to the emergence of Taliban militia. While the Arab world (52 countries) follows the policy of wait and watch, only one non-Arab Islamic neighbour Pakistan is behind them. Common people, especially the women in the Arab world, see the Taliban imposition as going back to pre-Islamic era. Out of all the Islamic countries, it is only Iran which still recognises the Rabbani government and reasserts its position regarding Afghanistan." "Our formula to the resolution of Afghan crisis is very clear," he reiterated. "We always kept open the doors for peaceful negotiation. Let us solve the problem politically, that is,

(a) Taliban must leave Kabul, we also withdraw from Kabul,

(b) to demilitarise Kabul,

(c) We both work on a broad-based formula of ceasefire, elections and elected government. In this interim period a neutral hand or third force or the UN should take over the administration of Kabul. The peaceful political negotiations should include all ethnic groups in Afghanistan (Pushtoon, Taziks, Hizarah, Uzbeks). Military conquest and destruction is no solution to the present crisis in Afghanistan," concluded Mr Khalili.

Many of the experts who came together at a seminar on the future of Afghanistan organised by the US Institute of Peace, felt that Pakistan's moves were detrimental to a resolution of Afghan crisis. Dr Marvin Weinbaum, senior fellow at the Institute, warned that "Pakistan in its support of the Taliban is playing with fire" and predicted that, "the worst possible outcome for Pakistan would be an incomplete Taliban victory." Dr Ashraf Ghani, senior anthropologist with the World Bank, warned that the war in Afghanistan is "likely to assume an increasingly ethnic and sectarian shape producing psychological scars to render a compromise less likely."[14]

Libyan leader Muammar Gaddafi recently warned that political systems based on religion were dangerous, particularly for women. In a speech in *Sabha* to mark a declaration of the rights and obligations of women in Libya, Mr Gaddafi said the recent experience of rule by the fundamentalist Taliban movement in Afghanistan showed that the first victims of religion-based rule were women. "Any political system which is based on religion or has justified being in power with religion, is one of the most dangerous systems for women's freedom," the Libyan leader said. Mr Gaddafi accused fundamentalist groups of being bankrupt and of wanting only to control the masses, saying that they used religion to achieve this because religion could not be debated or opposed."This is the worst exploitation of religion. These systems which are based on religion are the most dangerous of systems and the most atheistic, hypocritical and bankrupt from the economic, political and scientific point of view," Mr Gaddafi said.[15]

To Mr K.M. Singh of Delhi University, the emergence of Taliban fundametalist militia in Kabul is ominous. It is a reversion to the worst form of obscurantism. The piteous state of the women specially in Kabul can be imagined. They have to cover themselves fully as per Taliban's dictates. They are not even allowed to pursue their jobs or studies. This means depriving them of the benefits of civilisation."

The situation in Afghanistan still remains fluid. The whole country is teetering at the edge of a precipice. If it falls, it will plunge into greater agony than it has known before, and the consequences for the region as a whole can be far-reaching and tragic. There is little prospect of any one faction succeeding in gaining control over the entire country and providing the peace, stability, security and prosperity that its people desperately need. Absence of a unified set-up will lead to destruction. Over a period of time the fundamentalist Taliban is bound to provoke popular reaction against it, even if it is the dominant faction.

References

1. Ram Rahul, *Afghanistan The USSR and the USA Delhi*: ABC Publishing House, 1981, p. 53.
2. *Oxford History of India,* Vincent A. Smith, London 1923.
3. "Broken Window in Central Asia: Afghanistan" Richard Aspinall, *Australia an Outlook*, vol. 10, no. 1, March 1956, p. 47.
4. J.P. Sharma, "Uncertain future ahead of Afghanistan" in *National Herald* (Delhi) Friday, March 3, 1989.
5. Arkady Dubnov, "Where will the Taliban stop?" in New Times, November 1996, p. 56.
6. N.C.Menon, "US, Iran, Afghan policy" in *The Hindustan Times,* November 4, 1996.
7. Ali Khorram, "Afghanistan and the National Security of the Islamic Republic of Iran" in *Amu Darya* (Tehran) vol.I, No.2, Summers I all 1996, pp.225-230.
8. *National Herald* (Delhi) November 28, 1996.
9. Quoted in *The Asin Age,* Delhi & London, February 18, 1997.
10. Quoted in *The Asian Age,* February 24, 1997.
11. The Hindu (Chennai) Aug. 19, 1993.
12. Graham E. Fuller, *Algeria: The Next Fundamentalist state ?* Santa Monica: The Rand Corporation, 1996, p. 38
13. John Simpson, "Afghan cockpit" in *Index on Censorship* 4, 1996, (London, p. 164.
14. *The Statesman* (Calcutta) Nov. 25, 1996.
15. Quoted in *Asian Age* March 18, 1997.

11

WEAPONS AND NARCOTICS IN AFGHANISTAN: STRATEGIES AND AMBITIONS IN A LIGHT WEAPONS WAR

TARA KARTHA

The conflict in Afghanistan appears to have reached a crucial stage with the Taliban having captured most of the areas though it may be temporary. In Afghanistan, the fighting and the endless alliances and counter alliances are only a very small part of the whole as the Soviet intervention has proved in recent decades. The history of Afghanistan has never been written by war or victory, but by intrigue, diplomatic double entendre and the decisions of leaders in capitals several hundred miles away. Nothing much has changed in Afghanistan over the years, except that the bullet holes in the walls of houses in Kabul have been replaced by artillary cracks, even as the population is steadily decimated by war, disease and that peculiar legacy of today's wars—from injury from the several million landmines that are scattered about the country, especially between the Afghan-Pak border.

Afghanistan's geograhical location has, as always, had much to do with what seems to be an almost unending history of conflict, with ironically one of the main reasons for internal instability being that regimes in Kabul have been hamstrung by the lack of resources within the country itself, even as it sits across a vital trade route that could link the riches of Central Asia with the rest of the world. Tsarist Russia eyed the riches of the "Silk Route" (which had hardly any silk) and made it's way southwards, but during the Cold War, this picture was somewhat reversed with the Soviets accused of scheming to get at the oil-rich Gulf states, and that almost legendary desire for a warm water port, rather than any desire to open trade routes. That the Soviets hardly concentrated troops to the borders of Iran was immaterial to the Cold War players, nor the fact that Soviet entry had been hesitant and fraught with discord and governed more by the fact that Afghanistan has always been seen as a threat to the vital periphery of Russia—the Central Asian states. To a country that was almost obsessed with defence, this was a vital factor.

Today while this continues to remain part of the larger picture, the lure of "silk" has been replaced by the promise of oil and gas from the wells of Turkmenistan and "white gold" from Uzbekistan further north stretches the tempting possibility of a trade route into Turkey and beyond. This is a temptation to all countries in the region. But to Pakistan, whose Sui gas field is due to run out by 2010, (or earlier) this is more than a temptation—it is a vital, national security concern. If General Zia was determined to "pray at the mosques of Kabul" he and his generals had other objectives in mind. As the "Islamisation" of Pakistan followed and foreign policy began to be tinged with green, it was obvious that Zia hoped that the unifying factor of Islam would erode the fitful and dangerous tendencies of Pushtoon nationalism that threatened the cohesion of the Pakistani state. To the US administration (especially to the CIA chief) the driving need to avenge Vietnam was almost an obsession, while among Afghanistan's neighbours, there were few who could view the Soviet invasion without concern. India particularly saw the dangers inherent to such a policy, and the advantages that would accrue to Pakistan as a "frontline state" against the Reds. But these and all other considerations were only contributory factors. The seed of unending conflict were sown quite literally in 1979 as the systematic cultivation of poppy for the purposes of funding a war began, and as billions of dollars of weapons aid began to seep into the country. Today it would not be erroneous to say that whoever controls the narcotics fields of Afghanistan, rules the region. At a street value that has been variously estimated as between 4 billion US dollars (in 1989) to around 30 billion US dollars a little less than a decade later, this is a "strategic" relationship that has many facets—from the fact that drug revenues constitute almost double that of the annual budget, to the fact that the major political figures continues to be involved in the trade—the reported involvement of Asif Zardari is only one such instance. Apart from this is in the intimate relationship between the ambitions of the Intelligence Services and its financial needs to fulfil those ambitions.

Which leads to another facet peculiar to the conflict in Afghanistan. Today, from a rather backward country that few knew anything about, it is possibly the largest warehouse of light weapons anywhere in the world not produced by itself. Having said that a caveat needs to be added. The thousands of tons of light weapons—the assault rifles, mortars and rockets which are the primary weapons of war in this conflict have one basic requirement to keep up their deadly onslaught—the ammunition. While weapons are plentiful in the international blackmarket, ammunition is another matter altogether. There is nothing to indicate that any blackmarket anywhere, can provide ammunition in sufficient numbers to can keep the rapid firing weapons active—a Kalashnikov after all has a rate of fire of 600 rounds a minute—in a conflict that slips repeatedly into high intensity 'virtual war' conditions. In essence, the conflict would rapidly grind to a halt without neighbouring sustenance. The story of the war in Afghanistan is about systematic and sustained weapons infusions into the country, about short-sighted policies, and not least about the fragmentation of a country by vested interests that are involved in the continuation of narcotics production.

Background

Afghanistan formally entered the state system after the second Anglo-Afghan war (1878-80). Its unfortunate geographic location between the two expanding powers of that era—Tsarist Russia and Imperial Britain—allowed it only a limited sovereignty over its territory and the conduct of foreign policy. The country emerged as a buffer state, and remained so after the Second Afghan War, under the tenuous control of the Mohammadzai clan of the Barakzai tribe of Durrani Pushtoons, who presided over a country that was in effect, a grouping of fiercely independent and fractious tribal republics, where the control of the centre was often challenged by feisty local chieftains. During the Cold War, the rulers of Afghanistan attempted to maintain a fragile non-aligned policy, even as they continued to accept considerable aid from both blocs. Once, Pakistan was co-opted into the American bloc system, its neighbour turned more and more to its nearest superpower. The Soviet Union sponsored the equipping and sustaining of a 100,000 man army, and from 1956 to 1978 provided the country with 1,265 million US dollars in economic aid and roughly 1,250 million US dollars military aid.[1] The United States also provided economic aid and military training, together with India and Egypt.

In essence both powers competed for influence over the one regime (King Zahir Shah) even as palace intrigues, and ethnic rivalries continued to simmer. The overthrow of the monarchy, and the establishment of Daud (1973), a cousin as President changed this trend, leading to a competition to patronize different groupings, which added to the uneasy brew that was already fermenting. Iran, rich in oil and firmly in the western camp offered aid and an opening to the sea, as it attemped to woo Afghanistan into its circle, while Pakistan sponsored a number of Islamic uprisings against the regime. In the same year, according to the former governor of NWFP, Pakistan began to arm and train batches of 30-40 disaffected elements to man operations that were carried out with help from the Central Intelligence Agency (CIA), according to General Fazle Haq.[2] The former Governor of the Frontier provinces Maj. Gen. Nasirullah Babbar also confirms that Pakistan began training and arming of disaffected Afghans in 1973, additionally keeping at the ready a small Mujahideen manned armoured force that could be airlifted for surprise guerrilla attacks at a crucial juncture.[3] Between 1973-77 Pakistan trained an estimated 5000 dissidents and channeled aid to the Hazaras located in Central Afghanistan.[4] The involvement of the CIA appears to be supported by the accounts of Brezinski, who as national security advisor was urging more "sympathetic" treatment of the Afghans in early 1989.[5] The failure of the most ambitious such uprising in 1975 led to a split among the Islamists leading to one group led by Burhannudin Rabbani of the original Jamiat Islami (Islamic society) and the other of the

Hizb-i-Islami (Islamic Party) led by former student leader Gulbuddin Hekmatyar. Bases were established at Miran Shah, Parachinar, Mohmand, and Bajaur Agencies inside Pakistan, with financial help provided by the Saudi-based organisation the Muslim World League, channeled through the Pakistan political party Jamaat-i-Islami, a political party that was staunchly Islamic, and a puppet creature of the Pakistani intelligence network, the Inter-Services Intelligence (ISI). Neither of the two groups were at all ethnically homogenous, both were made up of leaders and cadres from secular backgrounds and education, and neither could claim to represent all the ethnic and tribal groupings within Afghanistan. Of the two, the Rabbani group was the more moderate, and had eventually the best commanders within its ranks, which included traditional tribal *ulema.* Pushtoons from outside the tribal areas tended to gravitate towards the Hekmatyar group, which in time turned to more extreme religious views and tended to antagonize the hierarchies of tribal politics. The policy of creating guerrilla camps was expanded by the military regime that followed in Pakistan, at least seven to eight months before the Soviet invasion, in an apparent attempt to 'solve' the border issues that bedevilled relations between the two countries.

After the military coup of 1978 which led to the establishment of the Democratic Republic of Afghanistan, the country became totally dependent on Soviet aid, and American aid was terminated. In February, following the overthrow of the Shah of Iran, a group of military officers under Ismael Khan attacked and briefly took control of Herat, even as attacks from bases in Pakistan increased in tempo. In Moscow the alarm at the progress of events led to the moving in December, 1979 of a 'limited contingent' into Kabul, an event that was to cast its shadow over the next decade and more in the history of the subcontinent. Reports of journalists carried accounts of the swift operation, that was carried out with an initial troop movement by air (roughly 5000) followed by tanks crossing the Amu Darya.[6] By 1981 there were roughly upwards of 100,000 troops in the country.

There is now nothing to show that the Soviets ever envisaged a prolonged stay, nor that their motives were at all influenced by a thirst for a warm water port, nor even a planned invasion of the oil rich Middle East. As noted by analysts, the Soviet intention was to make sure that the state remained a buffer, and did not fall into the steadily increasing number of countries that firmed up the policy of encirclement.[7] However, in the United States, National Security Advisor Brezinski was already warning of a threat to the integrity of Pakistan and leaned to the dominant feeling in the US that the Soviets pay a price for their invasion.[8] The State of the Union Address of President Carter (January 23, 1980) reflected prevailing fears as he warned that any adventures against the Persian Gulf would be considered an "assault on the vital interests" of the USA which would be met with "all means necessary including military force."[9]

The costs of intervention

The events of December 1979 were equally of epochal significance to the Soviets. That decision was to lead to a long and costly engagement whose end was followed rapidly by the annulment of the Soviet Union itself. From 1979 to 1991 the Soviet Union suffered, according to some sources, an intervention cost of around 3 billion US dollars a year according to Soviet figures.[10] The same study also inferred that Soviet expenditure on conflicts supportive of 'friendly' regimes was six to eight times higher than that borne by the US to support the resistance forces. Clearly the option of creating 'proxy' groups and arming them with guns, rocket propelled grenades, mines and other so-called 'small arms' constituted the infinitely cheaper option than shoring up a regime with expensive aircraft, tanks and air defence screens. In Afghanistan, the billions of dollars that the Soviet Union spent on the regime, was in terms of quantity far less than the millions that was spent on the resistance that brought in tons of assault rifles, rocket propelled grenades (RPG), and mortars. Other sources have put the costs of the conflict at 5 billion US dollars which was about fifty times the yearly aid that had been given till 1979.[11] American aid started at about 30 million US dollars in 1980, (as compared to roughly 20 million US dollars annual economic aid) previously going up to 50 million US dollars in 1981-82. Under the Reagan Administration this amount jumped to 80 million US dollars in 1983, and 120 million US dollar in 1984 (FY). The US Congress doubled the administration's requested funds to 250 million US dollars plus an extra allocation for anti-aircraft weapons in 1985. This figure climbed to 470 million US dollars in 1986 and 630 million US dollars in 1987 remaining thus through

1989. With Saudi Arabia aid matching US contributions, total aid from 1987 exceeded one billion a year to 1989.[12] Total aid from all sides has been put by other sources as around 8.7 billion US dollars (1986-90) far exceeding the legal weapon imports of most countries during the same time period. By the end of 1992, Afghanistan had a minuscule airforce, tanks and enough small weapons within to equip the armed forces of both India and Pakistan.

The Operation

In Pakistan, the military regime under General Zia took the undoubtedly difficult decision to ally itself with the US in systematically providing assistance to the rebels. This was something more than the fitful aid that had gone on previously, but nonetheless the decision to be part of the containment strategy had been taken at least a decade earlier when Pakistan joined the Central Treaty Organisation (CENTO) and South East Asian Treaty Organisation (SEATO). With Iran out of the circle, Pakistan became in American eyes the lone state that would be the springboard to protect the Persian Gulf, besides providing a convenient location to "keep an eye on what the Soviet were up to." As is wellknown now, and hardly needs reiteration, that policy bought for Pakistan a 3.2 billion US dollars aid package, a blind eye to its nuclear programme, and what is less known—the weapons and finance that allowed it to wage its own proxy war in the region. A somewhat less than attractive legacy was the fact that by the time the Americans and the Soviets quit the region, Pakistan has become a nodal centre of an entire network of drug syndicates that flourished within the country, even as they systematically used the conflict in Afghanistan to make it the second largest producer of opium in the world.

The Americans entered the fray prepared to "punish" the Soviets. That the US apparently did not expect that the Mujahideen would be able to actually push out Soviet battle hardened troops is evident in the fact that no thought was apparently given to the possibility that the 'Resistance' might well be the government of the future in Afghanistan. The Americans interfered not at all in the actual distribution of the weapons and aid that it so meticulously provided in what was essentially a 'holding' operation (though the CIA was actively involved). This indifference is perplexing, since many within the government were warning of the unhealthy tilt towards fundamentalist elements, who's ideology was frightening even to the Afghans themselves. Selig Harrison and Representative Ritter had commented on these aspects, as well as warned that the Peshawar elements were far from representative in character.[13] By admission of the Pakistanis themselves, aid was heavily tilted in favour of the more 'fundamentalist' and extreme elements. (67-73 per cent of aid[14]). The moderates were more or less left to fend for themselves, with their commanders' loyalties tied firmly to weapons aid, while mainstream nationalists were completely cut off (in fact many respected figures were simply killed in suspicious circumstances). Attempts by these groups to convene a traditional *Loya Jirga* of tribal leaders, were hindered with members forced to move out of Quetta and harassed by Pakistani security. These policies had important repercussions on the future of conflict resolution. As present day Pakistanis complain, the US realised all its goals in the area, and then left it to Pakistan to handle the troublesome legacy of a chaotic state. However, as Afghan Mujahideen observe, the very policies of Pakistan were angled to prevent such a national consensus or a true government-in-exile'.

The stepmotherly treatment meted out to groups not immediately under the Pakistani wing, led to the commanders of the mainly Tajik forces in the north growing independent of their would be 'controllers'. Dependent on local sources to some extent, they were forced to create an administration and a resource base that took local loyalties into account thus creating a force that had the implicit support of the people. By the same policy, groups based in Peshawar (especially the Hezbe of Hekmatyar) and dependent totally on Pakistani whims, remained a 'rented' revolutionary with no power base of his own within Afghanistan. Moderates and well respected men like Sayid Ahmed Gailani, leader of the NIFA were sidelined, while non-Sunnis turned to Iran bringing in yet another entrant to the Great Game being played inside Afghanistan in addition to the United States, Soviet Russia, Saudi Arabia, Pakistan and China. To this list could also be added a wide variety of private sponsors like the Muslim Brotherhood funded by Saudi money, "Islamic Salvation Foundation" funded by construction millionaire Osma Bin Laden, and European NGOs.

Recent research suggests that China, Egypt and the United States began covert aid to the Mujahideen well before 1979[15] while Pakistani assistance, as noted, began in 1973 with CIA assistance. The CIA's role was limited in the initial stages to the scouting for weapons that ensured deniability, and later in routing weapons from all over the world including the United Kingdom, West Germany and other allies. Weapons arrived by ship and sometimes by air, after which they were then effectively under the control of the ISI. Weapons were then trucked from Karachi to arms dumps at Ojhiri, and Peshawar. From there ISI passes ensured that a steady stream of trucks pushed the weapons to the border, from where again they were moved on by various sources of transport (by mule, truck or human loads) by contractors who were often known to supply all sides in the war.

Seepage and diversion started at the very first stage according to Pakistani sources who allege that weapons meant for Afghanistan were often diverted to other locations.[16] Certainly, it is also equally true that weapons from other locations were sent in to Afghanistan. For instance captured weapons of the Iraqi army were sent into the pipeline. The haphazard storage that marked the second stage was not surprising since given the fact that the ISI and the Pakistani Army were simply unable to handle such vast quantities of weapons. The committee that went into the causes of the massive explosion at the Ojhri arms dump in 1988 testifies to negligence and neglect of basic safety procedures.[17] The several transfers which marked third stage was the most susceptible to theft, accident and plain corruption, as a variety of actors were involved in trucking the weapons across mountains and desert to the Mujahideen fighting the war in Afghanistan. Analysts have noted several factors that were prevalent in the progress of the pipeline. Representatives of the various parties were prone to sign for more weapons than they had actually received, with the difference being sold to local markets to the enrichment of both parties involved—the party persons and Pakistani officials. Brigadier Youssaf who was in charge of the operation in a later period, testifies to the endemic corruption that was apparent at every leg of the route, while various other sources commented on the fact that the Mujahideen seemed to benefit very little from the massive aid a mounts that were being pumped in.

Between 1980-84 a majority were still fighting with old weapons,[18] and a few captured ones. A correspondent from Christian Science Monitor covering Afghanistan for instance cites the practice by Pakistan of replacing new Kalashnikovs with old Chinese made Pakistan Army issue rifles.[19] The former Director of the Fulbright Foundation after a visit observed that the fighters had nowhere the amount of equipment that had been credited to them. He observed "there is some indication that the Pakistanis have interdicted some of the weapons, especially the SAM-7 kind of weaponry that is so important."[20] A Rand study done in 1987 called for a counter-air capability as also the fact that aid needed to be supplied directly to the Mujahideen "which will alleviate politicisation."[21] With over 50-60 trucks a day moving around 65,000 tons of weapons through the Frontier provinces, the arms bazaars were overflowing with the latest in weapons as the many actors at all concerned levels with the pipeline began to sell weapons to the highest bidders.

Apart from these were freewheeling blackmarketeers who supplied weapons from across the Amu Darya, from China and from diverse other sources. Journalists report of an unending convoy of mules entering Afghanistan from the north leading to a pot-pourri of an amazing variety of weapons flowing into the markets of the Frontier regions of Pakistan. Resistance leaders are believed to have stolen or sold hundreds of millions worth of weaponry, while at least 20-30 per cent was assessed to have been skimmed off with Zia's forces claiming a fair share.[22] Pakistani Foreign Office personnel reportedly put this at as much as 60 per cent going astray, a figure upheld by other sources who maintain that Pakistan generals were siphoning off millions.[23]

By 1989 prices of weapons took a plunge, according to reporters with the AK-47 falling from Rs. 30,000 to a mere Rs. 17,000. The arms bazaars of Pakistan began to swell with anything from multi-barrelled rocket launchers, the famed Stalin's Organ, rocket propelled grenades (RPGs) sniper weapons, and gelatine sticks sold by the gross and ammunition sold by weight.[24] The Frontier areas of Pakistan were soon a meeting point for militants of all hues, who came to avail themselves of this largesse that was sold to (almost) anyone with cash in their pockets. A lot of this began to move into Pakistan as political groups and drug dealers began to arm themselves. As drug barons entrenched themselves, a symbiotic relationship was established between sections of the Mujahideen and the drug cartels. In a few years it was unclear whether the drugs were the driving factor in the continuance of the conflict, or vice versa. By this time, the fact that Mujahideen were trading with all comers, including their supposed enemies was obvious (one reason why they disliked the idea of bombing Kabul which was the main business area) and millions were being made.

Drugs and Weapons

One factor that was to add to the continuation of the conflict was the rise of drug cultivation and trafficking in Afghan-Pak region. Several factors aided this movement. The advent of the Khomeini regime led to the moving out of narcotics organisations from Iran into Afghanistan basically into Peshawar due in part due to the better infrastructure, (banking, finance, money laundering etc. and partly the obvious fact that the Soviet invasion made such operations difficult). Cultivation was however encouraged in the vast tracts of the Helmand valley, an operation that may have been partly encouraged by the CIA in its objective of demoralizing the Soviets on all fronts. In a repetition of Vietnam, the use of narcotics appears to have increased substantially within the Soviet forces as also the attractive possibility of smuggling out the opium for large profits. Heroin production however took off in the late 1970's with Pakistanis accusing Germans and Filipinos of bringing in the chemical processes necessary for refining opium. According to some sources even Chinese organised crime syndicates were involved in selling drug refining tools, even as they 'swapped' drugs for guns.[25] This process was immeasurably helped by the institution of the "Hudood laws which banned narcotic use and cultivation, and promptly sent the price soaring. Heroin labs sprouted along the Pakistani frontier regions (170 according to General Fazle Haq, the governor of the region[26]) leading to a rather mysterious operation whose stated aim was to destroy these facilities, and retrieve massive number of Soviet weaponry that were supplied to rebellious tribals. A massive security operation against the Kuki Khels (Khyber region) is said to have razed a number of heroin labs, and unearthed 300,000 Kalashnikovs of Soviet and Chinese make.[27] Pakistani journals however noted that nothing was heard later about the mysterious operation, which apparently had little effect on narcotics production. The General himself died one of the wealthiest men in the country.

The movement of drugs and weapons were closely intertwined in the operation of the pipeline. Trucks moving in weapons brought out the raw opium (or heroin) and eyewitness accounts in the couragious Pakistani journal *The Herald* (September 1985) observed drugs and weapons being moved into government warehouses from 1980 onwards. Not surprisingly this gave a fillip to the drug cultivation inside Afghanistan. Between 1986-88 drug cultivation nearly doubled (roughly 400 to 800 tons[28]).

The fact that the superpowers were on the road to dialogue (and therefore a possible cut-off of aid) was obvious to key participants in early 1986. Rubin notes that by 1988, that Hekmatyar was already systematically funding his operations through drug refining in cooperation with Pakistani-based syndicates[29]. The warlord's fortunes were on the decline, as Washington reacted to increasing criticism of the copious amounts that this lone actor was receiving at the expense of other commanders. Various analysts have noted the almost symbiotic relationship between the Hekmatyar group and the ISI, leading to the conclusion arrived at by some that the relationship prospered because he was privy to most of the ins and outs of the ISI and Army operations. Certainly, it would have been impossible for the warlord to carry on his narcotics activities without the knowledge and assent of his 'controllers'. The election of the new government under Ms Benazir Bhutto (Pakistan People's Party) could have been another factor. It was wellknown that the PPP was for distancing itself from the Afghan conflict, a move that was wholly repugnant to the Army (and its COAS Gen. Aslam Beg) and senior ISI officers. Narcotics cultivation therefore may have been a source of almost unlimited funding, even as Washington began to cut back on new equipment and trying to retrieve those sophisticated arms that were known to be flowing out of the country.

By 1989, large parts of Afghanistan were under the control of the "mullah warlords" who with the clout and money from narcotics cultvation, took over from the traditional leadership[30]. Local farmers were often forced to grow poppy, while the rest of the process (transport, sale, refining, etc.) were contracted out to organised crime networks in Pakistan. The narcotics operations thus spread a long way and with immeasurable consequences—from the cultivator in Afghanistan (local warlord), to the transporter (largely Pushtoons and refugees based in Karachi and subcontracted by the Army) via routes controlled by various petty warlords to the refining (controlled by nouveau riche in the Frontier regions) to local markets (the refugee areas in Girdi jungle, and urban "Goths" run by Punjabis) to the international outlets in Karachi and the Makran coast. Profits were unevenly distributed (in the typical inverted triangle model) with a large part of it going to a 'non-actor'—the politicians and the security force. With their own sources of funding, petty warlords were soon independent of outside direction, and apparently uninterested in the factional fighting that brought all pretenses of a *jehad* to a close.

Weapons and the Rise in Technology

From the jezail and the flintlock, Afghan Mujahideen were given access to newer and more sophisticated weapons as more countries became involved in the operation. From the .303s that they managed to cull from the Pakistani arms bazaars of the Frontier in the early 1970s and the G-3s supplied by Pakistani intelligence, they graduated rapidly to the assault rifles and rocket launchers that were provided to them from diverse sources. Initial supplies included Chinese, East European, and Soviet type weapons—the dependence of Chinese supplies marked by at least one instance when a fire at a Chinese weapons factory held up shipment of weapons—and later including weapons of all kinds and makes. East Europe, as Gen Schwarkopf's testimony notes, continued to be a source of weapons at least till February 1990[31]. A kind of weapon bonanza seems to have emerged, as CIA personnel and arms dealers scouted the world for Russian weaponry. In 1980 the Americans contracted with Egypt to supply AK-47, SAM-7 as well as surface-to-air missiles and anti-tank grenades from its factories. These weapons were however found to be unsatisfactory and many items like anti-aircraft guns and heavy machine-guns were upgraded in American factories[32]. China had been supplying SAM-7s from June, 1980 but these did not prove effective either. The Hughes Aircraft company was assigned to develop improved warheads for the Egyptian missiles, but eventually in late 1980s the British 'Redeye' was supplied[33]. The Saudis, in return for the supply of five AWACS agreed to step up assistance to the rebels. Weapons supplied included the 7.62 Kalashnikov (AK-47) as well as the 5.56 mm AK-74. Largely Chinese mortars and RPGs together with the RPK and RPD Russian heavy machine-guns (HMG) were also supplied in the initial stages. Evident also are G-3s, a few M-16s, a wide variety of pistols and revolvers the Egyptian 'Sakr' shoulder-fired missile, the British Blowpipe, the Igla, Strela and anti-personnel mines from China, Czechoslovakia, Egypt, the UK, the USSR, and Yugoslavia[34].

The RPG-18 was first sighted in June, 1985 along with other disposable light anti-armour weapons. The effect was striking, causing the almost total decimation of the 444 Commandos Brigade of the Afghan Army in the narrow valleys of Konar and Herat.[35] The first Chinese 107 mm high explosive rockets were seen in Mujahideen hands after March, 1985, used singly instead of being fired from multiple launchers (107mm Type 63). With a 1.2 kg warhead they were propped up on a wooden cradle and wired to a battery detonator with surprisingly effective results.[36]

The piece de resistance was of course the extremely accurate Stinger SAM. From the initial preoccupation with ensuring 'deniability' and thus restricting itself to collecting Soviet weaponry, the CIA as the coordinating authority was soon under pressure from different quarters (not least from the US congress) to increase both the quantities and sophistication of weapons provided. This was especially apparent after Presidential Directive 166 called for help for the "freedom fighters" and committed the US to unequivocal support for their cause. The 'Rollback doctrine' allowed the use of American air defence weapons that had never previously been given to any non-NATO ally and perhaps not even to some NATO members. The Stingers marked a quantum leap in technology, and hundreds began to arrive in Afghanistan by late 1986. The actual numbers supplied are not clear. Reportedly 900 were supplied (1985) and 340 fired. Other sources attest that 250 launchers and 1000 missiles were provided. At least 2-300 are missing though there were reports of 'Stingers' available in the arms bazaars of Pakistan, Tajikistan and at least 16 were found in a captured Iranian gun-boat. After boarding, authorities seized power batteries and launch tubes in poor condition. The missiles themselves are thought to have been either sold by corrupt Pakistanis, or as alleged was the result of Iranians waylaying a particular consignment on its way past the Iranian border. There are many accounts of 'Stingers' available in the marketplace for between 100,000 US dollars per missile[37] while others maintain that the high prices that the CIA is offering has driven it up to double that figure.[38]

As Selig Harrison noted, "Experience suggests that for every improvement in American supplied weaponry, Moscow would be likely to counter with its own escalation."[39] Not surprisingly the first transfer of Scud-Bs and possibly Scud-Cs were made in 1988, with the first showing on parade on 1st November of two Scud-Bs. The Scuds were fired the same evening, and were used heavily in the defence of Jalalabad, with approximately 438 fired between March and June 1989, In a single day (6 July) more than 11 Scuds were fired into Mujahideen positions.[40] Used also in the battle for Khost (12 March 1990) though on a much reduced scale, the firing of missiles from Mazar-e-Sharif seems to indicate that the missiles were Scud-Cs since the distance of 460 km would have been beyond the earlier missile. The US reaction to the spotting of the Scuds was predictable with the US State Department spokesman declaring "our support for Pakistan and the Mujahideen are unshakable".[41] However, with the adverse publicity on the conduct of the war, and the expectation of a quick military victory, funds began to dip in 1989 and 1990. The disaster that was Jalalabad (8 March, 1989), and the eventual success of the Najibullah regime in keeping every inch of its territory, led to a. severe (though expected) cut in congress budgeting. A cut of nearly 60 per cent over previous levels was however equalised out by Saudi contributions which came with 435 million US dollars and Saudi and Kuwaiti princes contributed 100 million US dollars from 'private' funds.[42] Up to 1991, Saudi and Kuwaiti governments and private sources are said to have supplied another 1 billion US dollars.

With the shift to conventional warfare, weapons supplied included heavy artillery, rocket launchers, and other weapons suitable for a move to the offensive. After the dismissal of the Bhutto government in Pakistan in 1990, the hawks were once more on the ascendant, and Hekmatyar is reported to have received a consignment of arms that included forty thousand rockets and seven hundred trucks of ammunition.[43] Hekmatyar is also said to have received funds from Libya and Iraq.[44] From 1990, aid began to go directly to the commanders, (at least publicly) to the detriment of Hekmatyar, and Ahmed Shah Masood at last getting a comparable level of weaponry from the American and other western sources. The wrangling over 'positive' and 'negative', asymmetry (which was diplomatic speak for a cut off or carrying-on of weapons aid) led to a continuation of American and Soviet aid up to 1992. This aid was accelerated or encouraged by the successful conclusion of the Conventional Forces in Europe (CFE) Treaty of 1990, the withdrawal of forces from Mongolia (55,000) and the overall reduction of half a million announced by Gorbachev as a confidence building measure. The CFE Treaty also led to the 'cascade' of weapons from the Treaty limited areas to countries that were outside it. The Treaty while putting in place clear restrictions on the heavier weapons made no mention at all of infantry weapons, which were transferred to all manner of countries.

The first tanks were used in battle at Gardez (September 1991). About 50 were used by the Mujahideen and appeared to be T-62's. They appeared to make little difference to the battle (which saw heavy involvement of Pakistani intelligence in operation and logistics), and was severely depleted by ambushes and air attacks.[45]

The Soviet Union till 1991 was still supplying what Gen. Schwarzkopf described as "an unbelievable amount of modern weaponry" at a Senate Armed Services Hearing on 8 February, 1990, as tanks, armoured personnel carriers and aircraft were transferred. Not only were the quantities considerable, but there appeared to be distinct rise in quality, with the new BM-22 Multiple Rocket Launchers, the SA-13 SP Surface-to-air missiles, R-17 and R-300 Scuds and the Luna-M FROG-7 were also transferred during this period. According to resistance sources, the flow of small weapons, particularly the Kalashnikov series was so heavy that the weapons were beginning to move out to other parts of South Asia.[46] Soviet aircraft flying from Chimkent, Mary, Ferghana and Dushanbe were delivering supplies at the rate of about 20-40 sorties a day, according to some sources (the Soviets put this at 10 flights). Resistance sources also reported the movement of 700-1200 trucks a week across the Amu Darya, and from Torghundi, in a resupply effort lasting throughout the winter of 1990-91 up to 1990, Eastern Europe remained a source of arms. East Germany supplied the coveted 7.62

Kalashnikovs, while Czechoslovakia supplied the 12.7 HMG, and the Kalashnikov. Bulgaria is reported to have transferred some 20 million US dollars in arms (mostly small arms) in 1983-85.[47] Arms and ammunition dumps were also created at the strategic border town of Hairatan. Less is known about American and western arms supplies. A huge arms dump exploded in April, 1988 at Ojhri sending sharpnel and rockets for miles around. Hundreds died, and the actual reasons for the blast has never been fully explained, with assumptions that the blast was intended to hide from increasingly intrusive US liaison officers, the amounts of weaponry that had been spirited away by the ISI (Inter Services Intelligence).[48] Hundreds died in the ensuing chaos, and angry legislators demanded the resignation of those responsible. The only assessment of the dollar value of the weapons seems somewhat low, but Ambassador Raphael in a reportedly exhaustive inventory considered it to be worth 130 million US dollars. The lost supplies were promptly replaced from West Germany.[49]

Closing Chapter of an Era—An Interregnum

As the last Soviet soldier crossed the Amu Darya, the various commanders were taking control in their respective areas. Masood moved into Taloquan, the Hazaras, backed heavily by Iran took parts of Central Afghanistan and Kunar fell to the rebels. Hekmatyar further blackened his reputation by allying with Khalqi Defence Minister Shahnawaz Tanai in a coup attempt that failed dramatically. The incident caused much diplomatic profit for President Najibullah, even as it underlined the 'unholy' war that was being waged by the ISI and its commanders. The US was annoyed when food aid intended for refugees was found to have been cached by the ISI ostensibly for the Hekmatyar forces. The continued favouring of the warlord, the intransigence of the Intelligence men led to the total suspension of all food aid by concerned authorities in the US. Hekmatyar meanwhile added to the confusion by looting a 64 truck weapon convoy and killing the top ten commanders of Ahmed Shah Masood, creating what has been to date an irreconcilable divide between the two. US weapons aid began to be routed directly to the commanders, with special envoy Peter Tomson liausing, with the objective of ensuring less pilferage and more weapons to "operational" commanders. Hekmatyar and his chief backers, the ISI were temporarily in the shade as the new government of Benazir Bhutto was sworn in. Her attempts to regain a control over the Afghan policy by sidelining the hardline Chief of the ISI (General Hamid Gul) plan backfired when he was reinstated as the commander of the prestigious Multan Corps even as she herself was dismissed (August 6, 1990) leading to a greater role for the fundamentalist ISI created party the Jama'at-i-Islami, a political ally of the new government of Nawaz Sharif.

All curbs instituted by the previous government were removed, and fresh supplies of weapons began to move to the Hezbe, even as bribes were spread around to "assist" other parties to cooperate. Simultaneously, around 30 million US dollars worth of captured weapons from Iraq were transferred to Pakistan to assist in the attack against the almost permanently besieged town of Khost.[50] The town fell in March, 1991, but provided little cause for celebration as Mujahideen groups once again fell out with each other. The Saudi Intelligence Chief was reported to have visited Hekmatyar and Haqquani, healing the breach which had developed, leading to Saudi funds once again flowing to Hekmatyar.[51] But it was increasingly clear that the '*jehad*' was over and the petty politics of the Peshawar "government-in-exile" had alienated most of the commanders. Masood called his own field commanders conference, thus effectively bypassing Pakistan (a process assisted by the supply of high power communication sets). Wrangling among commanders and those loyal to them had reached an all-time high, with the battle itself stagnating to intermittent rocket attacks on the capital. Infighting among commanders, led to more than 300 deaths, with the most bitter fighting between the Hezbe and Masood's forces, leading to a breach that played to the advantage of the Kabul regime.

The years 1990-92 have been called with justification the years of the 'petty warlord' as the country fragmented into pockets of control, even as Pakistan continued its efforts to push Hekmatyar forward as the best option. Drugs production meanwhile climbed rapidly as Mujahideen realising (especially after the Hekmatyar-Tanai combine) that the *jehad* was well and truly over, returned to their provinces to cultivate the new cash crop. Violence erupted in the four socalled "liberated zones" as bigger groups sought to swallow up smaller ones, and vied with each other to control the trade and drug route from Pakistan. The rest of Afghanistan was controlled by what could at best be called government funded militia, where conditions were little different from the banditry and greed that marked the Mujahideen 'controlled' areas. Commanders in Herat and Kandahar maintained what to outsiders may have seemed a dangerous liaison with the Kabul regime. Turncoat Mujahideen were heavily supplied with weapons, ammunition and food, even while on the outskirts of Herat, the 'frontline' continued to see exchanges between Mujahideen and "government forces." With a reported 60,000 former guerrillas in government ranks it was difficult to make distinctions.[52]

With the end of the USSR in 1991, the US congress began to lose interest in the war in Afghanistan. The new fiscal year budget allotted no funds for the cause, (much to the dislike of the CIA) and Russia was engrossed in her own internal instability. In September, 1991, Foreign Minister Boris Pankin and his counterpart at last agreed on ceasing all aid, and withdrawing major weapons systems from the crisis area. By September 30, 1991, all weapons supplies from the US ceased. In Pakistan, General Asif Nawaz alarmed at the chaos and violence in his own country as a direct fall-out of the Afghan war, moved resolutely to push the enthusiastic General Gul into retirement. The Pakistani foreign office was heard to say that the country supported the peace plan put forward by the Secretary General of the UN De Cuellar. The Zahir Shah option was being explored, even as the whole process was scuttled by the resignation of President Najibullah (18 March, 1992), a move that predictably led to all groups rushing to take over the capital. For Afghanistan's friends and neighbours, the war had begun again. This time the agendas were considerably changed.

The Rise of Regional Actors

In Pakistan, the re-election of Ms Benazir Bhutto led to a re-evaluation of foreign policy priorities in the light of the immeasurably extended strategic canvas now extending on the country's hinterland. The CAR states, rich in resources, and looking for a way to escape the Russian stranglehold on communications, obviously welcomed Pakistani overtures to economic cooperation, just as they welcomed Iran's hand of friendship. However, both countries were left in no doubt that none of the states welcomed either one's brand of political Islam, nor did they evince an interest in a bloc based on religion or ethnic commonality. The chief concern here was for economic outlets—pipelines, roads, railways—all leading to the markets of the world, an access heretofore denied to them by circumstance and geography. With what was assessed to be the next largest oil and gas reserves, the region did not suffer unduly from a lack of foreign interest. Western oil men were soon to be seen in all the newly independent states, but the problem that confronted them was that faced by the states themselves—the lack of a reliable access. Iran in a remarkably swift adjustment to changed circumstances, managed to project herself as not only the ideal route to market, but also restrained any attempts to woo Shia minorities in CAR states. Allegations of Iranian help to the rebels in Tajikistan has not been proved, though the influence of Iran in that country remained considerable.

Thus by 1994, there were several new or recycled actors with vital interests in the future of Afghanistan. Russia after following a policy of neglect, during the period when the Europeans dominated foreign policy, however, returned to the breach for the same reasons that had pushed her into the country in 1979. Russian military doctrine identified the spread of 'fundamentalism' (a word that was closely identified with western fears) and missile proliferation in the south as a cause for concern. The instability in the Ferghana valley, the near civil war conditions in Tajikistan, and the fact that neither states were at all able to police thier *porous* borders, all led to a conviction that instability in Afghanistan boded ill for the Russian 'first circle of security' the Commonwealth of Independent States (CIS). As far as that country was concerned, the borders of the CIS were to be protected as before, a policy that was reinforced after Tajikistan's conflict flared after 1993 (though the CIA had launched the *jehad* into the then Soviet territory was early as 1987). The border, never one that could be policed easily (especially towards the mountains) proved to be ideal guerrilla territory with Opposition forces given shelter mainly by the Tajik groups led by Masood (though initially they seemed to have been patronised by all groups, a period when Quazi Hussain was calling for a '*jehad*' carried into Chechnya, and further afield). Saudi Arabia continued to provide funds through '*private*' sources, though however, they now tended to favour the Rabbani group (which included Rasool Sayyaf). Whether this resulted in a cut-off to Hekmatyar is unknown. Pakistani Foreign Minister Assef Ali was declaring (during a visit to Central Asia) that

Hekmatyar is nothing. He is neither a political nor a tribal leader, just an average student leader picked up by Mr Z.A. Bhutto.[53] Even as these cutting statements were being made a 14 truck convoy was stopped at Torkham with weapons bound for the self same warlord. Investigations revealed that authorisation signatures of top officials had been faked, and there were rumours that the weapons were part of the stocks of a 'certain religious political party' from Lahore who had seized nearly a fourth of the arms aid from the pipeline[54]. Since no subsequent investigations have been made, it may be assumed that the weapons were made available by the ISI through the Jammat without the knowledge of the Foreign Office, or that the Pakistanis were still pinning their hopes on Hekmatyar on whom so much had been invested. The recalcitrant chief of the Hezbe thwarted from entering Kabul, contented himself with shelling the unfortunate city even as it was more than obvious that in the patchwork of Afghanistan in 1994, his group was most minimally represented—in essence he did not control a single important city. As the Interim Government was formed in 1992, with Rabbani as President and Hekmatyar as Prime Minister, the arrangement fell through as groups fought for preeminence in the capital. Alliances shifted with rapidity, and it became increasingly difficult to get group leaders to sit together let alone evolve a consensus.

A new figure was added to the meleë as General Rashid Dostum defected from the Kabul regime to ally himself with the Rabbani group, bringing with him over 100,000 soldiers of the former Afghan Army. However, by the time 1994 dawned General Dostum, finding his ambitions unfulfilled, switched to an unlikely alliance with the Hezbe (who had once called him the greatest enemy of the revolution while Dostum had called him "the greatest threat to peace in the region"[55]. Meanwhile this massive force was reported to be receiving its aid from Uzbekistan who saw this as a "great wall against fundamentalism." Since Uzbekistan's defence industrial capacity and financial resources were both extremely limited, it is apparent that it remained a conduit for aid rather than a primary backer. Spareparts for aircraft were reported to be coming from Tashkent[56] while electricity has been supplied from across the river. Reports of fleets of trucks crossing into this area, aircraft landing in Uzbek territory to refuel[57], and the sight of fresh uniforms for this men, all contributed to the theory of generous outside help. Uzbekistan was also reported to be printing currency[58] a practice that had been common when the Soviets supplied Najibullah with the almost entire currency required for Kabul. Rand analysts Zalmay Khalilazad notes that the General has channels of communication with the UK and the US, and confirms that he receives military supplies (tanks, aircraft and military personnel) from Uzbekistan. Under his control, Mazhar-e-Sharif thrived, with Russian and European goods flowing in, and a cosmopolitan style of living that was more to the liking of those who had grown used to the relatively egalitarian society of Kabul. A new airline "Balkh Air" (registered in Liberia) has regular flights to Sharjah and other countries. The General was also rumoured to be the biggest opium smuggler in the country, though there is no evidence to support this. The most remarkable aspect of the renamed Jumbesh Milli, was also that Dostum managed to keep his troops happy, allowing him to retain a fairly dependable force, rather than one prone to defections. He himself, with no precise ideology was able to shift sides according to his own preferences. Whether he also shifted patrons is a question that must remain in the realm of conjecture, though reliable journals reported that by 1995 he was getting funds from the Pakistanis as well as the US aid via the Uzbeks[59]. Dostum has been used to carry out attacks against the Tajik Islamic resistance in Masood areas, but Dostum and his men fight for themselves, rather than any ideology. In 1996, he and his immediate patron—Uzbekistan—seemed to have shifted back to a pro-Rabbani stance.

Another new group was the Hezb-e-Wahdat formed in 1990 under the umbrella of Iran. Till then occupied with more pressing matters on its other flank, Iran had at best maintained a careful watch on the war, without taking any drastic steps. Iran's policy objectives are diverse—aimed partly at keeping out Saudi influence, and partly desirous of keeping the Persian speaking Tajiks in power. The influx of drugs and weapons from Afghanistan has been serious enough to step up surveillance on the border as well as the construction of a electrified fence on the Pakistani-Iran border. Iran has also given refuge to over a million refugees, and additionally has seen a drastic rise in drug addiction among its population, especially in Khorrassan. Iran's desire to emerge as a regional stabilizing influence, as well as the transit country for the resources of the CAR states has led her to keep assistance at a low level, thus refraining from exacerbating a conflict that it was clearly in her interests to defuse. The relations between the Wahadat and the Saudi backed Ettehad have been particularly violent though neither are particularly important actors. The Wahadat, basing its membership on the Hazaras have not been any more easy to control than the other parties sponsored by different actors. Some of its moves often ran contrary to Iranian interests, besides being prone to factional fighting—reinforcing the dominant feeling among analysts that ethnic considerations have very less to do with the conflict than commonly assumed.

Masood's forces remained the most disciplined and effective under its commander's expert direction. The Jamiat in 1992 seemed to have the largest administrative base, and had its people in Kandahar. Herat and the alliance with the Ettahad of Rasool Sayyaf has proved useful in getting arms through. Rasool Sayyaf has been generously funded by Saudi Arabia, a circumstance that allows Sayyaf a greater leverage than otherwise. The Rabbani group was also informal alliance with the 'neutrals' like the Nangarhar Shoora, who managed to put together some administration and an airline in a remarkably short space of time. The airline has been accused of being the conduit for a 'pipeline' into Kabul from India. However, no aircraft of the company has been seized with arms. The Ettahad is virulently anti-Shia, and had its own university in Peshawar—the Da'wat'ul Jehad University which has been consistently linked to terrorist activities[60].

Even as Kabul suffered casualties of over 1000 killed and 12,000 injured in factional fighting, the rest of Afghanistan was quiet, but effectively out of anyone's control Commanders with their own personal militias supplanted the main commanders who were still in Kabul. Ismael Khan in Herat was a power unto himself, and to some extent managed to bring in some stability to the region. In other areas, rather more dubious personalities reigned, Parts of Kandahar (Spin Buldak) were under the control of Mullah Rocketi who achieved notoriety by kidnapping a team of Chinese engineers from Baluchistan, and was well known as a professional and competent arms dealer, Another "mullah warlord" Nasim Akundzada was reported to be one of the chief drug producers, who set production quotas for farmers, and imposed severe punishment if they were not fulfilled. His produce went to Pakistan for refining or onward transport[61] Journalists reported on the vast fields of poppy in Nangarhar which was under the control of a Shoora and an airline reported as the "Khyber Afghan Airline" which was reported to be the main carrier for a range of smuggled goods. Thus Afghanistan, entered the end of 1994 virtually fragmented and with no end to conflict in sight.

Meanwhile, the UN special envoy Mestiri was putting forward imaginative proposals that addressed all sections of those affected by the war, and more importantly called for a local peacekeeping force that, it was said, would be in keeping with Afghan traditional suspicion of any foreigners attempting to impose a peace upon it. Whatever the merits of such a proposal, it was accepted warily by most commanders.

Escalation—A New Force

It appeared that a "peace keeping force" was already on the way. As the battle got bogged down in the now regular pattern of shelling Kabul, Pakistan's Foreign Ministry under the premiership of Ms Bhutto was moving to consolidate Pakistani influences in Central Asia.The visit by the new Foreign Minister Sardar Assef Ali, and later by the Prime Minister to Uzbekistan proved fruitful. Talks with Ismael Khan and Rashid Dostum on allowing feasibility studies to open a road and rail link to Central Asian states met with immediate approval from the energy rich states striving to break the stranglehold of Russia. The Interior Minister, Gen Nasirullah Babar, arranged for a convoy of thirty plus trucks to travel to Central Asia loaded with supplies, organised by the Army's National Logistics Cell (the same department that had organised the arms pipeline) it set forth in October crossing into Afghanistan on the 1st of November, was rather predictably stopped by free wheeling armed bandits. The convoy, with Pakistan intelligence officers accompanying it, was freed by a group of "students from the Isamic schools—the—Taliban—who then proceeded to take over Kandahar itself. According to other sources, the Taliban first made an appearance after a local warlord raped two women, earning the wrath of the students headed by a Mullah Omar, who then set upon and killed the errant fighters. Whatever the truth, the fact remained that the romance and idealism that was associated with their birth stood them well in the coming months. The original student group soon swelled to the most amazing numbers. From July to September, 1994, the force had swelled from a few hundred to some 25,000 and acquired a formidable arsenal of some 200 tanks, aircraft and combat helilcopters. From Kandahar, the force swung to the Logar province from where they routed weakened warlord Hekmatyar from Charasyab in a fireless fight. With ten out of 30 provinces under their control, the Taliban were òutside the gates of Kabul by February, After its "tour de force"of Pushtoon areas, it was now up against the Tajiks.

The belief that the Taliban were yet another creation of the ISI was strong, even within Pakistan itself, where commentators warned against yet another bout of interference. The leader of the movement Mohammed Omar is said to have founded the movement from his mud-hut in Mewand (a town significant for its history where an Afghan girl Malalai fought the British alongside her brethren) Wounded four times in the war against the Soviets, he returned to his religious school (which is part of the JUI network of schools run by Pakistan's Fazlur Rahman and virulently opposed to the ISI creation the Jamaat. He is described by his compatriots as an expert marksman, and credited with destroying a number of Soviet tanks when fighting with the Hezbe Islami (Khalis) The number two man Haji Muawain like his chief was from Kandahar, and together with Maulvi Ehsanullah said to be in charge of administration in captured provinces, Maulvi Mohammad (military commander) and Maulvi Abbas (Mayor of Kandahar) were appearently the inner council of the Taliban. None however were clear on the exact hierarchy, and even knew nothing of the composition of the Shoora which was said to decide all matters. Believed to be dominated by Kandaharis, some effort was made to coopt others—including some strange elements like Mullah Rocket, who claimed that he had brought a vast store of weapons (including Stingers) to the Taliban leadership.[64] The Taliban are reported to have been allowed access to an old arms dump on the Pakistan-Kandahar border on the clearance of the Pakistani Interior Minister. This may account for a part of their arsenal, but the brand new Kalashikov's and weaponry has been the envy of other groups. Additional funds were reported to come from the transporters and allied mafia, with at least one group paying Rs. 6 million to open roads to Herat and through Mazar, where both commanders had levied heavy tolls.[65] Taliban leaders also claim that their coffers have been filled by influential leaders or those who have chosen to leave the field in a hurry. One local commanders' war chest is reputed to have yielded over Rs. 10.3 mn while the most significant amount of Rs. 30 million seems to have come from an unnamed member of the Jammat-e-Islami. Another Mullah Warlord from Helmand is also reported to have left behind around 50 million Clearly the profits from the drug business was nothing if not considerable.[66] Expenses are also considerably heavy. Taliban sources say that Kandahar alone is said to cost around Rs. 40 million rupees a month and this mainly only for security.

As the group progressed, it began to seem less like a 'peace keeping force' and more like the others that has gone before it. The Shia Wahadat leader Mazari and his top commanders were killed by the 'students' thus earning the hostility of the Saudis backers. Mazari's death was believed to have been ordered after he announced an alliance rather than the 'surrender' that the Taliban wanted publicly announced The wahadat rank and file refused to be disarmed, as the Talibs demanded they should. Most of the 'victories' notched up by the Talibs against the smaller commanders appear to have been motivated by the now time honoured tactic of striking a deal where no other option presents itself, or when confronted with a group that is temporarily at a better fighting strength Iran denounced the 'martyrdom' of Mazari[67] and was thereafter predictably hostile to the new force.

The operations of the Taliban have had a strong element of 'stop-start' tendency. For instance, it's headlong rush (believed to be against the wishes of the ISI) against seasoned commander Ismael Khan I was rudely defeated and the students were driven back to where they had come from—Kandahar. However, in what was to prove a pattern—the Taliban appeared to rally, new weapons, and leaving behind the "mass attack" strategy it had followed previously, attacks were organised with military precision leading to the fall of the target. Thus the second time round, Herat was taken, and Ismael Khan had to leave for Iran. Not surprisingly the Iranian press (known to reflect the views of the establishment) charged that the attack had been handily assisted by special Pakistani ground units, air strike flown out of Quetta, and military planning coordinated by Pakistan, and the CIA and the Mossad[68]. Another journal, commenting on the situation termed Pakistani denial of support of the Taliban as a "joke"[69]. Alliance after unlikely alliance emerged as the Taliban moved towards the Hezbe which in turn attacked the Ettahad base in Gawisar (Paktia). The base which has a massive arms dump was the target of attack, and for the first time since the Mujahideen "victory" aircraft intruded into Pakistani airspace and bombed villages on the border (Teri Mangal). The Gawisar base was believed to have been supplying weapons to the Rabbani regime. During October especially, several convoys of trucks laden with weapons like multi barreled rocket launchers, rocket launchers and ammunition, (besides volunteers) were making their way to the frontline[70].

According to observers, the operations for Kabul was tactically a brilliantly planned operation. Keeping to pattern, the Taliban appeared to gather strength even as veteran Mujahideen supported General Gul was warning of a "dangerous game" (in backing the Taliban) and predicting that the fall of Kabul would be an impossible mission[71]. In September, the Taliban had taken Jalalabad without a fight, cutting off Kabul's primary supply route, and moved on to Sarobi, Pul Charki and Gumruk. These were essentially "stand off" operations using heavy artillery and 122 mm mobile rocket launchers. Aircraft which were used by Taliban though not heavily enough caused a major difference to the battle. Kabul fell as its defenders withdrewl in good order. The former President Mr Najibullah was not so lucky. Dragged out of the UN consulate and shot, his body and that of his brother were strung up in public, and subjected to abuse. This one act, internationally televised, heaped opprobrium on the fundamentalist group, who had already begun to impose the most stringent "Islamic" laws on the hapless. Kabul residents.

The Afghan Vice Minister Ghafoorzia, for the first time, directly accused Pakistani and the United States of arming the Taliban, even while claiming that his government had captured 123 officers and personnel of the Pakistan Army earlier, (with Hekmatyar) and another 50 in later operations. He also accused the Taliban of using chemical weapons presumably in artillery shells[72].

Drugs and the Taliban

The other acts of the Taliban set off criticism especially within

Pakistan after its commanders later began to 'tax' traffic as they cashed in not only on the thriving consumer goods smuggling network which was assessed by the Pakistan Institute of Development Economics as worth Rs 100 billion[73], but also the spiralling drug trade which the United Nations Drug Control Programme estimated to be worth Rs 50 billion annually[74]. In March, the Taliban reportedly taxed a convoy, a fee of Rs 200,000 in Kandahar. Even more damning was the fact that after an initial spurt of anti-narcotics enthusiasm, drug cultivation had actually increase in after the advent of the Taliban. The INCR noted a 33 per cent increase in drug cultivation in 1996 from previous figures, particularly in the areas under the control of the Taliban[75].

As the UNDCP notes in its annual report for 1996, for the first time, refineries have opened up in the Afghanistan-Pakistan border, though the drug flow continues towards Pakistan. Refineries and new routes have opened up towards Central Asia. As the shadow of the Taliban fell on Herat, Toghundi on the Turkmenistan border opened up as an exit route. While consolidations had led to the opening of new labs along the Central Asian border it has to be stated clearly that the rise of the Taliban has been extremely beneficial for the drug trade.

Meanwhile, the redoubtable former arms merchant Rocketi was reportedly appointed Deputy Army Chief even as there were reports of internecine fighting that killed at least two top Taliban commanders apparently at the hands of supporters of Mullah Rabbani, the trusted lieutenant of Mullah Omar[76]. Worse still, as far as the western world was concerned. AFP reported that around 400 Islamic terrorist figures were sheltering under the Taliban protection including Osma Bin Laden, who is alleged to be the main financier of terrorist groups[77]. Taliban spokesmen, while confirming the existence of the Arabs, bypassed the question as to their legalisation as citizens.

The Alliance—Weakness From Within

At Kinjan, after a tense standoff, the forces of Dostum, Hekmatyar and Masood decided to fight the Taliban, to be joined later by the Wahadat and Pir Gailani. On 22 October, the Afghanistan High Defence Council was formed, composed of the forces of the Hezb-e-Wahadat (three groups of a total of around 10,000) the Hezb-e-Islami (around 2-3000), Harkat-e-Islami (led by Ayatollah Mohseni) and Hezb-e-Mahaz-e-Melli (Pir Gailani) apart from the Dostum, Masood and Rabbani combine. Altogether around 150 military and *jehadi* commanders were grouped within this umbrella. With Dostum's troop strength put at 50,000 and that of the Rabbani and Masood at between 50-70,000, the new alignment seemed to have the potential to change the balance. Yet there were enough indications of the disagreement among the factions. While observers were predicting that Masood was more likely to lose than gain aligning himself with such fickle partners. As the Taliban attacks on the Alliance area began, this fickleness was soon apparent as 'fronts' held by individual commanders collapsed in the face of a lack of cohesion and will. Commanders began to 'defect' to the Taliban with their troops. Gen Dostum was accused of having killed off rival commanders, which appears to be in part responsible for the latest and most dramatic defection of Gen Abdul Malik which occurred at a strategic point in time. This single incident served to underscore the fact that the term 'rented revolutionaries' was still operative, with ethnicity and such like taking a back seat. Clearly, the ability of Gen. Dostum to pay top dollar, as well as his ability to appoint future Prime Ministers (or equivalent) were in doubt. When the Taliban leader (who appear to have no less a taste for power than anybody else) balked at this, the General turned traitor.

International Reactions

International reactions were indicative of the strange alliances that were being forged. The United State's muted reaction was received with astonishment even by Pakistani commentators who commented that it was contradictory to the Washington's stand on human rights and extremism[78]. The Associated Press quoted a US official as saying that the Taliban followed a different brand of Islam (from the Iranians) and that this would not affect fundamentalism elsewhere was derided, while others wrote scathingly about Ms Bhutto's comment to the BBC that it was a "welcome development"[79]. The reaction from US oil companies were even more positive. UNOCAL Executive Vice President Chris Taggart told *Reuters* that it was a positive development, and urged the USA to extend recognition to the new rulers in Kabul, and thus lead the way for international lending agencies to come in[80]. These sentiments were backed by President Richard Keller in *Newsweek*, which also reported that the oil company, was later seen to be consulting with various groups. The emissary came away with 'enormous support' especially from northern warlord Dostum[81]. In Iran, President Rafsanjani termed the advance as a 'disaster' while Russia and the CAR states (less Turkmenistan) hurried into a meeting at Almaty to warn of direct consequences of any attack on their territories (in compliance with clause 4 of Collective Security Treaty) while the State Duma deputies issued a statement calling the situation one that directly affected the national security interests of Russia. Uzbekistan, even while calling for an arms embargo stressed that the Taliban needed to be stopped short of Salang[82], a requirement that General (now Pasha) Dostum seemed eager to comply with. The Taliban reaction was terse. It called upon the US to ask the CIS not to 'interfere' and continued to try to push north. In Pakistan, a series of developments were taking place. On the 26th of September the government formally approved the laying of the 2.6 billion US dollars worth 1,609 km long pipeline from Turkmenistan (Chardzhou) to a marine terminal in Baluchistan, receiving the formal terminal site optimization study from UNOCAL officials[83].

Pakistan rapidly improved communication lines, postal services and other links, and with the rush of the Taliban towards Mazar, decided to extend recognition. Above the skies a helicopter shot down revealed that it had been carrying ISI personnel[84].

Conclusions

It is a wonder that this 'war' that has been waged for so long and that has caused unprecedented destruction with so little result, has been all in all one that has not seen the use of any high technology weapons, or massed armies or brave speeches. It has remained akin to one of the 30 odd dirty little wars that are mushrooming across the globe, and in this sense it is no anomaly at all. For all these wars display a dismaying pattern—ethnic groups using cold war weaponry in the form of massive tonnage of what are basically light weapons. i.e., assault rifles, mortars, RPGs, shoulder fired weapons, etc. to kill, maim and destroy population and large swathes of territory in a senseless barrage of violence. Civilians everywhere have suffered the most either in terms of the dead or the injured or the displaced. Whole regions have been destabilized—witness Central Africa—

leading to the possibility of open war. Everywhere the supply of weapons goes on regardless of the fulminations of human rights groups or political analysts. Few within neighbouring countries seem to realise that these actions would rebound on their own security as weapons, crime and ethnic animosities spreads outward from the conflict zone. In Afghanistan, other factors immeasurably complicate this dangerous brew—the spread outward of narcotics movements and the apparently vital need of moving Central Asian oil out to world markets bypassing Iran.

The sheer extent of the arms supply and its nature—designed as it was to benefit the most extreme groups is nothing, if not wanton. Inexplicably, it now known that in spite of Hekmatyar's waywardness and cruelty, and Khalili's reputation as a dichard fundamentalist and patron of terrorism, the United States continued to siphon aid to these groups till 1993. Even stranger still is Washington's tolerance of the extreme Taliban, unless there was a clear indication that these were the forces of the moment—holding vital territory till another power could take over. Even should a regime with the former (Pushtoon) king as its head come in. The fact that the large part of vital territory is held by one group of like ethnic sympathy should make it easier for any future 'peace keeping force' to deal with it as such. The dangerous supposition that Iran will simply give in to such an arrangement is dangerous, and as long as the Heratis are kept under the thumb of the Taliban more trouble can be expected.

The crux of the problem arises from a rather dusty answer to the question as to who constitutes the Taliban—while the peaceful (if reactionary) credentials of the top leadership cannot be questioned, the vast majority of the men at the bottom are the same actors who have been battling it out since the end of the *jehad* against the Soviets—the traffickers, the arms dealers, the mercenaries and the hundreds of others who have their own diverse interests in keeping the war going. At the war planning levels are those who have served in regular armies in neighbouring countries, who have little patience with Islamic doctrine and theology. The last dash on Mazar was after all on a day when Muslims everywhere were engaged in prayer. In short, the old men of Kabul are not the Taliban and never were. Now its up to the international community (or those sections that are intensely involved in the 'oil great game' to give it an identity that would be suitable for the country as a whole.

Meanwhile, as the Taliban treatise with Uzbek leaders, another ethnic war bites the dust. There was never any ethnicity operating in the Afghan war, though western analyst continue to lay the roots of conflict in the historical hatreds caused by that loose and malleable term ethnicity. A closer look at most conflicts reveal that ethnicity has usually been injected into a conflict to suit someone's strategic interest. In Afghanistan, ethnicity, religion and narcotics all form part of a mosaic that has ruined the country, killed more than 100,000 unfortunate civilians and has very little to do with the realities on the ground. No one speaks for Afghanistan—not the Pakistanis or other regional actors who claim to be interested in the welfare of its citizens—and as time wears on the voice of Afghanistan becomes weaker, even as those of others become more strident. Once the United Nations was supposedly the last succour for war ravaged countries—today UN representative Norbert Holl is just another voice in the mêlée ? Few countries would be prepared to send troops into the country, while the only men who seem to be shuttling back and forth busily are the oil men.

Apparently, these groups and Central Asian states have atouching faith in the ability of the Taliban to secure areas for the construction of a pipeline, an exercise that is beyond the capability of the Taliban or anyone else—as long as the weapons continue to proliferate, any local warlord would be able to effectively stop the construction and functioning of a pipeline or even traffic along a road.

India has so far played a low key role in the conflict, (except for the rather surprising energy it displayed in hastening to Mazar-e-Sharif) and would be wise to continue to do so. In essence this means making as few public statements as possible even while keeping in mind that the stability of Central Asia is vital for peace in the entire area, especially Kashmir. This is not to be taken in the narrow sense of the Afghan fighters invading the valley. While this is undoubtedly a frightening prospect (as certainly Pakistan is not at all ready to have them turn upon her as they so easily might) in the larger context, peace in the heartland of Asia is inextricably intertwined. Peace is unlikely to be brought in by the Taliban, and regional security demands that all actors be given a say in drawing the conflict to a close. If however the Taliban are able to hang on and maintain a certain rude presence, and if this helps to bring about stability, then their presence must be encouraged in terms of not the usual food aid, and medicines but strong NGO support in revitalising agriculture and traditional cottage industry. To help itself, Afghanistan has to be first got to her feet. It is unwise to react to events in Afghanistan on the sole calculation of what Pakistan sees as beneficial for herself. Apart from the fact that these ideas have not always proved so, regional peace is vitally necessary for handling our own militancy related problems.

Keeping the last factor in mind, a full fledged disarmament and demobilization programme should be proposed by the Security Council for Afghanistan as soon as possible. The importance of such an initiative cannot be overemphasized, and may be vital to our own security. Religious bigotry and motivations to terrorism thrives on poverty and the lack of secure alternatives. The potency of this factor may be beyond even what Pakistan can control, even should she see the wisdom of doing so.

The power of the narcotics industry is another dimension that is linked to our own circle of crime and political patronage. The sheer reach of organised crime has not yet been fathomed in this country, but the first signs are already apparent in the increasing number of "money laundering" scandals, armed crime and shoot outs in urban areas, and above all the steady dilution of our borders, as militants, drugs and guns slip across with ease. In Pakistan, the Durand Line has ceased to exist for all practical purposes, and while this may seem a triumph in some circles in Afghanistan, it is precisely the fluid nature of the border that has eroded the stability of the country.

Clearly, even if the Taliban 'control' all or most of Afghanistan, this state of affairs is unlikely to hold, and will ultimately rebound on Pakistan herself. More sectarian instability in Pakistan can be expected, as Shia and Sunni battle it out in Afghanistan and the streets of Lahore. Whether Pakistan can then 'control' the Taliban, when she maintains scant control over her own internal security is doubtful and an unstable Pakistan is dangerous for India in diverse ways. In the medium term, a 'replacement' of the middle level leadership of the Taliban can be expected, as also a dilution of most of the extreme policies. What can clearly be said is that there will be no reduction in narcotics production or the flow through Pakistan. After all, even the 'gun and Koran' group has to kept happy, and Pakistan's fragile economy can hardly take the load, unless she is prepared to let foreign intelligence and oil agencies to once again take the role they once had—provider but not the distributor. The Mujahids have demonstrated many times that they are not always grateful to the hand that feeds it (especially when the other hand carries a list of conditions) and they may yet do so again. As Gen. Malik takes over from Gen. Dostum, nothing has changed in Afghanistan. Actors have been recycled, but the game remains the same.

References

1. Barnett Rubin, *The Search for Peace in Afghanistan* Yale University, 1995, p. 22.
2. See Robert G. Wirsing, *Pakistan's Security under Zia 1977-78*, Houndmills, Macmillan 1991, and also see Christina Lamp, *Waiting for Allah*, Hamish Hamilton, London, 1991.
3. Robert G. Wirsing, *Pakistan's Security under Zia, 1977-78*, Macmillan, London, 1991, p.30.
4. Edward Girardet, *Afghanistan: The Soviet War*, St Martin's Press: New York, 1985, p. 166.
5. Zbeigniew Brezinzski, *Power and Principle*, Weidenseld and Goldwonn: London, 1983, p. 420.
6. Kuldip Nayar, *Report on Afghanistan*, Allied Publishers: Bombay, 1981.
7. See L. Raymond Garthoff, *Detente and Confrontation: US-Soviet Relations from Nixon to Reagan* (Brookings Institution, 1985).
8. See n. 5, p. 423.
9. *Ibid* p. 426.
10. *Mezhhdunarodnaya Dzhin* in *Jane's Defence Weekly*, 5 November, 1988, p. 1156.
11. n. 1, p. 29.
12. n. 1 p. 30.
13. Testifying at a House Foreign Affairs Committee Hearing in 1990, quoted in *World Policy Journal*, Vol. II, No. 4, Spring, 1994.
14. See Mohammed Youssaf and Mark Adkin *'The Bear Trap' Jang*: Lahore, 1992.
15. Youssaf and Adkin, n. 13.
16. Youssaf and Adkin, n. 7.
17. General Imran's Report in *Muslim* 20 April, 1995.
18. Edward Girardet, *Afghanistan, Select*: New Delhi, 1986, p. 55.
19. *Ibid.*

20. See Tara Kartha, Spread of Arms and Instability in Pakistan, *Strategic Analysis,* Nov. 1993.
21. Alex Aliev, *The War in Afghanistan: Strategy and the state of the Resistance,* Santa Monica, Rand Corporation, Nov. 1986.
22. Marvin G. Weinbaum, *Pakistan and Afghanistan: Resistance and Reconstruction,* Westview Press, Boulder 1994, p. 31.
23. This figure is cited by Christina Lamb, *Waiting for Allah,* Hamish Hamilton: London, 1991, p. 223.
24. Emma Duncan, *Breaking the Curfew,* Penguin: London, 1989, p. 156.
25. See n. 6, p. 32.
26. See n. 23.
27. See Tara Kartha, Spread of Arms and Instability in Pakistan, *Strategic Analysis,* Vol. XVI, No. 8, Nov. 1993.
28. Figures from the *International Narcotics Control Strategy Report 1986,* 1990.
29. Barnett Rubin, *Fragmentation of Afghanistan,* Yale University Press 1995, p. 257.
30. See also Selig Harrison, *Containment and the Soviet Union in Afghanistan* in Terry L. Diebel, John Lewis Gaddis (ed) *Containment: Concept and Policy,* Vol. 2, National Defence University Press, Washington, DC, 1986, pp. 457-480.
31. *Jane's Intelligence Review,* Aug 91, p. 352.
32. Selig Harrison, Diego Cordovez *"Out of Afghanistan, The Inside Story of the Soviet Withdrawal,* Oxford University Press, 1995, p. 69.
33. *Ibid.*
34. *Jane's Intelligence Review* September 1994, p. 426.
35. *Jane's Defence Weekly,* 20 July, 1985, p. 109.
36. *Jane's Defence Weekly,* 17 August, 1985, p. 295.
37. Jane's Intelligence Review, October, 1996, p. 264.
38. *Electronic Telegraph,* 3 November, 1996, Issue 529.
39. Diebel, Gaddis, p. 475.
40. *Jane's Intelligence Review,* February 1992, p. 51.
41. *JDW,* 12 November 1988, p. 1189.
42. Rubin n. 1, p. 105.
43. *Herald,* October 1990, p. 32 see also Rubin p. 115.
44. *Ibid.* p. 106.
45. See Edgar O'Ballance, *Afghan Wars: What the British Gave and the Soviet Union Lost,* Brassey's : New York.
46. *Jane's Intelligence Review,* August 1991, p. 350.
47. *Ibid.* p. 353.
48. This view is put forward by Marvin Weinbaum as a possible cause of the explosion, n. 17.
49. *Nation,* 26 January, 1992.
50. Rubin n 1, p. 110.
51. *Herald,* October, 1991, p. 53.

52. See *Herald*, December, 1989, p. 96.
53. News, 1 September, 1992.
54. *Muslim*, 3 September 1992.
55. *Newsline*, Karachi, February, 1994, p. 56.
56. JDW, 15 January, 1994.
57. Reportedly at Termez, See Giles Dorronsoro, Afghanistan's Civil War, *Current History*, pp. 37-40.
58. Uzbekistan printing fake Afghani, *Khaleej Times*, 11 June, 1995.
59. On Pakistani funding see *JDW*, 22 April, 1995.
60. The University was closed following the attack on Pakistan's embassy in Kabul, *News*, 4 October, 1995.
61. n. 27 (Fragmentation).
62. To cite one "nothing less than the latest strategy of proxy war in Afghanistan through a third force..." *Nation*, 7 February, 1995.
63. *News*, 3 March, 1995.
64. *Ibid*.
65. *Nation*, 29 April, 1995.
66. *Herald*, March, 1995 p. 50.
67. *Frontier Post*, 14 March, 1995.
68. *Khayan International* quoted in *Herald* October, 1995, p. 34.
69. Following Foreign Minister Assef Ali's visit on September 16 *Iran News*, September 18 1995, in *Public Observer Trends* Afghanistan, October 19, 1995.
70. See *Herald*, October, 1995, pp. 25-35.
71. *Nawai-i- Waqt*, 15 September, 1996.
72. *Frontier Post*, 16 October, 1996.
73. See Ahmad Rashid in *Nation*, 29 April, 1995.
74. United Nations Drug Control Programme, International Narcotics Control, Vienna.
75. *International Narcotics Control Strategy Report*, US State Department, 1996.
76. Mullaj Borjan, top eastern commander, Abdus Sattar Niyazi (member of the leadership council, *IRNA* in *SWB/FE/2751* A/4, 24 October 1996.
77. AFP in *Pakistan Times*, 6 October 1996.
78. Eqbal Ahmed in *Dawn*, 15 October 1996.
79. For comments see Mushadid Hussain in *Nation*, 13 October, 1996.
80. In POT (Pakistan), Vol. XXIV, No. 245.
81. *Newsweek*, 4 November, 1996, p. 25.
82. Interfax in *SWB/FE/2736* A/3, 7 October, 1996.
83. *Dawn*, 26 September, 1996.
84. *Times of India*, 31 May, 1997.

12

AFGHANISTAN CRISIS: GEOPOLITICAL ASPECTS

NASSER SAGHAFI-AMERI

The crisis and disturbances in Afghanistan started from the occupation of Soviet troops in December, 1979. However the roots of this unsettlement could be traced to the gain of power by the communists through a Coup d'êtat.

The government of General Mohammed Daud, who deposed King Zahir Shah in a palace coup in July 1973, was brought down by Noor Mohammed Taraki in 1978, at the instigation of the Soviet Union. This in fact was a measure by the Soviets to prevent the spread of American influence and also the Islamic movements in Afghanistan and at the doorsteps of Central Asian republics.

Eventually, the Soviets became dissatisfied with Taraki because he could not overcome the problems which had come into being of his various development plans. The Soviets therefore intervened by sending their forces to Afghanistan. In reaction to that Soviet policy, the regional countries and the USA attempted to give Mujahideen military support in order to stop Soviet influence and its extension to the Persian Gulf and its rich oil resources.

Consequently, a new 'Great Game' started in the region. This new game was conceptually different from the previous 'Great Game' of the nineteenth century between the Tzarist Russia and the British empire. That game was based upon colonialism and military competition between those two rival empires. The two empires were afraid of each other. The British empire was concerned that the Tzarist Russia wanted to weaken its domination over India, while

Russia felt that Britain was engaged in sabotaging its programmes for occupation and domination of Central Asia.

In pursuance of these policies, Britain once in 1839 and on another occasion in 1878 occupied Kabul and Kandahar and part of eastern Afghanistan. On the other side, Russia frequently invaded the utonomous areas of Central Asia. Finally, in 1880, the two powers agreed upon creation of an independent and neutral country in a region between Hindukush mountains and Khaibar valley. Later in 1893, the British signed an agreement with Afghan government defining the boundary between Afghanistan and British India. Neutral status of Afghanistan continued till 1973 when the Soviet Union in support of People's Democratic Party (PDP) and for the creation of 'Republic of Afghanistan' jeopardised the neutral status of Afghanistan.

The Soviets, meanwhile exploited every opportunity to increase their influence in Afghanistan. Under this circumstance it is suggested that the 1978 events, which were defined as 'Saur Revolution' by the communists in Afghanistan was pre-eminently a response to the American attempts to grab Afghanistan for setting up its advance Cold War base after losing the foothold in Iran when the Shah's regime fell".[1]

The Soviets, fearing "a CIA take-over to undo the Afghan revolution", marched in as a pre-emptive move in December, 1979. This brought Afghanistan overnight into the vortex of the Cold War.

With the collapse of the Soviet Union and independence of Central Asian republics in the latter half of 1991, attention was once again drawn to this strategic region. Central Asia and Caspian sea basin have rich deposits of hydrocarbons which are largest in the world, second only to the Persian Gulf region. Recent studies indicate that the Caspian basin alone possesses more than 178 billion barrels of oil[2] which amounts to one-sixth of the total oil deposits of the world that have been discovered so far.

Thus in the new 'Great Game' access to this strategically important and land-locked area and its transit routes gained importance. In this regard Afghanistan has been considered as part of the transit route through Pakistan and therefore this country has once again become important in the 'Great Game'. Pakistan, by virtue of its geographical location and its close links with Taliban finds itself in a position to offer access through its ports to Central Asia via Afghanistan.

In the competition for access to Central Asia, regional as well as extraregional countries have become involved. For instance, the creation of Taliban and support rendered to it, despite its intransigent policies and its bad record of human rights could only be interpreted in the context of the 'New Great Game' theory.

In this competition, the USA has apparently closed its eyes from the activities of Taliban. Americans have given an indication to the effect that they favour opening of transit route through Afghanistan and laying down of oil and gas pipelines for Central Asia across that country. This policy of the USA is also in consonance with the Washington's declared intention of containing Iran and reducing the dependence of Central Asian countries to Russia. Besides Pakistan, Saudi Arabia has been named as supporters of Taliban.

A pro-Taliban journalist says that "Saudi Arabia was among the most generous donors which contributed to the religious schools (Madarsas) in Pakistan where the Taliban received their education is some evidence that Saudi Arabia is sympathetic to the Taliban cause and would offer help should the need arise."[3]

In the Central Asian countries, the real threat to the security of the region is considered coming from the Tajik-Afghan border. Afghanisation of Tajikistan and the whole of Central Asian region is considered potentially dangerous not only for the Central Asian states but for Russia as well-especially given the fact the Russian Federation considered this region as her "soft under-belly".[4]

For Iran, having close historical ties with Afghanistan and sharing 600 kms. of borders, the crisis has caused great concern. The problem of more than 2.5 million Afghan refugees in Iran as well as the problem of drug trafficking and related social and security issues are considered as the effects of crisis and instability in Afghanistan.

Iran has proposed the following a three-point plan for solving the Afghan crisis. First, the decision making in Afghanistan should be by the people of Afghanistan. Second, foreign countries should not interfere in the affairs of Afghanistan. Third, any government in

Afghanistan should be a broad-based one, consisting of all the ethnic and religious groups of the country.

It has now become more evident than before that the continuation of present trend in Afghanistan not only causes great losses to that country but would bring that country to the verge of disintegration. If this ever happens it would have regional ramifications. Many of the neighbouring countries of Afghanistan have similar ethnic population which also exists in Afghanistan. Therefore, disintegration of Afghanistan might not necessarily be limited to that country and would not proceed along calculated national geographical lines. The crisis might spread to the neighbouring and even other regional countries. With this prospect the situation tends to aggravate if the present crisis continues.

The Afghans have incurred more than their share of suffering and devastation. Afghanistan is in dire need of peace and tranquility, a factor that is congenial to national interests of all countries of the region including Pakistan. Taliban must therefore put aside unrealistic expectation and take part in the peace negotiations.

References

1. D.R. Goyal "Impact of Ethnic Conflict in Afghanistan on Adjoining Countries", in *Genesis of Regional Conflict: Kashmir, Afghanistan, Cambodia, West Asia Chechnya* (edited by V.D. Chopra and M. Rasgotra), Gyan Publishing House, New Delhi, 1995, p. 204.
2. See, the *Wall Street Journal*, May, 1977.
3. This is quoted from an article written by Nabi Misdaq on Afghanistan who heads the Pushtoon language service of the BBC See *Asian Affairs*, Dec. 1996, pp. 11-13.
4. See Oumersevic Kasenov, *Military Aspect of Security in Central Asia: National and Regional Strateges*, Amu Darya, Summer-Fall, 1996, p. 241.

13

OIL FACTOR IN AFGHANISTAN CRISIS

V.D. CHOPRA

One of the crucial reasons for Asia's strategic position in American, European and Japanese policy is its tremendous oil and uranium resources. These two resources have become more and more important since the Second World War. Dependency of these countries on oil becomes clear from cold statistics.

Although the American oil companies had lost some of their old positions, after nationalisation of oil in the 1970s, they captured new ones They began consolidating their grip on several adjacent energy fields. It is very revealing that the energy crisis which hit the developed world in the 1970s did not result in lower profits for the Big Five oil cartels. Even though the price of oil went up 400 per cent between October 1973 and the middle of 1975 it did not have an overall negative effect on the cartes profits. This becomes clear from Table 1.

Table 1
Profits of major US oil companies
(million dollars)

Company	1975	1976	1977	1978
Exxon	2,503.0	2,640.0	2,443	2,716
Texaco	830.6	869.7	890	852
Mobil	809.9	942.0	999	1,124

Gulf	700.0	716.0	752	792
SOCAL	772.5	880.0	1,004	1,106
Total	5,616.0	6,147.7	6,088	6,633

Sources: *Fortune,* May 1976, p. 318; *Petroleum Economist,* March/ 1977, p. 92; March 1979, p. 121.

Besides most of the Big Five's net profit, the United States received a great deal of money in the form of short-term credits and long-term investments from the oil producing countries. The income of the 13 members of the Organisation of Petroleum Exporting Countries (OPEC) members rose from 12,500 million dollars in 1971-72 to 113,000 million dollars in 1976, and it reached 128,000 million dollars in 1977.

In 1976 they conducted foreign commercial transactions worth 122,000 million dollars. A lot of money remained in the United States as investment in government bonds, in accounts in commercial banks, as corporate shares and as real estate. Most of that money came from four Arab countries—Saudi Arabia, Kuwait, the United Arab Emirates and Qatar. At the same time a lot of money came from its trade with the oil producing countries: in 1977 the OPEC countries, mainly the Arab ones, paid the United States 12,900 million dollars for its exports (arms sales not included).

Secondly, there was another factor which became more and more important for the United States. This is not just the transfer of profits by the American companies from Middle East oil, but the import of the oil itself. The Middle East is the developed world's largest reservoir of oil.

Developed world's dependency on oil becomes clear from Table 2.

Table 2
Energy consumption and import dependency, 1990

Country	*Consumption (millio n metric tons oil equivalent)*	*Per capita consumption (metric tons oil equivalent)*	*Dependence in imports %*	
			Total	*oil*
Japan	428	3.5	85.4	99.7
USA	1,906	7.6	17.8	43.9
Germany	278	4.4	53.6	95.7

UK	210	3.7	2.5	-14.7
France	221	3.9	55.0	96.1

Sources: *Facts and figures of Japan* (Tokyo: Foreign Press Centre of Japan, 1993 edition).

There are clear indications that oil reserves of the Gulf countries will start declining during the next two to three decades, though there are conflicting opinions among the experts Nevertheless one thing is certain that the American economic experts have already begun to look at reserves of the Central Asian republics. Though Afghanistan may not have as rich oil reserves as the Central Asian republics, however, the north Afghanistan has rich oil and gas reserves. Above all Afghanistan is a link among the various oil rich Central Asian republics.

Despite serious economic problems currently faced by the region, it is generally believed that the economies of Central Asia are likely to witness an upward trend in a few years. This will largely depend on natural resources of this region and how they are developing and on what terms and conditions foreign investments are made.

The second most important pre-requisite is the provision of infrastructure facilities for transit to the outside world. It is herein that importance of Afghanistan and its future have strategic importance for Central Asian Republics.

Economic prospects are especially bright for the four hydrocarbon rich states around the Caspian Sea—Kazakhistan, Uzbekistan, Turkmenistan and Azerbaijan. In these four republics energy sector holds the key to all future economic development. Prof. Arif Husain Rizvi of Aligarh Muslim University has provided this table which shows the estimates of oil and gas reserves for these republics.

Table 3

Oil and gas reserves of central Asia

Country	*Proven oil reserves*	*Potential oil reserves*	*Proven gas reserves*
	Bn. bld	*Bn. bld*	*tr. cu.m.*
Azerbaijan	1.2	15.0	0.1
Kazakhistan	5.3	20.0	1.8
Turkmenistan	1.4	4.2	2.9
Uzbekistan	—	3.2 MT	42.8 bn m^3

Sources: *OPEC Bulletin,* Nov./Dec. 1996; For Uzbekistan Adelphi Paper, 288.

This statistics proves that Central Asian republics will push themselves ahead of oil rich Gulf countries. At the end of 1993 the reserve production ratio for these four republics indicates that oil will last for 92 years in Azerbaijan, 124 years in Kazakhistan, 30 years in Turkmenistan and 78 years in Uzbekistan. Turkmenistan with its 2.4 tr.cu.m. gas will compensate for limited oil reserves.

According to a study of OPEC, Azerbaijan, Kazakhistan and Turkmenistan will have very substantial levels of exportable oil surpluses.

Ironically, like Afghanistan, all these republics are land-locked.

Let us look at the Central Asian republics from another angle. Kazakhstan was the second largest republic of the erstwhile Soviet Union and is presently the ninth largest state in the world. Its area is 2,71,330 sq. km.. With a total of about 17 million people today, its population density is the third lowest in the world, after Canada and Australia. Almost one-third of population of this republic is of Russian origin.

It has enormous quantities of livestock. Its mineral resources are very extensive, especially iron ore, lead, zinc, bauxite, gold, uranium, cadmium and copper. What is of far-reaching significance is that in the coming decades it may become one of the biggest oil producing countries, perhaps one of the top five countries.

Major oil sources are to be found in the vast Tenghiz fields which alone have a recoverable reserve of at least 6 to 9 billion barrels and at the north-eastern segment of the Caspian Sea. Huge natural gas reserves are located at Karachaganak. The Chevron Oil Company of the USA has the rights to the Tenghiz oil fields where it is proposing to spend 20 billion US dollars over the next 40 years in its development. By 2010 the peak output is likely to be 700,000 barrels a day. British Gas and Agip are negotiating for Karachaganak which is expected to contain 20,000 billion cubic feet of natural gas, plus 2 billion barrels of oil. These facts are revealing in themselves.

Kyrgyzstan

Kyrgyz Respublikasy (Republic of Kyrgyzstan), a former Soviet Republic that became independent in December, 1991 is situated on the eastern part of the Central Asian republics, bordering Kazakhstan in the north, China in the east, Tajikistan in the south and Uzbekistan in the west, Kyrgyzstan is a nascent democratic republic desperately trying to establish itself. Its population is nearly 4.6 million with just a shade over 50 per cent being ethnic Kyrgyz. Russians are around 20 per cent and Uzbeks about 13 per cent.

This republic has small amounts of oil, natural gas, gold and uranium. It is hardly enough for substantial exports. There are few other assets to fall back upon.

Tajikistan

Borders of this country are Afghanistan in the south, China in the east and Kyrgyzstan and Uzbekistan in the north and west. Of a total population of around 5.7 million, Tajiks are about 65 per cent and Uzbeks 25 per cent. Areas adjacent to Uzbekistan have over 50 per cent Uzbeks. Of the remaining 10 per cent the Russian number about a third.

Tajikistan is grossly underresourced. It was the poorest republic of the USSR. It depended overwhelmingly on Soviet subsidies to sustain its economy. It has in addition small quantities of petroleum, uranium, coal and mercury.

Uzbekistan

The most populous and centrally located republic, Uzbekistan holds the key to stability and prosperity in the Central Asian republics from several perspectives. About 33 per cent of the Central, Asian republics, 50 million people are Uzbeks. Uzbekistan's population of 21.6 million is the largest in the Central Asian Republics, with over 71 per cent Uzbeks and about 8 per cent Russians. This republic has an excellent record in the field of agriculture. Before independence it produced 65 per cent of the total cotton, 50 per cent of the total rice and 60 per cent of the total lucerne grown in the former Soviet Union.

Tajiks are an important minority at 4.7 per cent mainly around Bukhra and Samarkhand. It has considerable natural resources, though perhaps not as much as in Kazakhstan and Turkmenistan. These include petroleum, gas, coal, gold, uranium, silver and copper. Till recently it was the fourth largest producer of cotton in the world. Its oil and gas reserves are still not fully established but there are possibilities of large reserves.

Turkmenistan

This land is blessed with enormous riches and has very low population of around 4 million people. About 2 per cent are Russians who almost entirely live in the cities and approximately 9 per cent are Uzbek. National resources include petroleum, natural gas, coal, sulphur, salt and magnesium. Some estimates suggest that its natural gas reserves may be the third larges in the world, next only to the United States and Russia. This would make it potentially another Kuwait. However, it will take many years for this potential to be realised. The reason is simply that all pipelines and supply routes lead north to the Commonwealth of Independent States who are unable to pay for this in hard currency.

In the past Turkmenistan supplied enormous quantities of cotton, natural gas, petroleum and electric power to the USSR and received in return all its other requirements.

Supply of gas to the Central Asian republics remains a delicate issue. Ashkhabad claims that it sells this well below the world prices and less than what Russia charges. But it has to import 70 per cent of its own requirements for which the other republics are now asking for world rates. Recently an exit route by rail through Iran has been negotiate.

This shows geoeconomic importance of this region. However, the picture will not be complete without taking into account oil wealth of other countries in the region.

China

China is a big nation which is rich in energy resources. In 1949, the country's total production of raw coal was only 32 million tons, crude oil 120,000 tons, natural gas 7 million cubic metres, and power generated 434 billion kwh. By 1992, however, annual raw coal production totalled 1.12 billion tons, crude oil 142.1 million tons, natural gas 15.79 billion cubic metres, and power generated, 753.9 billion kwh making China the third largest energy producer. Technological levels have been markedly improved in the energy industry.

Iran

The picture about the oil wealth of this region will become complete if, we take into account the oil wealth of Iran. Among all the states on the periphery of the Central Asian region and Afghanistan, Iran is one country which has been vigorously seeking to establish close economic and commercial linkage with this region. This in turn had its own impact on the whole of West and the Arab World. Iran now seems to have come to the conclusion that stable Central Asian region and a united Afghanistan is in its economic and strategic interest.

It is pertinant to mentioned here that economic progress and expansion of markets in the Central Asian region and in Afghanistan depends largely on the development of their oil resources. This in itself is a time-consuming process. It may take another one decade before the economy of this region begins to change after harnessing its oil wealth.

This potentially oil rich region is confronted with a number of problems.

Firstly, all the Central Asian republics and Afghanistan are land-locked countries. That being the position for export of their oil wealth they need outlets. At the moment they can export their oil through Iran or Russia. However, Pakistan too can provide them an export route provided it has political hold over Afghanistan. Since there is no convergence of interests on this specific issue between Russia, and West the United States in particular, political hold of Pakistan and on Afghanistan is their bestbet. That explains the political policy of the West and the United States on Afghanistan.

Secondly, the economic potential of oil wealth can be developed with massive investment and modern technology. Russia at the present state is unable to undertake this work. However, if Russia, India and Iran pool their resources they may partially meet this challenge. Nonetheless, the ground reality is that American capital at the present stage is most active in this particular field.

In September, 1994 for instance a major deal worth 8 billion US dollars was signed between the Azerbaijan State Oil Company (Socar) and a nine-member western-led consortium to develop Azeri, Chirag and Guneshli oilfields. In that Socar gave away 5 per cent share to Iran out of its own 20 per cent share. However by March 1995 the Iranian participation was set aside. This was due to American firm's objection. Later on Azerbaijan gave that 5 per cent share to Turkey in addition to its original share of 1.75 per cent.

Whatever may be the assessment about this development, this clearly brings out how a cold war for controlling oil wealth in this region has already begun and that too in the neighbourhood of Russia—a former superpower.

Notwithstanding this development, Iran is anxious to participate in developing oil resources of Central Asian republics. Iran has offered to take oil from Azerbaijan for its Tabriz refinery and provide in return the equal amount of crude from its Gulf outlet for export by Azerbaijan. For this arrangement, Iran would just require an additional 80 km pipeline from Bandar Anzali port in the Caspian to the main Tabriz-Tehran line.

Again Iran entered into another deal with Azerbaijan on 4 June 1996, for the development of Shakh Beniz oilfield with a potential of 400 billion cu.m. of gas, 200 million metric tons of gas concentrate and 100 million tons of crude oil. The total value of the deal is 4 billion US dollars.

In May, 1996 Iran signed a deal with Kazakhstan. Under this deal Iran will receive initially 2 million tons of oil from the Kazakh port Aktan and ship it to Caspian port of Neka for use in Tehran and Tabriz Refineries. The quantity is expected to rise to 6 million tons in the next decade.

Turkmenistan which is a major producer of gas has offered to supply Iran natural gas for its northern provinces through an onshore gasline which will connect with the existing 30-Inch Iranian line with a capacity of 8-9 billion cubic metre per year. This project will cost 200 million US dollars.

Besides cooperation in the energy sector Iran is visualizing great potential in its role as a transit route to Central Asia. Iran has a well-developed railway and road network which can help transport goods from and to Central Asian republics via the Gulf. With the completion of 129 km Mashhad Sarakh's -Tajan railway line, Iran now has a direct connection with China via Turkmenistan, Uzbekistan and Kazakhstan to the Persian Gulf. Work is underway on another new railway line from Bafgh to Bandar Abbas in the southern Persian Gulf. It will provide another route for Central Asian's trade with south, south-east Asia and the Far East. This railway network has the capacity of 500,000 passengers and 2 million tons of goods, which in a year will go up to one million passengers and 10 million tons of goods.

Recent reports indicate that traffic via Sarakhs-Mashhad railway line has already started. Kazakhstan has sent its first consignment of gas, oil and fertiliser to Iran through this route. Goods originating from Uzbekistan to international markets have also been transported through the new railway link. All these facts have been compiled in a paper by Prof. Arif Husain Rizvi, Reader, Centre of West Asian Studies, Aligarh Muslim University.

This valuable information brings into sharp focus the new importance which the oil factor has assumed in the stability of this region.

14

RELIGIOUS FUNDAMENTALISM AND ETHNIC CONFLICTS

V.D. CHOPRA

In recent years, particularly in the post Cold War period, a new phrase, the "Rise of Fundamentalism", religious and ethnic conflicts have entered into the currency of political jargon, and academic discourse though the term 'fundamentalism' has not yet acquired a precise definition. The current crisis in some of the developing countries including in Afghanistan too are being examined within this framework.

To examine this problem and its relevance to the crisis in Afghanistan, it will be relevant to mention that after the end of the Second World War in about 3 decades more than 150 instances of major inter and intra-state violence took place and under 40 of them surface in the developing world. After the disintegration of the Soviet Union the intensity of these conflicts seems to have increased. Perhaps during the Cold War too superpowers did exercise some restraint on their allies. In the post Cold War period these conflicts have assumed a dangerous proportion and some of the countries have disintegrated.

However, one distinction should be made in these conflicts between the Cold War and the post Cold War periods. During the Cold War period for instance in two-thirds of the conflicts the developed nations directly or indirectly intervened. Many of them however, were anti-colonial was, only about a fifth of them were interstate conflicts, a number of them caused by religious, tribal and secessionist factors. On the other hand in the post Cold War period most of the conflicts can be traced to religious tribal and separatist factors.

Seen in this background the present crisis in Afghanistan should be examined in this context. In the present conflicts in Afghanistan religious, tribal, ethnic conflicts which were nursed, promoted, financed, materially equipped with lethal weapons, all these factors are playing a key role. Therefore, the crisis in Afghanistan as it exists today has a different dimension. It is no more a conflict merely between the two forces which want to modernise Afghanistan and those which are pitched against it. There is something more to it than meets the eye. The external forces are playing an important role in the present situation and this fact has been analysed in this book by various scholars.

After Afghanistan became a sovereign state, favourable conditions were created for tackling both its social and economic problems and matters connected with the acute problems of ethnic development as has been analysed in this study. The polarisation of political forces within Afghanistan, however, became complex because of economic, ethnic and religious factors. In fact, all these factors were intertwined. The position was also complicated by the interference of foreign powers and their policy of fomenting inter-ethnic friction and making use of conflicts, and of open or disguised support for separatist tendencies. Exaggeration of ethnic peculiarities, the erection of national barriers, often artificial, a morbid attitude towards national sovereignty, and the stirring up of old wrongs and of past mistakes in attempts to resolve ethnic problems-—all acquire in Afghanistan a new significance. They are employed by certain political circles in their geo-political interests.

Increasing attention has been paid in recent years to the ethnic problems of Afghanistan. The aspirations of people of Afghanistan, particularly among the new elite has been either ignored or underestimated. Nevertheless, one still finds that ethnic problems are understood only as inter-tribal hostility, and that the requisite significance is not always attached to them when concrete programmes are being worked out to eliminate actual inequalities in the levels of development of the different peoples. In many cases the national question is understood narrowly and out of context of social and economic processes.

Afghanistan and for that matter Pakistan provide much data for answering many questions, those associated with the processes of ethnic conflicts as compared to India.

What are these questions? What effect do ethnic problems have on the socio-economic development and political life of developing countries? What are the main trends in the ethnic development of such countries? Are there special features in the evolution of nation states in these countries? All these and many other questions call for all-round, thorough analysis.

A feature of modern nation-state building in developing countries, particularly of Asian countries has underlined the necessity of evolving transitional forms of political, economic, social and ethnic development.

This basic question can not be examined in this study. However, Afghanistan has its own specific features both about ethnic conflicts, rise of religious fundamentalism and above all their linkages.

It has to be recognised that ethnicity plays an important role in the political development and stability of both developed and developing societies. What is the importance of various ethnic nationalities in the power structure and the political framework of Pakistan? What are the constraints involved for participation and non-participation of the ethnic nationalities in the process of political socialisation in Pakistan? Does the national social studies curriculum taught at the secondary school level represent the values of major ethnic nationalities, and do the perceptions of the ruling elite differ from those of the indigenous ethnic nationalities? And in the light of the above, does the existing educational policy system correspond with the political culture of Pakistan; does it contribute to the process of national integration or does it destabilise the situation further?

These pertinent questions clearly bring out that in a multi-ethnic country like Pakistan which is supposed to be an Islamic country, ethnic conflicts are becoming sharp and that too after carving out of Bangladesh. This problem in Afghanistan is more acute.

An ethnic nationality is a group of people with common cultural traditions and a sense of identity. In this context the members of an ethnic group differ in regard to certain cultural characteristics despite the fact that they are a subgroup of a larger society. An ethnic group may have their own language and religion as well as certain distinct customs, and the term is applied usually, although not necessarily, to minority groups. But it came to refer to a dominant group as some writers do when there are a number of culturally different groups in a society. Various terms are used to refer to the dominated groups of society, ethnic groups, nationalities, or even minorities.

In the Pakistani case, the dominant army is called an ethnic army elite, because of its dominant Punjabi ethnicity; the same is true for the dominated Sindhi, Baluchi, and Pathan ethnic groups. An ethnic group should not be confused with a racial group, although it is possible for an ethnic group to be a racial group.

During the last two decades, particularly, after the Saur Revolution, the Soviet intervention in Afghanistan, overt and covert involvement of Pakistan in the Civil War in Afghanistan, deep involvement of the United States and the Western countries, an important change in the ethnic composition of both Afghanistan and Pakistan has taken place. If Tajiks and Uzbeks have migrated out of Afghanistan, a large chunk of Pushtoon population has migrated to Pakistan. Significantly, the ethnic and demographic composition of Baluchistan, North-West Frontier Province of Pakistan had undergone significant changes in 1947 with migration of 'Mohajirs'—refugees from mainly the two states of India—Bihar and Uttar Pradesh. The Pushtoon population too had migrated on both sides of the Durand Line. The migration of Afghan refugees, from Afghanistan made the problem complex. Though concrete statistics about this migration of population are not available, but it has created ethnic conflicts at least in 3 provinces of Pakistan, viz. Sind, NWFP and Baluchistan.

This trend has had its own political fall-out on the internal developments of both Pakistan and Afghanistan. The most important result of this development was the fostering of the culture of gun and drugs.

It will not be incorrect to say that the crisis in Afghanistan has created certain socio-economic and political problems at least in two provinces of Pakistan, namely, Sind and Baluchistan. "Mohajirs" agitation in Sind is too-well known. But it has escaped the attention of the outside world. Conflict between Afghan and

Baluchis should also not be ignored. The outbreak of the ethnic violence in Quetta during October, 1991 alone claimed 15 lives. That this conflict took place between Baluchis and Pushtoons conceals more than what it reveals.

It clearly underlines how developments in Afghanistan and Pakistan's present policy of Afghanistan have begun to destabilise both her two provinces namely, Sind and Baluchistan.

The intensity of ethnic conflict between Afghans and Baluchis in Baluchistan should not be underestimated because this province of Pakistan is more backward than any other province. Baluchis are divided between Pakistan and Iran.

What is more dangerous for Pakistan is that both in Sind and Baluchistan trade in sophisticated weapons is flourishing along with drug trafficking. These two factors have increased the intensity of inter and intra-tribal conflicts. Pakistani media has openly admitted that crime rate in Baluchistan has increased after the mass migration of Afghans into the cities of Baluchistan. According to some reliable reports 70 per cent of crimes in Baluchistan can be traced to these two factors. There is yet another aspect of the specific situation of Afghanistan.

Theory of "Civilisational Conflicts"—Ethnic-cum-religious Factor

The specific characteristic of the whole belt of Asia, in which Afghanistan has been described as at the crossroads, is that most of the societies in this region are multi-ethnic, multi-religious and multi-cultural. Turbulence and violence at the time when nation-states are being formed is not unusual. Nation-state as a concept emerged only in the sixteenth century and we have four centuries of history of evolution of nation-states, mostly in Europe and for the last one and a half century in the Western Hemisphere as well. That period of history was marked by extraordinary violence.

Another specific characteristic of this region is that geographical boundaries were carved out during the colonial period in such a manner that it laid the basis of religious-cum-ethnic conflicts.

In the late 1970s, political changes in Afghanistan and Iran, the intensification of democratic tendencies in the Persian Gulf countries and in North and North-East Africa, the rising prestige of the non-aligned movement, combined to challenge the position of developed countries—the former colonial powers. In this situation, the ruling circles of the NATO countries modified their "Muslim policy" by resorting to what they called a "dual strategy". The USA for instance set-up a special Muslim Department within the Central Intelligence Agency. They started to build up their armed forces on the borders of South and South-East Asian and North African countries. It is in this period that militarisation of some countries, which were considered to be friendly towards the United States were intensified. Inter-state conflicts among the Muslim countries began to show a new intensity.

On the other hand, the former colonial powers began to highlight their age-old respect for Muslim culture and Islamic civilisation, their sympathy and concern for the Muslims.

It is relevant to recapitulate these facts because in the new historical condition in the academic parlance of a leading member of American's foreign policy establishment, the differences now among various civilisations have become very acute. They do not leave at that. According to these experts, Cold War (I) was an ideological and economic conflict between "capitalism and communism". It is now turning into a Cold War (II) among civilisations. Some of them even have predicted that this may lead to Third World War.

Whatever may be the significance of this assessment one thing is certain that religious and ethnic conflicts are being promoted in those countries which do not fit into the strategic interests of the developed countries.

The crisis in Afghanistan needs to be seen in this context.

Rise of Taliban

Rise of Taliban—student force—between 1995-97 in Afghanistan, both as a political and military force is a major development in this country. The success of the Taliban among the various warring factions is primarily due to both internal and external factors. This faction controls about two-thirds of the Afghan territory and in the last week of September, 1996, it not only captured Kabul but also publicly executed Dr Najibullah who was taking shelter in the United Nations. This faction was armed and trained by external forces, particularly by Pakistan, Saudi Arabia and the United States. Which is well-known fact. It leads one to the conclusion that both religious and ethnic factors have become effective instruments of destabilisation. All those big or small nation-states, which are multi-religious and multi-ethnic need to draw appropriate lessons from this development, including India, Pakistan, Russia and Iran.

If one looks dispassionately at this trend perhaps not in a too distant future, Pakistan itself may have to pay a heavy price in terms of its unity and integrity.

The currents and under-currents in Sind and Baluchistan indeed are omnious developments for Pakistan itself. It is in this sense that one can draw the conclusion that the course of events in Afghanistan is becoming more and more a real threat to the stability of Asia.

What is of far-reaching significance is that some of the countries of Asia and Africa have already become victims of destabilisation in varying degrees by ethnic and religious conflicts, including Muslims majority countries such as Egypt and Algeria. The recent development in Chechnya too leads to the same conclusion.

It is pertinent here to mention that there is sufficient evidence to prove that a number of countries are suspected of developing and supporting the Taliban movement though this movement initially started operating from Pakistan.

According to some research scholars, there are about 50-60 thousand Afghan students studying in various 'Madarsas'-schools run by Muslim preachers in Pakistan. These students provide the recruiting base for the Taliban. They are educated in religious scriptures and also trained in fighting. Though it is difficult to assess the exact number of these students, according to one estimate nearly one-third of them are actively fighting in Afghanistan.

These Taliban are also active in the internal politics of Pakistan particularly in NWFP, Sind and Baluchistan. What is more it is, that their deep involvement in arms and drug trade, which gives them easy money and that too in massive quantities. Some of them have become more rich than the local population. There are others who control some sectors of economy such as trade and transport.

The reports have also appeared in the press to this effect that since 1994, the hardcore of Talibans are being given intensive military training by border frontier force and army of Pakistan.

Quite apart from this fact, many observers of Afghanistan believe that it is the Pakistani army, both retired army officers and servicemen who really do the fighting. The Afghan-Taliban are playing only a secondary role. It is the ISI which has master minded the entire operation of the Taliban. The ISI functions now as an independent outfit. This brings us to another question.

Who really has been financing and continues to finance Taliban?

It is not easy to answer this question. However, some researchers have alleged that three powers—Pakistan, the United States and Saudi Arabia have been giving liberal financial support to Taliban. It is estimated by some scholars that from 1994 to 1997, Pakistan mobilised about 200 million US dollars for the Taliban movement. In addition to this Taliban have raised huge funds through the illegal sale of arms and drug trafficking in the various Asian countries.

The trinity of Pakistan, Saudi Arabia, and USA has strategic interests in Afghanistan. If Pakistan is interested in trade with Central Asian republics through land route Saudi Arabia is fighting a proxy war against Iran and the United States wants to control the entire oil wealth of this region, of Central Asian republics in particular as has been discussed earlier.

This analysis shows that any study of the current situation in Afghanistan is like strip mining. The top layer consists of feudal and tribal character of the society. If you remove that strip you come across the problem of ethnic conflicts. Beneath these two layers is the religious affinities with its own peculiarities of conflict between Shias and Sunnis. Again the religious affinity of the Afghan people have their own characteristics.

Nevertheless, the bottom strip consists of the geopolitical location of this Asian country. That is why as long as Afghanistan remains in turmoil, it will continue to remain a destabilising factor in the entire region and some Asian countries have already begun to feel the pinch.

15

COMMON HERITAGE OF INDIA AND AFGHANISTAN

V.D. CHOPRA

No study of Indo-Afghan relations can be undertaken without a cursory look at the centuries-old common cultural and economic heritage of the people of India, Afghanistan and Central Asia. In fact this region has been birthplace of various philosophies. It is this factor which still plays an important role in the psychological affinity among the people of Pakistan. You cannot erase the past from the consciousness of people even through consistent efforts to distort history.

Mohenjo-Daro (Mound of the Dead) and Harappa are mere symbols of what was Indus Valley civilisation. This civilisation ranks with the antiquity of the valleys of the Nile, the Tigris, and the Euphrates, which had witnessed the growth of the ancient civilizations of Egypt, Assyria, and Babylonia. Its people knew how to build great cities and had a highly developed cultural life. Cotton and woollen fabrics were in common use; ornaments were worn by both men and women; beautiful pottery was produced; the sculptor's technique was perfect; the carpenter, the mason, the blacksmith, the goldsmith, the jeweller, the stone-cutter and the ivory worker had flourishing trade. Religion of a high order prevailed. The Indus Valley civilisation is believed to be older than even the culture of the Vedic period. While the Vedic Aryans were rural, the people of this valley possessed the amenities of a developed city life. Some hold that they were the same as the Sumerians, while others believe that they were Dravidians. Again, some are of the view that these two were identical with the Dravidians who at one time inhabited the whole of India including the Punjab, Sind and Baluchistan and even migrated to Mesopotamia. The Dravidian language is still spoken by the Brahui people of Baluchistan. This lends support to this view. But Mohenjo-Daro and Harappa maintain a serene silence, smiling like the Sphinx at the labours of the scholars.

Invader after invader for instance ravaged Afghanistan drowning it in blood and gore. Some invaders left only a bloody imprint; some integrated themselves totally with the indigenous population, while still others came as birds of passage.

Today, Afghanistan comprises some 121 tribes and nationalities including 21 big ethnic groups. The total population within the present political boundary of Afghanistan with an area of 6,52,090 sq.kms. was slightly over 15 million as per the 1979 census. The stone implements found in Ghazni province indicate that man appeared in Afghanistan quite early. The process of evolution has been akin to that in Central Asia. Man moved rapidly from food-gathering economy to food-production economy due to fertility of soil. He also became a cattle-breeder. With the prerequisities of settled life available civilisation thrived by 300 B.C. A number of ceramic items discovered in Afghanistan show similarity with those found in Harappa, the site of ancient Indian culture. It has been also established that Harappan towns received copper ore and lazurites from Afghanistan. It is obvious that Afghanistan had very old links with India and the emergence of civilised life both in Afghanistan and India was indigenous in origin. It appears that foreign invaders destroyed both the Afghanistani and Harappan civilizations of India.

The Aryans came to this region in several waves from the west and north-west. Afghanistan was the gateway to India for the successive waves of invaders, who wiped out the civilisations in the Indus Valley and the Gangetic plains and south of the Vindhyas. There are some historians who have come to the conclusion that indigenous civilisation in this region was more advanced than the Aryans.

Afghan historian Mohammad Ali, however, holds the opinion that it was in Afghanistan that "the oldest Aryan hymns and a great part of the Rig Veda were composed" (*A Short History of Afghanistan*). It was again in Afghanistan in the seventh century. B.C. Zoroaster was born who preached his monotheistic religion which later became the state religion of Iran. He upheld the banner of truth and spoke only of one God—Ahura Mazda. Zoroaster was born in Bactria, the "mother of cities", in north-western Afghanistan now called Balkh. This unique historical place has been the home of many great personalities. The great scholar and thinker as well as physician, Ibn-Sina, also known as Avicenna was born here. His mother, Sitara, was from Bukhara. Other prominent figure from Balkh included such scholars and historians as Alberuni, Jaber Khorassani, and Abu Musher. It was also the home of the first poetess of Islamic period, Rabia Balkhi, and perhaps of the greatest of the Sufi poets, Maulana Jalaluddin Balkhi, (Rumi). Balkh's glory was shattered by Ghengis Khan whose hordes devastated it in 1220. Let us leave this period at that and move into the next phase.[1]

Buddhism came to Afghanistan in the third century B.C. perhaps following in the wake of the traders passing through that land. The Mauryan Emperor Ashoka greatly helped the spread of Buddhism in many parts of the world. In Afghanistan, Buddhism took deep roots and flourished for about 1000 years. In and around Bamian which was the main monastery, Buddhism spread its message and soon became the faith of most people in Afghanistan. Remnants of thousands of caves and stupas and above all two huge statues of Buddha—53 and 35 metres high as well as a reclining Buddha statue in Nirvana pose, about 250 metres long, are a living testimony to widespread Buddhist culture in Afghanistan.[2]

Again Buddhism flourished after the Kushans established themselves and fanned out controlling the greater part of Central Asia, the whole of Afghanistan and northern India. Under Kanishka (120-160 A.D.) who embraced Buddhism, it spread out very widely. He organised the fourth council—the last of its kind—of Buddhist monks to settle the disputed points of the faith and founded the new school of Buddhism called the Mahayana. It was from Afghanistan that Buddhism penetrated into China via Central Asia. We will come to this point later on in this study.

Then began another phase in the history of Afghanistan. Afghanistan came under repeated attacks of the Arabs and defended their motherland from subjugation. However, slowly the Arabs made inroads. In 661 A.D. they conquered Lashkargarh-Bost, the citadel, in Helmand province. Kabul retained its independence till 871 A.D. Though the Arabs failed to conquer the whole of Afghanistan by force of arms, their religion, Islam triumphed and was voluntarily adopted by the population. After the destruction of Buddhism, there was really no main religion except dozens of cults, religious bigotry, and superstition. Islam's basic democratic tenets, concepts of equality and brotherhood without any special status being given to a person by virtue of birth were found to be attractive to the people. It broke down social barriers, provided social and political solidarity and for the first time linked the diverse people together by a common faith. There was a good deal of intermixing of cultures and both the Arab and Afghans benefited from it. Though the people had embraced Islam, they were at the same time steadfast in their opposition to Arab domination. Let us now step into the next phase.

Though darkness envelops for several centuries in the ancient history of Afghanistan, one thing is certain that Aryan migrations are supposed to have taken place about 1000 years after the Indus valley civilisation disappeared. We are told in Rig Veda that Yadu and Turvasa, two of the famous Aryan tribes, were brought by Indra from a distant land. Some tablets of the 14th century B.C. discovered at Boghaz Keui in Asia Minor bear references to kings who had Aryan names and used to invoke the blessings of gods Indra, Mitra, Varuna, etc. It is probably that the Aryans came from Asia Minor and adjoining areas and the Punjab was their earliest home in India. Their conquest of the Indus valley and penetration into the basin of the Ganges belongs to prehistory. The only evidence of their first settlement in India is to be found in the Vedas and the great epics. Max Müeller hesitatingly places the beginnings of the Vedic literature in the later half of the second millennium.

The Persian empire founded by Cyrus on the ruins of Assyria extended to the Punjab in the region of Darius (521-485 B.C.) and the territory round Peshawar and Rawalpindi which came to be known as Ghandara, became a big satrapy of the Empire. This territory was divided into two parts by the Indus. To the west of the river lay the kingdom of Pushkalavati in the modern distict of Peshawar and to its east was the realm of Taxila near Rawalpindi. Taxila was a very prosperous kingdom and served as an emporium of commerce between India and Central Asia. Tradition has it that the Mahabharata was first recited in the capital of Taxila. To the south-east of this kingdom lay the twin kingdoms of the Paurvas, the people already famous in Vedic hymns.

In 326 B.C. Alexander, the great Macedonian emperor, crossed the Indus and pushed his way to the river Beas. He wished to press forward to the Ganges valley but his war-worn troops did not like him to go farther. After erecting 12 tower-altars to mark the utmost limit of his march, he withdrew to Babylonia where he died in 323 B.C.

The Macedonian garrisons were soon swept away by Chandra gupta Maurya, and within a few years all traces of foreign domination disappeared from the Punjab and Sind.

Notwithstanding these historic events, one cannot ignore that Afghanistan, a country of magnificent mountains and fertile valleys, is a virtual archeological treasure-house of the Orient. The ruins of ancient towns, palaces and temples on its territory have long been world famous. The abundance of major monuments of ancient art is amazing. Suffice it to mention that during just a few years of investigating the religious complexes in the vicinity of Hadda more than 20,000 samples of ancient sculpture have been discovered some, of them real masterpieces. But what is more important is that it was precisely archaeological material that made it possible to disclose the whole epoch of Afghanistan's ancient history and to learn more about the country's past over many thousands of years and its relations with India and Central Asia.

At the same time, the basic elements of this highly developed culture were known in southern Turkmenistan where they took shape based on the cultural traditions of local early land-cultivating communities. It was in the second millennium B.C. that the main centres of this culture—Namazgha-tepe and Altin-tepe—fell into decline. Part of the population moved east to the Murghab delta, where new oases were founded with their centres in the form of rectangular fortresses surrounded by walls with semi-circular towers on the sides. Apparently, the movement of this population group with its high urban-type culture resulted in the development of fertile tracts of land in the north of Afghanistan. Simultaneously, settlements with an identical culture made their appearance on the right bank of the Amu Darya in southern Uzbekistan.

However, this was by no means a simple transfer of a stable set of cultural traditions. The presence in the complexes of the Dashly type of indisputable Mesopotamian features and the presence of grey-clay ceramics more characteristic of the south-eastern area near the Caspian Sea than of southern Turkmenia proper, point to the fact that the real transfer processes were complicated. One thing is indisputable: it was a time of sharp intensification of various contacts, which sometimes indicated the resettlement of tribal groups. It is not accidental that not far from north-Afghan fortresses of the Bronze Age camps were found with crude clay moulded earthenware typical of the steppe cattle-breeding tribes of the Bronze Age in Kazakhstan and the northern part of Central Asia.

By the middle of the first millennium B.C., certain progress had been made in the development of handicrafts, especially in the production of pottery; now all earthenware was made with the aid of a potter's wheel. Similar types of vessels were used in the north and south of the country, which testifies to the process of cultural integration. One can assume this was facilitated by Afghanistan's inclusion, in the sixth to fourth centuries B.C., in the Achaemenid power, which united almost the entire civilised world of the ancient East—from Asia Minor to the western regions of the Hindustan Peninsula.

Cultural integration was to some extent a reflection of an attempt at political stability and a trend towards creation of a large state. Nomad principalities that were at first at loggerheads with one another, were in the course of time united under the aegis of the ablest and luckiest ruler of the Kushan tribe, who proclaimed himself the king of kings. Next the Kushan armies headed south, across the Hindukush. As a result, a new world power came into being in the first century A.D., stretching from Benares in the Hindustan Peninsula to Syrdrya in Central Asia. A period of stability and prosperity followed. New towns were built, and monumental palaces and temples erected. External and internal trade were broadly developed, as is shown by the thousands of Kushan coins and goods imported from the far-off Roman Empire were discovered during excavations of Kushan monuments. Along with local religious cults, Buddhism became quite widespread. Through the Kushans, it reached farther east to China and Japan.

The variety of religious buildings discovered during the excavations of Dilberjin is important. Judging by the pictures on coins, Kushan kings were tolerant rulers. Kanishka being the most famous among them. As a result, Buddhism became widespread during the Kushan period and Buddhist monuments have been found in various parts of Afghanistan. As a rule, they were decorated with many statues and reliefs. The best known are the ancient monuments of the Hadda region, not far from Jalalabad. Remnants of Buddhist stupas, monasteries and other structures have been traced here. The statues of Buddha and the bodhisattavas, according to religious canons, recreate the ideally beautiful image immoile in self-contemplation. But in depicting faces, whose presentation was not restricted by tradition, Hadda sculptures were exceptionally realistic. Images of man are seen with strong-willed faces, thick moustaches, and wearing light tunics. The so-called head of an ascetic with sharp lines around the mouth and the stubbornly knitted brows is distinguished by a great inner force. Hadda sculptures with their realism and attention to the individual features of persons, penetrating in their psychology, are an outstanding achievement of Kushan art which creatively adopted the traditions of the psychological portrait of the Hellenic epoch.

Thus, the extensive materials charachterise the Kushan epoch as one of flourishing local urban civilization. The Kushans, who maintained close contacts with the largest states of the time, created a synthetic culture that creatively imbibed and transformed, on local basis, achievements of many countries and peoples. The decline of Kushan culture in the fifth century A.D. can be explained by unsuccessful wars with Sassanid Iran and the invasions of nomad tribes from the north, as well as an inner crisis. In any case, the majority of Kushan towns fell into decay. True, the Kushan heritage is an organic part of the culture of Afghanistan and Central Asia of the early medieval epoch, but that period has been studied more thorughly in the regions on the right bank of the Amu Darya than in Afghanistan proper. It can only be said that the Buddhist temples of the sixth to eighth centuries retained to some extent, old artistic traditions, although new features were already noticeable in sculpture, and especially in the fine arts, notable being the Buddhist complex Tapa Sardar near Ghazni. Through them, cultural achievements reach the Muslim Middle Ages as is convincingly shown by new researches conducted by art scholars and historians. The ancient civilisations that had existed on the territory of Afghanistan became part and parcel of the treasure-house of world culture.

The perfunctory survey of the rich cultural heritage of Afghanistan, its cultural and economic ties with India and Central Asia and above all, its emergence as the centre of the ancient civilisation of human beings speaks for itself. This survey, though imperfect and perhaps lop-sided has been included in this study with a purpose. The idea is to remind the present generation of sober-minded intellectuals that the present blood-shed in Afghanistan alone does not reflect their national character. They were a most civilised people. This intellectual and cultural achievement of Afghanistan took place when the modern nation-states were far more backward than the Afghans. It is pertinent to remind the world about it so that peace is restored in Afghanistan and the people of this ancient nation is allowed once again to mould their destiny.

References

1. *Afghanistan: From Tragedy to Triumph*. Sadhna Mukherjee, p. 6.
2. *Ibid.*, p. 7.

16

INDIA'S STAND ON AFGHANISTAN CRISIS

V.D. Chopra

The political developments in Afghanistan became an international issue on December 26th, 1979, when the Soviet tanks and troops rolled into Afghanistan, the traditional buffer between the Indian subcontinent and Russia. As mentioned earlier, in this country the 'Great Game' had been played very often during the British Raj. India had just competed a hard-fought election. The Congress had been swept into power. The Soviet invasion of a small neighbour virtually created a violent reaction in the world. A debate on Afghanistan was scheduled in the United Nations for early January. Instructions had to be sent to the Indian delegation to the UN.

Looking at the Afghan problem Prime Minister Indira Gandhi felt that while opposing the presence of any foreign troops on the soil of any country, India must not antagonise the Soviet Union over the Afghan issue. She also said that the Soviet military intervention in Afghanistan was not the start of the problem but a culmination, albeit an undesirable one, of a whole series of actions by the Shah of Iran, the US and others to wean Afghanistan away from its close relationship with the Soviet Union. She, therefore, ruled that New Delhi should call for a political rather than military solution of the problem so that conditions could be created for an early withdrawal of the Soviet troops from Afghanistan.[1]

From the Indian standpoint it was an unexceptionable position to take though it was bound to be unpopuiar with the West.

Indira Gandhi was quick to correct the distortion in the country's foreign policy by the previous regime. Thereafter, she held fast to the policy framework she had outlined in the first instance. Lord Carrington, the then British Foreign Secretary was in New Delhi within a few days of the UN debate. He did not fully agree with what Indira Gandhi had to say on the Afghan issue, but according to one of his aides who sat through the discussions Carrington was 'much impressed' by the logic of Indira Gandhi's presentation. President Giscard D'Estaing of France a week later, publically endorsed Indira's Afghan policy. The joint communique issued by them later became the basis of the consensus on Afghanistan at a meeting of the Non-Aligned Foreign Ministers in New Delhi, to which both Pakistan and Afghanistan were parties.[2]

If in her talks with Western and Non-Aligned leaders Indira stressed the inadvisability of joining the 'chorus of condemnation of the Soviet Union' orchestrated by the US and China, to the Rusians she spoke sharply about the need for an early Soviet withdrawal from Afghanistan. Andrei Gromyko, the veteran Soviet Foreign Minister (later President of the erstwhile Soviet Union) rushed to Delhi as soon as Giscard left. Indira patiently heard him but told him clearly. "On this I cannot help you." Later, she became the first and, so far, only head of government to demand the Soviet withdrawal from Afghanistan from a public platform in Moscow.[3] This historical fact has been forgotten by the critics of Indira Gandhi.

The Afghan conflict became a major threat to India's security. This assumed a new dimension within a period of two years if one recalls the developments in Punjab.

Since independence India had to fight four and a half wars with her neighbouring countries. Only one of them was with China and the remaining three and a half were with Pakistan. Though smaller than India, Pakistan had felt emboldened to attack it in 1965 because of American weaponry, generously given to it by successive US administrations since 1954, under a mutual security pact. The 1965 war had led to a US arms embargo on both countries but ways were found to get round in the case of Pakistan. American arms were therefore also much in evidence during the 1971 war which led nevertheless, to Pakistan being cut into two and the creation of the independent republic of Bangladesh.[4]

This shows that Indira Gandhi had a clear perception about the developments in Afghanistan. She rightly opposed the Soviet intervention. She was equally clear that Afghanistan was becoming a victim of a geopolitical game.

In any case, Indira Gandhi was more worried about safeguarding Indian security. The Iran-Iraq war, beginning in September, 1980 had brought superpower rivalries and military deployments too close to Indian shores. A greater source of perturbation was the US decision, in the wake of the Soviet military intervention in Afghanistan and the collapse of the regime Shah of Iran to pump highly sophisticated weaponry into Pakistan which had previously used US-gifted arms against India. This shows that Indira Gandhi and later Rajiv Gandhi were clear in their minds about the external ramifications of the Afghanistan crisis.

However, after bloodshed for ten years in Afghanistan, the US policy under the force of circumstances began to show some realism. It started moving towards the position of finding a political solution. By that time an interim government had been set up though Najibullah and his party was in command in Kabul and in large parts of the country. The joint communique of Shevardnadze and Baker of February 10, 1990 started that "The two sides had a constructive discussion on the conditions for a political settlement in Afghanistan, including the need for a transition period that provides for an intra-Afghan dialogue, a broad-based government which would ensure the peaceful, independent and non-aligned status of Afghanistan." However, US-Soviet perceptions still were conflicting.

Significantly, UN representative Cordovez took the position that both the Najibullah government and the interim government had not gathered sufficient support. He insisted that a genuinely broad-based Afghan government could not ignore the Peoples Demorcratic Party. He emphasised on its participation in government. At that stage, the US saw the proposal as premature.

However, Najibullah asked for UN supervised elections, and said that he would quit if he failed to get majority. On the other hand US officials were saying that Najibullah "may be allowed to participate" in a political transition if his ultimate departure from

Kabul was assured. Najibullah himself had said that he would even step down before the voting, but PDPA must be included in the new government.

The interim government had its own plans to choose a new government by May, 1990. This had the support of the US, according to some observers, "Pakistan-based guerrillas and Iran-based leaders were opposed to taking part in the selection of candidates." However, the shape of the interim arrangement was moulded by the bickerings of the resistance groups, solidity of the PDPA prestige of Najibullah, who presented himself as the champion of national sovereignty in a country long hostile to foreign meddling, and the attitude of the US and the USSR.

From an Indian point of view, a strong champion of national sovereignty would conform to non-alignment. New Delhi made it clear that it help in reconstruction. India's attempt to strengthen non-alignment was in keeping with the consensus of having a non-aligned status for Afghanistan.

The later period, however, witnessed the continuation of double-track policy of Washington. Najibullah had welcomed the proposal to entrust the UN peace-keeping forces with the task of supervising the cease fire for he believed that it could help establish conditions necessary for dialogue and negotiations for creating a broad-based government. He in fact came forward with fresh proposals.

He made it clear on a number of occasions that he wanted that a vastly representative coalition government should come into being in Afghanistan which would include representatives of all shades of opinion both within and outside the country including the various formations of Mujahideen, representatives of the emigrants in Europe and the United States, followers of King Zahir Shah and the PDPA and above all the representatives of various sects and leaders of the tribes. Thus he wanted to set up a pluralistic political system.

His stand on religion was based on the concrete reality in his country. In one of his statements, he had said: "Islam is more than a religion. It is a way of life for many millions of people." At his initiative an international conference of Muslims fighting for peace and security was held in Kabul in October, 1988.

He openly declared that he was willing to meet President Bush to discuss with him how to stop the civil war in Afghanistan. He further said that he would to cooperate with all the countries for the economic development of his country including the United States, West Germany and Japan.

Naturally, fundamentalist and dogmatic leaders did not share this perception. Unlike him they wanted to monopolise power for themselves. Najibullah, therefore, was the now emerging leader of all shades of political trends in Afghanistan. The West, the United Nations and the Mujahideen were being forced to talk to the man they once despised the most. Whatever inhibitions Islamabad and Washington might have had about him, Najibullah in the final analysis was an Afghan and a nationalist who loved his country and countrymen. All estimates about the collapse of the Kabul Government and all expectations that a coup against him could lead to anarchy had proved to be wrong. Practical politics demanded that both Washington and Islamabad should recognise him as the central figure in Afghanistan and talk to him. The reality was that within a short span of one year after the withdrawal of the Soviet troops, Najibullah had emerged as a popular leader to do business with, notwithstanding the conflicting estimates about his communist bearing. That in a traditional and tribal society revenge is the hallmark of the trait of an individual leader is a known fact. But Najibullah was confirmed by the fact that three Presidents before Karmal had been killed—Daud, Taraki and Hafizullah Amin by their successors. This was the traditional policy of Afghanistan. But Najibullah decided to break this inhumanistic tradition. That is why instead of killing Karmal he exiled him.

But there is also another aspect of Najibullah's personality. Slowly, he had taken out his party from the narrow grooves of what is called classical communism. He embarked on the path of rebuilding his country through national reconciliation and on the basis of a multi-party system and friendly relations with all the countries, particularly the neighbouring countries. That was the reason that though he was a hated figure in the guerrilla-held mountains, some of them began to regard him. They began to talk to him.

However, instead of starting a dialogue with him, the hawks in Pakistan started working on plans to dislodge him from power. The result was the bloodbath that continued in the country.

What was happening in Afghanistan was only one side of the coin. Its other side depicted developments in Jammu and Kashmir and Punjab. There was a growing feeling in the international community that the two sides of the coin might not remain apart for long. There was a linkage between the two, the linkage being resurgence of fundamentalism. This conclusion holds good even today. If this trend is not reversed, it may set the whole of Central Asia on fire as has been analysed earlier in this study. That is why India cannot remain indifferent to it. That also explains why India has been demanding that outside intervention and interference in the internal affairs of Afghanistan should be stopped for it has a direct bearing on regional stability and peace. India has already begun to feel the pinch of the fallout of development in Afghanistan on its own security and unity.

There is sufficient evidence to the effect that the Mujahideen have begun to take active interest in destabilising Jammu and Kashmir. This shows that the invisible link between Afghanistan and Jammu and Kashmir is becoming increasingly visible. In this sense, India is vitally interested in the peaceful resolution of the Afghanistan tangle. That also explains why India has an important role to play in resolving the Afghan conflict peacefully and through dialogue. If the bloodshed in Afghanistan stops and Afghanistan and Pakistan begin to live peacefully as good neighbours, it will have its own impact on normalisation of relations between India and Pakistan. Moreover, it will have a stabilising influence on other countries in the region.

Scondly, now that more than one decade has passed since all the troops from the erstwhile Soviet Union have been withdrawn, and the Soviet Union no more exists, all attempts to resolve the Afghanistan problem through dialogue and peaceful means should be intensified in a realistic and practical manner.

The important fact to underline in this connection is that this settlement will only be possible when overtly and covertly interference from outside is stopped and all efforts to impose a solution from outside are given up. As a first step in this direction massive supply of arms and sophisticated weapons to the Mujahideen should cease. It is a widely known fact that massive supply of arms to the Mujahideen has been continuing by Pakistan which in turn has been getting these supplies from Washington. It is anybody's guess whether all the arms and sophisticated weapons received from Washington for Mujahideen have actually been despatched to Afghanistan. A considerable part of this aid may have been diverted for non-Afghan purposes including for destabilising India.[4]

Even if one leaves aside this question for the time being what clearly needs to be understood is that India as a nation has a vital stake in the settlement of the Afghan problem because what happens in this country will have a chain reaction in the entire region.

A non-aligned sovereign, neutral and independent Afghanistan is in the interest of the stability and friendly relation among the countries of this region. In any attempt at arriving at a solution of the Afghanistan tangle elections will be a viable method. The question, therefore, is as to how to conduct a fair, free and peaceful poll. It is in this scenario that the specific role of the United Nations as an international agency which supervises these elections has to be seen.

The readiness of the Najibullah regime in Kabul to hold elections under the supervision of the United Nations should have been accepted. But this did not happen and a course was adopted, which led to the intensification of the civil war. Now one faction known as the Taliban has become a dominant force through its military strength.

Nevertheless, one thing is certain that in the name of fundamentalism, outside forces cannot be allowed to interfere in the process of national reconciliation in Afghanistan, whether it was a mistake or not and whether the demand of the international community that the Soviet troops should be withdrawn are no more living issues. They have now become part of history. There is no point in harping on the old mistakes all the time. The whole situation has to be examined in the context of the new realities and in the framework of the situation as it exists today. This is the only pragmatic and realistic manner of looking at the complex problem.

The public opinion on the global level should be mobilised to prevent the fate of nations to be decided by other countries and not by the concerned nations themselves. The attempts to shape the course of events or claims of other nations to mould the destiny of the people of Afghanistan have no place in contemporary international politics in the era of democratisation of international relations on the basis of equality and non-interference in the internal affairs of other countries.

The people of Afghanistan, therefore, should have been left to themselves to shape their destiny. But the tragedy of Afghanistan as we have analysed in earlier chapters is that outside forces gave arms and military training to certain elements. This in fact has made the Afghan problem more complex.

By the middle of this decade the developments in Afghanistan took a new turn qualitatively. The Taliban militants, to be precise in September, 1996, launched a major offensive. The Taliban's rocket attack on the Iranian Embassy in Kabul clearly indicated the change that had taken place in Afghanistan. Even Ms Robin Raphel, the US Assistant Secretary of State expressed anxiety over this development. She spoke of a 'deep concern' over the potential for continuing political instability in Afghanistan. This in her view might effect the bordering states and the region in a negative way. (Emphasis added)[5]

Significantly, the Rabbani-Masood regime came into power in Kabul after the Najibullah government accused Pakistan of supporting the Taliban, particularly when they entered Kandahar.

Mrs Raphel, who maintained that the US was not seeking to experiment with any new ideas on Afghanistan at that time wanted to familiarise herself with the thinking of such Afghan-oriented countries as Uzbekistan, Tajikistan and Turkmenistan in Central Asia that borders Afghanistan. However, one significant omission in Ms Raphel's diplomatic calendar and tour itinerary related to Iran. This is a Shite Muslim state which seemed to have come closer to Afghanistan than Pakistan in a geopolitical sense.

The US did not obviously wish to ignore the critical Iran factor in crisis-prone Afghanistan. However, Washington's dilemma was that it could not hope to decipher Iran's thinking through a direct dialogue with Tehran. Moreover, its relations with Pakistan stood on a different footing. The US recently has revived its pre-Reaganist world view. As a result Iran has at this time replaced the now-defunct Soviet Union as the centre of all evil and a virtual evil empire in Asia.

Washington, nonetheless, has been seeking to fathom the Iranian mind on this key question by banking on Pakistan which apparently knows more about this country's politics than many other countries. This apparent dependence is only designed to supplement Washington's own intelligence on Iran.

The Clinton administration has not so far been able to evolve an Afghan policy that might secure for it a decisive say over the evolution of a post-communist Islamist order in Afghanistan and other Muslim countries who are either hostile to it or suspicious about it.

The US had done so much in the past, wittingly or otherwise, to pave the way for an Islamic dispensation in Afghanistan. In that exercise, the US had utilised the services of Pakistan which was only eager to render help for a diplomatic reward. But one problem that Washington now faces is that Islamabad and Tehran have conflicting perceptions on the question of Afghanistan. Even in the past, when the US was seeking to oust the Najibullah regime in Kabul, Iran and Pakistan were not really looking at Afghanistan through the American prism. However, today's differences between Tehran and Islamabad on Afghanistan seem to be quite fundamental in content.[6] Their geopolitical and geoeconomic interests are conflicting. The situation has become more complex because of Shia-Sunni contradictions.

The US began to evolve its Afghanistan policy, when it came to believe that Rabbani-Masood government has clearly gravitated towards Iran. The Kabul regime's compulsions were traceable to its suspicions that Pakistan is fully backing the Sunni Muslim fundamentalist Taliban which wanted to capture Afghanistan.

When the Taliban took over Kabul in the end of 1996 and pushed further north, Afghanistan entered a new turbulent phase. India's last outpost in the North-West may be deemed to have fallen. This is said in a geopolitical sense and not in any hegemonistic manner. India cannot easily forsake or forget its history from the beginning of the third century BC when Chandragupta Maurya extended his domain up to the Hindukush mountains. The majestic rock-cut sculpture of the Buddha at Bamiyan in central Afghanistan reminds India and West Asia that the ties between the two regions were not merely territorial but also religious and cultural as has been mentioned earlier.[7]

It is in this context that notwithstanding the changes in the power structure in India, it has evolved a clear policy about the current developments in Afghanistan.

External Affairs Minister Inder Kumar Gujral, who now is the

Prime Minister, in identical statements to both Houses of Parliament said on November 25, 1996 that the Taliban were "obscurantists" with little respect for human rights and are not the legitimate government, even if they rule the capital, Kabul. He also, in so many words said they were a direct threat to India's security.

India, he asserted, has a "vital interest" in who rules Afghanistan and how, and, accordingly, a role in "restoration of peace there". Coupled with his statement of no place for a military solution, barely two months after the Taliban conquered Kabul, he made clear India's determination to get the Taliban's opponents back to power, even if they have to share it.

He specified how the Indian government was maintaining contact with Burhanuddin Rabbani, whom the Taliban ousted from Kabul. Calling him President Rabbani, Gujral told the House about his meeting with Prime Minister Deve Gowda during the latter's recent visit to Rome and about an official delegation led by his ministry's secretary for the region to General Abdul Rashid Dostum, a key (for now) Rabbani ally and Taliban opponent, at the warlord's headquarters in north-west Afghanistan.

I.K. Gujral also went out of his way, again and again, to refer to the "brutal and abhorent murder" of Najibullah, head of the ousted communist government from 1986-92, by the Taliban in their conquest of Kabul.

He also had strong words of condemnation for the Taliban's position on women, saying it was a "greatly disturbing denial of human rights."

On what should be done now, Gujral said an end to the ongoing civil war and the demilitarisation of Kabul was needed. Afghan leaders will have to "forsake the path of confrontation." And for this to happen, foreign powers. (meaning Pakistan, for one) must cease interference.[8]

Now that the Taliban seem to have an edge in Afghanistan, India is striving for a peaceful solution of the Afghan problem. Obviously in this effort, the Taliban factor will have to be taken into account.

References

1. Inder Malhotra, *Indira Gandhi: A Personal and Political Biography*, p. 218.
2. *Ibid.*
3. *Ibid.* p. 219.
4. Ibid.
5. Jaipal Reddy, (presently information minister), Superpower *Detente and Future of Afghanistan*, pp. 76-77.
6. *Hindu:* 9th May, 1996.
7. *Ibid.*
8. The Times of India: 28the November 1996.

17

CONTEMPORARY AFGHANISTAN

Fred Halliday

The Saur Revolution was a revolution from above, one that tried to enforce radical changes through a weak state relying on foreign help. It was therefore unable to contain the violent reaction caused by its reforms. Even at the beginning the state did not have a monopoly of the means of violence. Factional disputes and purges further weakened a state based on a delicate balance of ethnic and tribal forces. The regime was not about to collapse in late 1979 but its base of support was seriously eroded. The Soviet entry further exacerbated the situation. After 1980, the Peoples Democratic Party of Afghanistan (PDPA) regime, expanded, but such expansion concealed differences of intent. The armed forces grew, but they were riven by internal conflicts. With Soviet help the PDPA managed to establish a firm control over the state and to increase its military control over the country. It also managed to increase its influence over some areas of the countryside. But the overall balance was not affected. As Marshal Akhromeev put it in 1986, the military strength was not matched by political influence.

After 1986, changes took place in the military structure as well as in the PDPA, with the marginalisation of the old guard of the

SEMINAR ON AFGHANISTAN : Department of International Relations of the London School of Economics and Political Science organized an international seminar on Afghanistan, on 2nd July, 1997. The following is an abridged version of this seminar.

party, while non-party elements were brought in. In the countryside the stress was now on an inducement policy (National Reconciliation). This brought some successes in the North and North-East, but at the price of granting autonomy at the local level.

Lack of resources was one main source of the ultimate failure of the PDPA, but the real limit in the approach of the Afghan leadership was that every new policy led to new conflicts, with an ever stronger factionalism emerging within the PDPA. Belief in continued Soviet support finally made PDPA more reckless.

THE RISE AND FALL OF NATIONAL RECONCILIATION

Dr Antonio Guistozzi

"National Reconciliation" as a policy only came into being in early 1987, but it did not come out of the blue. Its origins can be traced back to as early as 1979, when Taraki and Amin armed as many as 200,000 tribesmen to fight on their behalf. A very large part of these "militias" melted away in the wake of the Soviet occupation, but their creation points to a recurrent pattern of behaviour of the Afghan leadership. At the same time, in the spring of 1979 the Soviet Politburo adopted the approach to Afghanistan which it maintained during most of the eighties; cautious reforms and peace with tribals notables and the clergy, but the ideological impetus was still strong and the PDPA was, contradictorily, invited to rely on land reform to win the support of the peasants.

From 1980 the Soviets pressurised the Afghan leadership to implement their vaguely defined policies. This allowed the Afghans some room for manoeuvre, which they often used to delay changes. The institutions supposed to implement the new policies (National Fatherland Front, *Jirgahs*) only became active in 1983-84. The notable policy (1980-86) was unsuccessful because precedence was still given to the strengthening of the PDPA and, on the other hand, the notables themselves were in decline in the countryside, as they were being replaced by Mujahideen commanders and warlords. At the same time the need to form local militias to consolidate the government influence in the countryside was increasingly emphasized. However, but in most cases only former Mujahideen commanders who at that time provided limited support to the government proved to be militarily effective.

When they introduced the "National Reconciliation" policy in Afghanistan in 1987, what the Soviets wanted was a pacification of the country, so that they could leave. Najibullah's solution was to switch the stress from the old notables to the new ones, i.e., Mujahideen commanders. The commanders were the real power in the countryside now. He devised a policy to bring them onto his side, offering them unprecedented degrees of autonomy at the local level, and not only scrapping the social reforms, but also allowing them to concentrate military, political, economic and judicial power in their hands. The Kabul leadership was now playing the same game as the Mujahideen parties, buying influence through the distribution of weapons.

This was fairly successful, particularly after the Soviet withdrawal, and by the end of 1990 as many as 100,000 former Mujahideen were on the government side. However, this reliance on warlords also led to the demise of National Reconciliation as it was initially intended. Warlords were not interested in peace; rather they wanted to expand their influence at the expense of their neighbours and rivals. The outcome was an unstable and weak regime structurally entangled in a low intensity conflict.

Discussion :

Questions and statements about the clergy in government policies, the absence of financially viable models of state in the various party programmes, the regime's behaviour towards political and intellectual opposition, the role of US responsibilities, the importance of women's issues.

Tanin and Giustozzi answer that the success of the government with the clergy was very limited. A real reconciliation and democratization were not the aims of the regime. US policies in Afghanistan had a very great effect indeed.

SOVIET CONCEPTIONS OF AFGHANISTAN

Academician Nodari Simoniya : *(IMEMO)*

The Afghan case illustrated an argument of *Engels*, that factional struggle among revolutionary groups tends to push them too far, till they realize they are losing their social base. A rollback follows, but some achievements of the previous phase are retained. This is exactly what happened in Afghanistan. Taraki thought he was going to repeat the October Revolution, but Afghanistan was too backward from the social point of view. The Soviet politburo did not see any problem either. Simoniya himself and many other Soviet specialists advised the Afghan leadership personally to moderate their views, in order to avoid the rollback, but they did not listen. A project to translate for the Afghan public the author's book on revolutions was blocked in the Soviet Union. The rollback duly occurred. It would have been still possible to save some of the achievements of the Revolution—a withdrawal from the previous radical policies was possible. Najibullah was the man who tried this and with Soviet support he would have stayed in power. Finally, foreign intervention always proves negative in revolutions, and external political factors are even today playing a very negative role.

MOSCOW'S DECISION TO WITHDRAW : INTERNAL FACTIONS AND EXTERNAL PRESSURES

Professor Fred Halliday, LSE

The passage of time, and a mass of new material from both Soviet and western sources, make it possible to reconstruct more accurately the pattern of Soviet decision-making on Afghanistan:

Phase I to April 1978, shows a general reluctance to become involved but unanswered questions remain about the role of the GRU and the death of Khaibar.

Phase II, from April, 1978 to December, 1979, shows the Soviet Union being drawn in refusal to send troops in March, 1979 and is followed by a change in September-November following the death of Taraki and a decision by four top officials to send in troops in an expectaion of rapid consolidation of the regime.

Phase III from December, 1979, is that of growing realisation by the Soviet leadership that a purely military solution is not possible. Until 1985 this involved above all military action combined with an attempt to reverse radical reforms, and engage in the UN negotiations process. Gorbachev initially tried to consolidate the PDPA by (i) military action and (ii) replacing Babrak with Najib. By the end of 1986, a decision in principle to withdraw was taken, but Gorbachev could only prevail and stipulate a date in late 1987. Throughout this period there were sharp divisions in the Soviet leadership compounding those in Kabul. After the Geneva accords Soviet arms and finance sustained the regime until the August 1991 coup attempt in Moscow.

Soviet policy on Afghanistan always was part of a broader Soviet view of relations with the West. In 1987-88 Gorbachev traded Afghanistan for an agreement on arms control. Even the US decision to continue sending arms did not halt the Soviet pullout. Afghanistan cannot be seen as the main factor in the Soviet collapse. It has rather been part of a much broader loss of strategic position and ideological self-confidence.

Discussion:

Questions and statements about the reasons for the April 1978 coup in Afghanistan, the existence of a real menace to Central Asia in 1979, the impact of the war on the common people.

Halliday answers pointing at the difficulty in the practice of dividing ideological motives from self-interest and at the exaggerated fear of American involvement by the Soviet leadership, while Simoniya stresses the non-involvement of the Soviet Union with the 1978 coup. Others detail the impact of the war on social structure of Afghanistan and how it changed the tribal structure, and provided information about the refugees and the effects of the war on society.

SOURCES OF CONFLICT IN AFGHANISTAN

Dr Barnett Rubin : Council on Foreign Relations, New York

The structure of conflict in Afghanistan is centred first of all on the lack of a state. The destructurisation of society is also of fundamental importance, as can be seen with the coming to power of a sector of the clergy (the Taliban) previously marginalised by other sections of the clergy and by the Mujahideen parties. The economy was also radically changed and was switched to opium production. Women are newly marginalised because of disappearance of the old economy. Refugee life also contributed to the destruction of former Afghan civilization; this is being replaced by territorially based and military oriented organizations which enjoy ethnic support although they do not display any ethnic ideology.

Competition among bordering states, however, reinforces ethnic politics in Afghanistan. Ideology is not very important even in the case of the Taliban, who in fact are not so much radically departured from the policies as most Mujahideen parties. The main obstacle to any settlement is the control of the security of Kabul. Furthermore, while agreements normally come into being when hurting stalemates are reached, in Afghanistan the alternative of asking for support from an external source is always available. In other words, stability in Afghanistan can only be reached within the regional environment.

THE REGIONAL DIMENSIONS

Dr Edmund Herzig : Manchester University :

Tajikistan considers Masood the main threat, although the Taliban threat is also acknowledged to exist. It was only after the increase of the Taliban danger that attempts at establishing a new relationship with the pro-Masood opposition began to be made.

The President of Uzbekistan, Krimov, deeply fears fundamentalist Islam and thinks prevention is necessary. He is trying to increase his independence from Moscow, but also wants Russian peacekeepers to stay in Tajikistan. He tries to avoid giving the Russians the opportunity to exert more pressure on him. Turkmenistan perceives no threat from the Taliban. All the Central Asian states complain about narcotics, as borders are permeable because of corruption.

Iranian officials often don't seem very well informed about Afghanistan. They tend to be more reactive than pro-active. They are however strongly anti-Taliban. Iran is also keen to remain the main Islamic vanguard state. Iran is, anyway, in no position to influence events.

With regard to the UNOCAL pipeline, it is just one among many projects in the area, and not the most viable one, as there are several difficulties. It will not be easy to have it financed. In the future even a pipeline through Iran might become feasible, if US policy towards that country changes. There are other schemes to bring energy to Pakistan and even a stable Afghanistan would not necessarily see the project being realized. There is today no tremendous rivalry to exploit Afghanistan. Everybody agrees peace is the best option, but they disagree about how to achieve it. In the short term there is no solution for Afghanistan—apart from everything else the hostility between US and Iran is at present an insurmountable obstacle.

Discussion :

Question whether Pakistan has a coherent strategy in Afghanistan. Rubin answered that Pakistan had several policies in Afghanistan as the decay of government institutions does not allow the pursuance of a coherent foreign policy. He also stressed that there is no public US policy on Afghanistan. Halliday wondered whether Pakistan really has no coherent policy or rather only pretends, so, to show an innocent face even when violating international agreements, as in the late eighties.

Questions and statements about the issue of Pushtoon chauvinism, the need for an international conference on Afghanistan the relevance of the economic motives of Pakistan, the real relevance of the ethnic issue, the possibility of a division of Afghanistan into two states, Karimov's ambitions in Afghanistan and the real chances of Islamic fundamentalism in Central Asia.

Rubin answered that today Pushtoons are more integrated than ever into the Pakistan state, the real danger to Pakistan is a Pakistani Taliban movement. An international conference is a remote option because such forums have never been used before to resolve military confrontations. Afghanistan's neighbours are against separate states, including Karimov who did not encourage Uzbek nationalism there, but in the future Afghanistan will have to acknowledge the desire for autonomous security among the minorities. It is difficult to say much about Islamism in Central Asia, as these movements are taking different roads in different countries.

Herzing pointed out that in fact Karimov is driving Islamic moderates towards the extremists. Existing international and regional organisations might have a role in bringing about an international conference on Afghanistan, but it will depend on the members of such organizations.

Roundtable with Michael Ignatieff, Laurent Corbaz (International Committee of the Red Cross, Geneva) and Barnett Rubin.

L. Corbaz : Apart from fighters, some farmers and some traders, nobody has got a job in Afghanistan. Smuggling profits are not redistributed. Out of 1 million inhabitants of Kabul 80 per cent cannot feed themselves. Families headed by women and handicapped men are the most destitute. Most people have already sold whatever they could in order to survive. There are roughly 1 million internally displaced persons in Afghanistan. There are also problems in Mazar-i-Sharif because of the closure of the Uzbek border. There are reported to be Hazara hostages in Kabul and Taliban hostages in Mazar.

M. Ignatieff : Afghanistan is not simply a humanitarian disaster, but a new state of existence—a society losing the capacity of reproducing itself without outside help. Only private organisations take care of Afghanistan today. Should a humanitarian organisation rule a country ? A mutual (perverse) dependency is being created between the ICRC (which has expanded enormously to face the task) and Afghanistan, which could be harmful in the future. Most of the international community have walked away.

Discussion :

Questions and statements were put forth about the dimension of the cultural castasrophe, the "image" problem of Afghanistan and declining international concern, the failure of the Afghan intelligentsia to address the problems of Afghanistan, the impact of narcotics production on the economic and social situation of women, the opportunity to support Taliban as the only faction capable of bringing peace and aid leaks to warring factions. A questioner points out that intellectual groups actually got together in 1992, but UN envoy B. Sevan failed to notice that, or consult them.

Rubin answered that the media was not responsible for disinterest actually there is scant interest in the world for Afghanistan. The media can bring some sympathy, but no solution to problems. If we support a Taliban government, reactions to it would make things worse, as in 1979. The only solution is to convince the regional powers to give up supporting the Afghan factions.

Corbaz noted that at present women are forbidden to work even in Mazar-i-Sharif. Women can still work in the countryside but only when accompanied by a man, which is a very strong limitation. For the Red Cross, withdrawal from Afghanistan is ethically impossible, but on some points it stands on principles: health care must be available to women too. As far as the ICRC is concerned, there have been only very minimal aid leaks to the factions.

Report compiled by Dr A. Giustozzi, LSE.

This seminar arose from a research project on the PDPA regime conducted by Prof. F. Halliday and Dr Z. Tanin with a grant from the Economic and Social Research Council. Fred Halliday is well known as an authority on international affairs. His books include Iran (1978) and, with Maxine Molyneux, The Ethiopian Revolution (Verso 1982) and The Making of the Second Cold War.

Report compiled by Dr A. [illegible], LSE

This seminar arose from a research project on the PDPA regime conducted by Prof. F. Halliday and Dr Z. [illegible] with a grant from the Economic and Social Research Council. Prof. Halliday is well known as an authority on international affairs. His books include Iran (1978) and, with Maxine Molyneux, The Ethiopian Revolution (Verso 1982) and The Making of the Second Cold War.

Index

Academician Nodari Simoniya, 227
Afghan Peace Conference, 75
Albright, Madeleine, 14
Alliance Weakness, 174
Aligarh Muslim University, 195
Amir-ul-Momineen, 110
Amanullah, Amir, 26
Amanullah's economic policy, 56
Ammanullah, Amir, 51
Amu Darya, 210
Anglo-Afghan Treaty, 26
Anglo-Afghan War, 149
Annan, Kofi, 117
Arms Embargo, 107
Army's National Logistics Cell, 170
Ashoka, King, 207
Asia Pacific Economic Cooperation (APEC), 31
Association of South-East Asian Nations (ASEAN), 135

Babar, Nasrullah, 124
Bacha-i-Sako, 58
Bahadur, Prof. Kalim, 20
Bahadur, Kalim, 63
Balkh Air, 168
Bandar Anzali Port, 194
Beg, Gen. Mirza Aslam, 121
Bhutto, Benazir, 67
Bhutto, Z.A., 67
Boghaz Keui in Asia Minor, 208
Buddhism, 207

Carpenter, T.G., 104
Carrington, Lord, 214
Carter Administration, 90
Central Intelligence Agency, 150
Central Treaty Organisation, 153
Chechnya, 18
China, 192
Chopra, V.D., 23
Civilisational conflicts, 201
Civil War in Afghanistan, 84, 200
Clinton Administration, 15
Clinton-Gujral Summit in New York, 14
Closing of Era, 163
Coldrin, Lee, 109
Cold War, 91
Commensurate measures, 83
Commonwealth of Independent States (CIS), 16, 166
Comprehensive Test Ban Treaty (CTBT), 14
Conventional Forces in Europe, 162
Conventional Weapons and Foreign Policy in South Asia, 96
Corbaz, L., 231
Costs of Intervention, 152
Council on Foreign Relations, New York, 229
Cultural integration, 210
Curzon, Lord, 25

Delta Oil Company, 111

Democratic Republic of Afghanistan, 30
D'Estaing, President Giscard, 214
Drugs and Taliban, 173
Drugs and Weapons, 157
Dostum, Abdul Rashid, 81
Durand Line, 49

Energy consumption and import, 188
Escalation—a new force, 170
Ethiopian Revolution, 233
European Security and Cooperation, 95

Fatva, 60
Firman, 60
Friendship and political unity, 54

Gandhi, Indira, 213
Gandhi, Rajiv, 215
Geneva Accord, 136
Ghazi, Habibullah, 59
Ghazni province, 206
Ghilzai tribes, 45
Giustozzi, Dr. A., 233
Gorbachev, Mikhail, 90
Gowda, H.D. Deve, 139
Great Game, 184
Great Geneva Agreement, 136
Gujral, I.K. 139
Gun and Koran, 180

Hadis, 65
Hank Brown Amendment, 120
Harappa, 205
Hezbe Islami, 171
Hikmatyar, Gulbuddin, 64
Hindukush, 24
Hizb-e-Islami, 119
Hizb-e-Islam of Gulbuddin, 113
House Foreign Affairs Committee, 104

Ignatieff, M., 232
Indus River, 38
International Committee of Red Cross, Geneva, 231
International reactions, 175
Inter Services Intelligence, 64
Iran, 192
Iranian-Taliban, 107
Islamic Conference Organisation, 135

Jamiat-e-Ulema Islam, 121
Jalilullah, Maulvi, 126
Jirga, 65
John Hopkins University, 74

Kattaghan Province, 52
Kaushik Devendra, 71
Kazakhstan, 80
Keller, Richard, 98
Kerim, Abdul, 53
Khan, Ahmad Ali, 59
Khan, Durrani, 42
Khan, Gohar Ayub, 87
Khan, Habibullah, 50
Khan, Ismael, 169
Khan, Mohd. Daud, 28
Khan, Nadir, 26
Khan, Nasrullah, 50
Khost, Ghilzai, 53
Kremlin, 81
Kuki Khels, 157
Kunnar Mohammed Agency, 128
Kushan Kings, 211

Lawrence, Colonel, 60
Leghari, Farooq, 84
Liberal Democratic Party of Russia, 82
Loya Jirgah, 28

Mahapatra Chintamani, 89
Mahmood, Mufti, 67

Malaviya, K.D., 25
Malik, Gen. Abdul, 68
Manchester University, 230
Masood, Ahmad Shah, 81
Maurya, Chandra Gupta, 209
Mazar-e-Sharif, 178
Mazar-i-Sharif, 74
Mc Namara, Robert, 90
Mehrotra, O.N., 79
Mohenjo-Daro, 205
Monroe Doctrine, 80
Moscow, 79
Moscow's decision to withdraw, 228
Mujaddedi, Hazrat Sibghatullah, 30
Mujahideens, 29
Mullah Warlord, 169
Muslim League, 28

Najibullah, Dr. M., 30
National Security Strategy of Engagement and Enlargement, 31
New Great Game, 118
New York's World Trade Centre, 105
Non-Aligned Movement, 135
Non-Proliferation Treaty (NPT), 14
Noori, Nateq, 139
North Atlantic Treaty Organisation, 32
North-Western Frontier Province, 26
North-West Frontier Province of Pakistan, 200
North-West Frontier of India, 134

Oil and Gas reserves for Central Asia, 189
Organisation of Islamic Conference, 143

Pakistan Military, 34
Pakistan Institute of Development Economics, 174
Palestine Liberation Organisation, 142
Panjsher Valley, 68
Pehlavi, Reza Shah, 134
People's Democratic Party, 184
People's Democratic Party of Afghanistan (PDPA), 29,135
Persian Gulf Work, 194
Peshawar seven, 102
Post Cold War Period, 27
Profits of major oil companies, 187
Purdah, 65

Quran, 65

Rabbani-Masood Regime, 220
Rabbani, President, 64
Rahman, Maulana Fazlur, 63, 67
Raphel, Robin, 93
Reagan, Ronald, 90
Regional Actors, 165
Regional dimensions, 230
Reisner, Igor, 37
Rekhmanov, Emamali, 72
Revolutionary Council, 29
Rise and fall of National reconciliation, 226
Rise of Fundamentalism, 197
Rise of Taliban, 202
Rocket Propelled Grenades, 152
Rollback doctrine, 160
Round-table with Michael Ignatieff, 231
Russian Federal Border Service, 86
Russian Federation, 73
Russian Heavy Machine-Guns, 160

Saghafi-Ameri, Nasser, 20,183
Saudi Arabia's Delta Oil Company, 84
Saur Revolution of April 1978, 23
Sayyaf, Rasul, 64
Second Afghan War, 149
Second World War, 27

Security Council for Afghanistan, 179
Seleznyov, Gennady, 71
Senate Armed Services Hearing, 162
Seraj-ul-Akhbar, 50
Seven Anti-Terrorism Conference, 105
Shah, Ahmad, 39
Shah, Mohd. Zahir, 27
Shah, Nadir, 39
Shariat, 66
Sharif, Mazar, 68
Sharif, Nawaz, 130
Shefag-e-Sorh, 54
Shoukars, 57
Singh, Uma, 117
Simon Commission, 134
Sources of conflict in Afghanistan, 229
South East Asian Treaty Organisation, 153
Soviet Conceptions of Afghanistan, 227
State of the Union Address of President Carter, 152
Stobdan, P., 101
Strategic depth, 102

Tajikistan, 191
Talbott, Strobe, 15
Taliban Movement, 85
Talibans, 35
Tanin, Dr. Zahir, 225
Tarzi, Mahmud-bek, 50
Trinity of Pakistan, 204
Turkmenistan, 192

Ulema Shura, 110
UN De Cuellar, 165
UN Drug Control Programme, 174
UN Drugs Control Programme, 111
UN General Assembly, 135
United Arab Emirates, 188
UN Security Council, 71
US Institute of Peace, 145
Uzbekistan, 80, 191
Uzbek High Command, 124

Waqf, 52
Waziri Community, 43
Weapons and the rise in technology, 159
White House, 31
World War II, 89

Yeltsin, President, 81
Young Afghan Movement, 50
Young Afghans, 26

Zardari, Asif, 149
Zia-ul-Haq, Gen., 30